History

THE JOHNS HOPKINS UNIVERSITY PRESS
BALTIMORE AND LONDON

History

*Professional
Scholarship
in
America*

JOHN HIGHAM

© 1965 by the Trustees of Princeton University
Johns Hopkins Paperbacks edition © 1983, 1989 by
The Johns Hopkins University Press
All rights reserved
Printed in the United States of America

Originally published by Prentice-Hall, Inc., 1965
Harper Torchbook edition, 1973
Johns Hopkins Paperbacks edition, 1983
Hardcover printing, 1986
Updated paperback edition, 1989
Second printing, 1990

The Johns Hopkins University Press
701 West 40th Street
Baltimore, Maryland 21211
The Johns Hopkins Press Ltd., London

Library of Congress Cataloging-in-Publication Data

Higham, John.
    History: professional scholarship in America / John Higham.
        p. cm.
    Includes bibliographical references and index.
    ISBN 0-8018-3952-1
    1. United States —Historiography.   2. Historiography
—United States.   3. Historians —United States.
I. Title.
E175.H64   1989   89-11045
973'.072 —dc20   CIP

For RICHARD SCHLATTER
who invented this book, sustained its
writing, personifies its commitment,
and shares its memories.

CONTENTS

PREFACE

History is one of the oldest and most protean forms of intellectual activity. Any story about human experience that tries to exclude fable and error in the interest of truth has a claim to the name of history. Our constant need to remember the jumble of experience in orderly sequence makes everyone a historian. In daily life historical thinking engages each of us, just as we must all be moralists in making decisions, actors in playing roles, and artists in arranging materials. The reconstruction of the past resembles each of these practical occupations. In fact, it incorporates all of them: in involves commitment, enactment, and design. History is common, but it is also complex.

Accordingly, it has stubbornly resisted codification. Historical thinking characteristically proceeds with a minimum of rules. It lends itself to all the cross-purposes of life. Historians have never elaborated their own special language. They have never agreed on uniform criteria for evaluating their own performance. Until fairly recent times, history was not taught as a distinct subject in schools or universities, and few men gave their whole careers to writing it. Before the nineteenth century history was generally assigned a secondary, though essential, place among the various forms of thought and expression. Thus Samuel Johnson could declare:

> Great parts were not requisite for a historian, as in that kind of composition all the greatest powers of the human mind are quiescent. He has facts ready to his hand, so he has no exercise of invention. Imagination is not required in any high degree; only about as much as is used in the lower parts of poetry. Some penetration, accuracy, and coloring will fit a man for such a task, who can give the application which is necessary.[1]

Yet the development of historical understanding, during the century following Johnson's summary verdict, was one of the most striking features of Western culture. Both historiography and historical thinking in a

---

[1] *Boswell's London Journal, 1762–1763*, ed. Frederick A. Pottle (1950), p. 293. For a compact survey see George H. Nadel, "Philosophy of History Before Historicism," *History and Theory* 3 (1964) : 291–315.

larger sense advanced as never before. We have come to realize that the historical movement of the nineteenth century was perhaps second only to the scientific revolution of the seventeenth century in transforming Western thought and shaping our modern mentality.[2] A historical point of view penetrated into art, literature, philosophy, theology, and the new sciences of man. Herder, Marx, Darwin, Tolstoy, and Weber, to name just a few, were all historical thinkers. Henceforth, no cultivated person could feel that history left the greatest powers of the human mind quiescent.

An adequate account of the historical movement is yet to be written, and I have not aspired to so large an undertaking. This book deals with one special aspect of the new historical consciousness: the development of professional studies of history in the United States. What I have written is primarily a synthesis, a variegated account of the work and thought of the American professional historian, rather than a sharply defined interpretation. Nevertheless, I have sought to trace the participation of professional historians in the whole historical movement and in the difficulties that movement has encountered. While scholarship progressed in refinement and comprehensiveness, history lost in the intellectual life of the twentieth century some of the importance it had in the nineteenth. How historians responded under the particular conditions of American culture is one of my concerns.

The book grew from intentions that were initially quite modest. In 1959 Princeton University's Council of the Humanities asked me to take responsibility for producing a critical description and evaluation of historical scholarship in America in recent decades. I contemplated a small book of essays dealing with the last twenty-five or thirty years. I had already written some highly opinionated articles on the current historiographical scene, and I supposed it would not be hard to flesh them into a more rounded appraisal.[3] As I dug into the records, however, I discovered that the striking features of my own era had deeper roots and more complicated relationships than my polemical essays had allowed. The trail led back, step by step, to the very beginnings of systematic historical study in American universities in the 1870s. Instead of a con-

[2] Herbert Butterfield, *Man on His Past* (1960), p. vii.
[3] "The Cult of the 'American Consensus'," *Commentary*, XXVII (1959), 93–100, was the most influential of these.

temporary survey and critique, I found myself writing an intellectual history.

Constructing a well-rounded intellectual history of the scholars occupied with a body of knowledge as diversified as history posed some formidable problems. I needed to explain, of course, the ideas, social circumstances, and cultural aspirations that motivated them. But I should also examine and try to account for the changes that occurred over time in the range and quality of their achievements. Yet I could not myself master the inner structure of the many kinds of history studied in the United States. I adopted, therefore, the strategy of organizing my history as a series of concentric circles, only the innermost of which would receive a full assessment. The largest circle, embracing the entire historical profession as an organized body, would establish the external relations of historians with one another and with the world in which they lived. This outer circle should prepare the reader to enter a second, more subjective realm. The second circle would mark out the general conceptions about the nature of historical knowledge which American scholars have held, irrespective of their special fields. An understanding of those general ideas about history, and of the institutional setting treated in the first part of the book, would in turn lead the reader into the narrower circle of writings about American history. There alone I might hope to penetrate underlying conceptions about specific historical experience and relate those conceptions to the contexts I had already described. This book takes the form, then, of three parallel, interconnected narratives, each moving through the same successive phases of development but each probing a deeper level of intellectual activity.

One of the great pleasures I received from working on this book was the experience of correcting, from what seemed to be a more inclusive perspective, the partisan formulations I had earlier given to some historiographical problems. I discovered among America's professional historians, past and present, a wider network of affinities and a more continuous intellectual connection than I had previously suspected. Critics duly noted the irenic (though not uncritical) tone these disclosures gave to the book. What troubled them was the optimistic conclusion the book reached—its final judgment that a revitalization of historical thinking, beginning after World War II, was modestly going forward. My optimism left skeptical readers unconvinced.

More than two decades have now passed since the book was written, and the record of those decades supports the critics. In place of an embattled polemic, I had substituted a wider affirmation that can still in important respects be defended; but it did not take enough account either of what was deficient or of what was vulnerable in the historiography of the postwar era. Clearly the special mood of the early 1960s—the vanity and pride of the Kennedy years—had left too strong a mark on the more hopeful passages at the end of Parts I and II.

I would phrase those passages differently if I were writing *History* today, but to tamper with them now would surely violate the integrity and coherence of the book. I have therefore simply added a fourth part. It carries down to the 1980s the story of the writing of American history and then, in a Postscript, comments briefly on recent developments in the debate over objectivity that is traced in Part II. This concluding comment amplifies a review of Peter Novick's *That Noble Dream: The "Objectivity Question" and the American Historical Profession* (1988), which is to appear in the *Journal of Modern History*, LXII (1990).

The new Part IV of *History* should make clear what has changed in my own perspective. I hope that what has not changed is also apparent. I should like to think that the basic spirit in which the book was conceived remains intact. Its affirmation of the historical vocation, its conviction of the irreplaceable worth and perennial charm of historical writing, its commitment to historical thinking—none of these needs to be recalled.

In producing the original version of this book I had the inestimable advantage of collaboration with two extraordinary intellectual historians of modern Europe, Leonard Krieger and Felix Gilbert. Krieger contributed a masterly section on the study of European history in America. Gilbert summed up with a concluding essay on the different ways in which historians in Europe have done their work. My own efforts were clarified by their advice and enriched by their criticism. Of the many colleagues at home and abroad who responded generously to personal inquiries, I remember especially Miriam and Alfred Vagts and Boyd C. Shafer, then executive secretary of the American Historical Association. I also benefited greatly from a critical reading of various chapters by my friends Bradford Perkins and Trygve Tholfsen and by my esteemed teacher, the late W. Stull Holt, who was himself an accomplished historiographer. Three of my students—Stuart Samuels, Raymond Detter, and Susan Brimm—contributed research assistance for which I am still grateful. My principal institutional debt was to the University of Michigan, which offered the stimulus of an exciting department of history and the time I needed to complete the manuscript. Now, for invaluable criticism of Part IV, I am also indebted to my colleagues in American history at the Johns Hopkins University and to the students in my seminar, among whom Mark Kornbluh and Michael Sewell deserve a special salute. In producing this new paperback edition I have been the grateful beneficiary of a Mellon Foundation Senior Fellowship at the National Humanities Center.

Research Triangle Park, North Carolina   J.H.

❧ I ❧

THE HISTORICAL PROFESSION

❧

From the time of the earliest English settlements in America, men and women of many sorts have been writing history. No one group has ever had a monopoly of the production of competent histories. Leadership in setting standards, however, has usually belonged to a particular class. Twice this leadership has changed hands.

During the seventeenth century the best history was written by Puritan clergymen and by lay officials associated with them in creating a new Zion in the wilderness. They wrote hastily, in whatever moments they could spare from active labors in behalf of the Puritan cause. Their history was a further extension of scripture: a chronicle of God's inscrutable will working within their own community. Clergymen long remained one of the most numerous species of historical writers, but their importance diminished as the church ceased to form the cultural center of American life.

In the eighteenth century, patrician historians came to the fore. The growth of private wealth allowed a margin of leisure time for their studies. The weightiness of history appealed to the strong sense of social responsibility that characterized many American gentlemen; to them the historian was the ultimate human judge of men and events. They strove—without always succeeding, of course—to play a judicial role fairly and impartially, for the patrician, untrammeled by religious orthodoxy, prided himself on his independence of mind. He participated in a wide, transatlantic literary culture and wrote for an unspecialized, cultivated audience.[1] During the greater part of the eighteenth and nineteenth centuries the patrician historian held the center of the stage, and in the works of Thomas Hutchinson, Charles Gayarré, Francis Parkman, Henry C. Lea, and others, his history reached a high level of accuracy and distinction.

After 1870 a new social type appeared, and by the end of the cen-

[1] The most detailed studies are Michael Kraus's *The Writing of American History*, rev. ed. (1953); David D. Van Tassel's *Recording America's Past, 1607-1884* (1960); Kenneth Murdock's *Literature and Theology in Colonial New England* (1949), pp. 67-97; Richard S. Dunn's "Seventeenth-Century English Historians of America," in *Seventeenth-Century America*, ed. James Morton Smith (1959), pp. 195-225. For social origins see also George H. Callcott's "Historians in Early Nineteenth-Century America," *New England Quarterly*, XXXII (1959), 496-520.

tury it was becoming the dominant figure in American historiography. As the Puritan gave way to the patrician, so the patrician at length yielded leadership to the professional historian. Unlike any of his predecessors, the professional historian devoted substantially his entire career to teaching and writing. Earlier scholars, largely self-taught, usually turned to serious historical studies in their mature years. The professional learned his skills and fixed his course as a student at a university, there imbibing precept and example from established scholars.

Two signal developments in higher education made this possible. First, the breakdown of the old classical curriculum and the rise of the elective system created a new need for college teachers of history. College curriculums until the 1870's had room for very few history courses, and these were generally taught by professors primarily interested in the classics or in philosophy. As late as 1884 the four hundred American institutions of higher education had about twenty full-time teachers of history. At Princeton the sole professor of history also taught political science.[2] A decade later nearly a hundred college teachers devoted full time to history, and the demand was growing steadily.[3] Meanwhile the modern university, conceived as a center for research and graduate training, became at last, after many abortive antebellum attempts, the capstone of the educational system. The opening of The Johns Hopkins University in 1876 and the transformation of Harvard during the same decade pointed the way. The university supplied an institutional setting for professional scholarship, and, by the requirements for its Ph.D. degree, transmitted an incentive for research to the college teachers whom it trained. The professional historian materialized in the guise of a teacher-specialist. After a long intervening period of free-lance scholarship, historians again became, as they had been in Puritan New England, servants of an institution.

Although the university provided a new institutional basis for historical scholarship, it could not alone supply the discipline and esprit de corps a profession requires. A profession is, among other

[2] Charles W. Eliot, *Educational Reform: Essays and Addresses* (1909), pp. 105-106; G. Stanley Hall, ed., *Methods of Teaching and Studying History* (1886), pp. 49-50; J. F. Jameson, "The American Historical Association, 1884-1909," *American Historical Review*, XV (1909), 2.

[3] J. F. Jameson, "The American Historical Review, 1895-1920," *American Historical Review*, XXVI (1920), 2.

things, a body of individuals with a particular skill, who by coopera-tive action establish and maintain their own standards of achieve-ment instead of obeying some external authority. While universities furnished professional training and opportunity, the new type of scholar also needed his own nationwide organization for the promo-tion of his collective interests and the regulation of his work. This he secured through the American Historical Association, founded in 1884. The reciprocal relations between this emerging Association and the existing world of amateur scholarship constitute the central theme in the formation of a historical profession.

FORMATIVE YEARS

It is clear in retrospect that amateur and professional historians operate very differently, and that the shift from one kind of leadership to the other has not been all clear gain. The most conspicuous advantage of professionalism inhered in the coordination of many individuals' efforts. "Scholars and students can no longer afford to live in isolation," insisted the chairman at the organizing session of the American Historical Association.[1] By working together, professionals pooled their knowledge and collaborated with more or less success in assembling materials, facilitating research, organizing collective projects, disseminating ideas, criticizing results, and multiplying the number of historians. One result was an enormous quantitative increase in sound historical writing. Moreover, the professional spirit of coordination required, in theory at least, that every individual investigation should reach outward toward a larger organization of historical knowledge; every local inquiry should relate itself to a general pattern of development. Thus the professional made war on the disconnected nature of amateur scholarship.

A cooperative ethic had, however, the disadvantage of putting more emphasis on attainment of a general level of competence than on the creation of unique achievements. The cultivation of talent discouraged to some degree a quest for genius. One of the founders of the American Historical Association, J. Franklin Jameson, grasped very early the nature of the choice that was being made, and accepted it. "Now it is the spread of thoroughly good second-class work," he wrote in 1891, ". . . that our science most needs at present; for it sorely needs that improvement in technical process, that superior finish of workmanship, which a large number of works of talent can do more to foster than a few works of literary genius." [2]

The standards of craftsmanship for which Jameson spoke took on

---

[1] Quoted in David D. Van Tassel, "The American Historical Association and the South, 1884-1913," *Journal of Southern History*, XXIII (1957), 466.

[2] J. F. Jameson, *The History of Historical Writing in America* (1891), pp. 132-33.

such importance in professional eyes that content could easily suffer at the expense of technique. Moreover, the guild-enclosed historian could not escape the standardization of goals and activities that is inherent in organizational life. In spite of a self-critical spirit built into professional history, the insular and fraternal habits of professional association tended to perpetuate the high level of mediocrity that Jameson regarded as a necessary but temporary stage in preparing the way for truly great and profound work. Perhaps the teaching function of the professional historian also sustained a good-natured tolerance of routine performance. In the protected atmosphere of the classroom a man continually responsible to others younger and less mature than himself does not easily hold to an extravagant and selfish ideal of achievement.

The amateur historian, on the other hand, cherished his independence. John Bach McMaster, a self-made historian who secured a professorship at Pennsylvania because he wrote an outstanding book, a scholar who was notably absent at the founding of the American Historical Association, illustrated the amateur spirit in opposing the Carnegie plan for pensioning retired professors. "I believe that in this and in all professions, as in business, each man should stand on his own basis, and on that alone," McMaster announced in his highly unprofessional way.[3] Similarly, the amateur historian expected his work to survive or perish on its individual merits; he was little concerned about its status as a "contribution" to some continuing collective inquiry. Having no feeling of corporate identity (except in a local or ethnic sense), the amateur historian did not write primarily for other historians. He chose his subject for its intrinsic interest and wrote either for his own satisfaction or for a public that would accept him on his own terms. He might have too little knowledge and appreciation of technique, but he never had too much.

So, in time, many amateur historians grew contemptuous of their professional brethren. "After a while," Theodore Roosevelt recalled, "it dawned on me that all of the conscientious, industrious, painstaking little pedants, who would have been useful in a rather small way if they had understood their own limitations, had become because of their conceit distinctly noxious. They solemnly believed that if there were only enough of them, and that if they only collected

[3] Eric Goldman, *John Bach McMaster, American Historian* (1943), pp. 70-71.

enough facts of all kinds and sorts, there would cease to be any need hereafter for great writers, great thinkers." [4]

One might suppose, in view of this sharp divergence, that the professional summarily thrust the amateur aside, that lines of battle were drawn from the outset, and that the victory of one meant the defeat of the other. Things were not that simple. Neither a professional ethic nor a mature professional organization came into being overnight in 1884. These developed gradually and did not become distinct until the twentieth century. The new school of Ph.D.'s, although quite self-conscious in the eighties, had not yet found its place in American culture. It needed the help and sought the aid of everyone seriously interested in history. Aid was readily extended, for the better amateur historians fully shared the professionals' interest in raising the standards of cultural activity in America. Much of the character of modern American historiography will remain obscure unless we appreciate that it sprang from the combined efforts of independent gentlemen and professional scholars, who comprised initially a homogeneous class with a common mission.

The rise of a professional outlook in the field of history was an integral part of a broad movement for the establishment of authority in American intellectual life. In almost all fields of cultural endeavor, associations that defined standards and goals appeared in the late nineteenth century. The American Historical Association was one among a great number of such bodies. The American Philological Association made its debut in 1869. At least 79 learned societies were organized in the next decade, and 121 in the Eighties. The new universities not only introduced graduate schools of arts and sciences but also multiplied and immensely invigorated the nation's professional schools. Beginning in the 1870's, physicians underwent increasing regulation by state examining boards. The spread of state and local bar associations and the organization of the American Bar Association in 1878 strengthened the professional consciousness of lawyers.[5] The National Education Association (1870) tried to do the same with teachers.

[4] Quoted in Howard K. Beale, "The Professional Historian: His Theory and His Practice," *Pacific Historical Review*, XXII (1953), 228.
[5] Merle Curti, *The Growth of American Thought*, 2nd ed. (1951), pp. 586-88; James Bryce, *The American Commonwealth*, 2nd ed., vol. II (London, 1891), p. 502; Richard Harrison Shryock, *The Development of Modern Medicine* (London, 1948), p. 284.

Other agencies stepped forward to exercise custodial jurisdiction over literature and the arts. The great metropolitan art museums, most of which were established in the 1870's, served as weighty arbiters of taste. New nonpartisan, nondenominational magazines—the *Atlantic Monthly,* the *Century, Scribner's*—labored to elevate and guide a national middle-class audience in the pursuit of culture and respectability. The *Nation,* edited by E. L. Godkin, was the most distinguished and influential of these journals. Throughout the last third of the nineteenth century it was the authoritative voice of the patrician and academic intelligentsia. In 1868 Godkin had complained that all groups in America were organized except "the chaotic mass of persons scattered from Maine to California to whom mental culture is one of the great objects of this mortal life."[6] By the end of the century the chaotic mass had undergone an organizational revolution comparable to the trust movement in American business. There was even, after 1898, a National Institute of Arts and Letters, an honorific, self-appointed body modeled on the great European academies.

Scholars inevitably participated prominently in this movement of consolidation, since it blended with a long-term trend toward specialization and technical refinement in intellectual life. It also enlisted the cultivated patrician class, for the movement represented a profound reaction against the democratic openness and rawness of the pre-Civil War era. America in the midnineteenth century had had a paucity of effective intellectual institutions. Its strikingly undisciplined culture had thrown off institutional restraints on the individual. It valued the omnicompetence of the common man above the tutelage of any elite. In the late nineteenth century, urbanization, conservatism, and a general weakening of democratic values contributed to a reassertion of leadership by established authorities.

Thus patricians readily joined professional scholars in enterprises calculated to uplift and codify American culture; they could not anticipate how far the codification would go, or how much their own intellectual pre-eminence would ultimately suffer. The academic men, for their part, felt at home in patrician circles. James Bryce noticed in the late Eighties that American professors, in spite of modest salaries, seemed always to be among the local social aristocracy. They were dignified, frock-coated gentlemen, and at Columbia Uni-

[6] E. L. Godkin, "The Organization of Culture," *Nation,* VII (1868), 486-88.

versity before the turn of the century professors were almost automatically listed in the New York *Social Register*. (At the best universities even the salaries of the top professors were substantial. A
few exceeded $5,000 in a time when many school teachers earned
$500 and maids were available for $3.50 per week.) [7] As if to sym-
bolize the alliance of academic authority with aristocratic traditions,
universities in the late nineteenth century adopted ceremonial robes
for formal occasions, and enclosed their new laboratories in ivy-
covered Gothic.

Moreover, most academic scholars shared the social ideals of their
patrician associates. Both groups conceived of themselves as guides
for a democratic society that overestimated material success and un-
dervalued "the higher ideals of life." Both felt a common mission to
civilize the masses on the one hand and subdue the upstart nouveaux
riches on the other. Both echoed the *Nation* and the *Atlantic* in calling for "an educated class amongst us, to be the guardians of the traditions and feelings and aspirations of high culture, and the diffuser
of an atmosphere of thought and study—a kind of barrier, too,
against the gross materialism of the time, the growing tendency to
estimate the value of everything in dollars and cents, and to despise
or shirk all discipline of mind or body which does not promise a
speedy return in hard cash." This class would constitute, said William T. Harris, U.S. Commissioner of Education, an "aristocracy of
culture," disputing alike the claims of mere wealth and the preroga-
tives of birth.[8]

Accordingly, the early professional historians regarded their

---

[7] Bryce, *op. cit.*, p. 549; John D. Davies, "The 'Old' Faculty," *Princeton Alumni
Weekly*, LXI (November 25, 1960), 6-9; W. R. Harper, "The Pay of American
College Professors," *Forum*, XVI (1893), 96-109; Hugh Hawkins, *Pioneer: A
History of the Johns Hopkins University, 1874-1889* (1960), pp. 42, 129. M.
Halsey Thomas, to whose knowledge of New York social history I am much in-
debted, has checked his recollections of faculty conversation by looking up the
Columbia faculty of 1900 in the *Social Register* of that year. He found nearly
all of the full professors listed, leaving aside three Jews and the notoriously un-
conventional Harry Thurston Peck.

[8] *Nation*, IV (February 21, 1867), 151-52; Thomas Wentworth Higginson, "A
Plea for Culture," *Atlantic Monthly*, XIX (1867), 29-37; William T. Harris,
"The Use of Higher Education," *Educational Review*, XVI (1898), 160. See
also G. Stanley Hall, *Aspects of German Culture* (1881), p. 307; James Russell
Lowell, *Representative Selections*, ed. Harry Hayden Clark and Norman Foerster
(1947), pp. 436-51; Henry Dwight Sedgwick, "The Mob Spirit in Literature,"
Atlantic Monthly, XCVI (1905), 14-15.

scholarly activity as an essential component of the whole movement for consolidating American culture. In Germany, where many of them in the 1870's and 1880's went for training, they acquired an austere conception of specialized research that would before long separate them from amateur connections; but they also found in Germany the example of a professoriat active in civic enterprise. The German idea of the professor as the conscience of the state corresponded roughly to the American ideal of an aristocracy of culture. John W. Burgess, German-trained historian who inaugurated graduate work at Columbia in history and political science, hoped to produce statesmen and public officials as well as scholars. The first American guidebook to historical scholarship, Charles Kendall Adams' pioneering *Manual of Historical Literature* (1882), contained a long digression on current national problems that would require historically informed leaders. Early meetings of the American Historical Association reverberated with pleas to historians to serve society, raise the level of political debate, and restore integrity in public life.[9]

The chief architect of the American Historical Association exemplified and fostered the union of professors and patricians. Herbert Baxter Adams, director of historical studies at Johns Hopkins during the Eighties and Nineties, though not a noteworthy scholar in his own right, was the first indefatigable promoter of professional history. Through his outstanding students, through the *Johns Hopkins University Studies in Historical and Political Science* (1882-   ), which he founded and edited, and through his secretaryship of the American Historical Association during its first sixteen years, Adams probably did more than anyone else to Germanize American historical scholarship. Yet he took special care to involve amateur historians in the Association and thereby make it a broadly national institution.

A New Englander "of sound Puritan stock" though unrelated to the more famous Adamses, Herbert Baxter was a product of Phillips Exeter Academy, Amherst College, and the University of Heidel-

[9] Charles Kendall Adams, *A Manual of Historical Literature*, 3rd ed. (1889), pp. 19-23; Herman Ausubel, *Historians and Their Craft: A Study of the Presidential Addresses of the American Historical Association, 1884-1945* (1950), pp. 38-39; Andrew D. White, "European Schools of History and Politics," *Johns Hopkins University Studies in Historical and Political Science*, V (1887), 471-546.

berg. He worshiped his Heidelberg master, Johann Bluntschli, who (Adams thought) had arrived at a truly historical jurisprudence by participating in the politics and legislation of his time. Adams' own enthusiasm for public service expressed itself through his connection with the U.S. Bureau of Education, for which he wrote and edited a long series of pamphlets on the history and current state of American education. His favorite project for a time was a scheme for a national academy at Washington to train professional civil servants as West Point and Annapolis trained officers. Adams all the while enjoyed the pleasures of Baltimore and Washington society, particularly the Cosmos Club and the Saturday Evening Literary Club that met at the home of a wealthy and cultivated lawyer, Horatio King. In 1891, when Adams was offered a lucrative post at the new University of Chicago, he drew up a balance sheet, comparing the two situations, which presents a revealing profile of patrician values. Among other, more personal considerations, he listed: [10]

East	West
Quiet	Rush
Continuity	Broken
Society	New People
Conservatism	Boom
Duty	Advantage
Settled	Moving
Identification	Lost

Not surprisingly, Adams decided to stay at Johns Hopkins.

Privately, Adams had a rather superior attitude toward the many local historical societies and the amateur historians of the country. But he realized keenly, as he told a friend, "the importance of corporate influences, of associations of men and money." [11] So he launched his plan for a national historical society with the aid of the American Social Science Association, a kind of clearing house for knowledge about social and educational issues that concerned the aristocracy of culture. The President of the Social Science Association, John Eaton, who was also Commissioner of Education at the time, joined

10 W. Stull Holt, ed., *Historical Scholarship in the United States, 1876-1901* (1938), p. 157. See also *Herbert B. Adams: Tributes of Friends* (1902).
11 Holt, *op. cit.*, p. 469.

Adams and two other professional historians in summoning an organizational meeting of historians, to be held in conjunction with the annual meeting of the social science group. Of the forty-one people who answered the call and constituted themselves the American Historical Association (AHA) only a minority had any professional historical training. The charter members included patrician historians, like William B. Weeden and Charles Deane, and men of affairs, like Carroll Wright, Rutherford B. Hayes, and William T. Harris. Nevertheless the professionals controlled the organization from the outset; and at the second annual meeting they declared their fundamental allegiance by electing Leopold von Ranke, then approaching his ninetieth birthday, as their first and only honorary member.[12]

Determined to bring all the historical resources of the nation within the purview of his Association, Adams continued to direct its energies outward. For two decades he and his cohorts on the Executive Council rarely selected a professional historian as their annual president. (The only clear exceptions were Andrew Dickson White and Charles Kendall Adams, both university presidents.) Sometimes the AHA recognized a great patrician scholar like the revered George Bancroft, heavy with years and honors. Sometimes it honored a distinguished clergyman with historical tastes, like Richard Salter Storrs. Sometimes it chose a conservative and cultivated man of affairs, like Simeon Baldwin, chief justice of the Connecticut Supreme Court and one-time president of the American Bar Association. Meanwhile, Adams took pains to gather the state and local historical societies under the Association's paternal wing. When in 1889 some of them seemed on the verge of creating their own federation, Adams headed them off with a special invitation to participate in the Association's work. He also initiated an elaborate bibliography of their publications.[13]

Just as Adams associated himself with the U.S. Bureau of Education, so he strove to attach the American Historical Association to the federal government. American governments, in contrast to European, had shockingly little interest in subsidizing research, publishing historical documents, or maintaining usable archives. Adams was de-

[12] American Historical Association *Papers,* I (1886), 22-23, 483; J. F. Jameson, "Early Days of the American Historical Association, 1884-1895," *American Historical Review,* XL (1934), 1-5.
[13] Holt, *op. cit.,* pp. 126-28; A. P. C. Griffin, ed., "Bibliography of American Historical Societies," AHA *Annual Report* (1905), vol. II.

termined to rouse Congress to a consciousness of its historical responsibilities. Reciprocally, he wished to clothe the AHA with the
dignity of the national state. After the first two annual meetings at
the headquarters of the Social Science Association in Saratoga, New
York, Adams shifted the base of operations to Washington. For a
decade the AHA met there regularly, except one year when it went
to Boston to honor Justin Winsor and another when it met at the
World's Fair in Chicago. Adams delighted in the attendance of a few
Congressmen and governmental officials at these meetings. Furthermore, he prevailed upon their good will to secure from Congress in
1889 a federal charter for the American Historical Association. This
unusual act of incorporation fixed the principal office of the Association permanently in Washington, and authorized it to report annually to the Smithsonian Institution. The latter was directed to
transmit to Congress the AHA's proceedings and its reports on the
condition of historical study in America. Adams thereby secured at
government expense both office space and the printing of his annual
reports.[14] More important, he opened a channel through which the
aristocracy of culture might, in historical matters, exert a vigorous,
uplifting influence on national policies.

These expectations proved false. The governmental connection
never matured. In America, unlike Adams' beloved Germany, professors and other guardians of culture did not succeed in establishing
a solid partnership with the state. During the Jacksonian period the
intellectual class in America had lost its political eminence, and all
efforts to recover that eminence in the late nineteenth century were
unavailing. In the early 1890's committees of the American Historical Association began memorializing Congress to take heed of the
nation's scattered and neglected historical records. The scholars
wanted a unified management of the national archives; they also
pleaded for a Historical Manuscripts Commission that would—like
the British agency of that name—inventory important papers in
private hands. Congress did nothing. Any prospect that it would seriously notice the annual reports it still receives from the Association
soon vanished. The arrangement continues today as a useful economy in scholarly printing expenses and as a memorial of the forgot-
ten hopes of Herbert Baxter Adams.

14 The story may be followed in the annual *Papers* and *Reports* of the AHA and
in the articles by Jameson cited above.

Another, greater Adams also tried vainly in the 1880's to close the gap between government and culture. While Herbert Baxter used the new device of a professional organization, Henry Adams relied on his own brilliant salon. He established himself at Lafayette Square in Washington in 1877, partly to pursue historical research and partly to be where he expected political, scientific, and historical talent to converge in a new concentration of national energy. Washington failed to live up to these expectations. It never became a genuine capital in the sense in which almost every European country had a national center of wealth, knowledge, intellect, fashion, and political power. Nor did Henry's personal circle become a society. Instead, it contracted as his life darkened. Even the presence of a fellow historian in the White House after 1901 did not unite the world of learning and the world of politics.[15]

In the absence of a political system capable of binding the patrician intellectual and the academic teacher to a common center of authority, the two groups eventually drifted apart. Each was thrown too exclusively on its own intellectual resources. The drive toward a stricter professionalism gradually pulled the academic men away from patrician associations and from the wide culture that patrician life at its best embraced. To this trend the patrician offered little effective counterpressure. After the 1890's the number of amateurs producing important historical books diminished drastically. There is no reason to suppose that professionals crowded them out; they quit of their own accord. James Ford Rhodes, speaking to the Harvard undergraduate History Club in 1908, advised young men of ample means to devote their lives to independent historical scholarship; [16] but very few took such advice, and Rhodes himself had in the early twentieth century no real successor. A similar disengagement evidently occurred in other fields of cultural endeavor. One thinks of Edith Wharton's literary isolation in upper-class New York, her descriptions of delicate American dilettantes in Europe, and her own nostalgia. The aristocratic revival in American culture during the post-Civil War decades had spent much of its force by the turn of the century. In the increasingly democratic atmosphere of the Progressive Era the aristocracy of culture very largely went to pieces; and

[15] A. Hunter Dupree, *Science in the Federal Government* (1957), pp. 296-300. On Henry Adams see Ernest Samuels' *Henry Adams: The Middle Years* (1957).
[16] James Ford Rhodes, *Historical Essays* (1909), pp. 77-78.

many of its patrician elements became—like Henry Adams himself in his later years—peevish, precious, and aloof.

We can observe the other side of this separation beginning in the American Historical Association in the 1890's, as the professors moved to take full charge. After a decade of Herbert Baxter Adams' leadership, dissatisfaction broke out in 1895. On the surface the issue was simply one of where to meet. A group of professors, led by George Burton Adams of Yale, William A. Dunning of Columbia, and Albert Bushnell Hart of Harvard, complained that the annual meetings were dull and poorly attended because Washington was not an adequate center of literary and academic life. The protesters demanded and won a new policy of rotation that would bring the Association each year to one of the major university communities.

Behind this specific change it is not hard to see a broader professorial rebellion against Herbert Baxter Adams' careful balancing of academic and nonacademic interests. The programs to date had included a large number of papers by nonprofessional historians, mostly light and trivial performances. The Association had largely avoided discussion of pedagogical problems and had maintained on its Executive Council an even balance between professionals and amateurs. In all these respects the emphasis now shifted decisively in a professional direction. More professional historians were elected to the Executive Council. Their papers henceforth dominated the annual meetings. And in 1896 the AHA appointed its famous Committee of Seven (all professors) to improve historical instruction in the secondary schools. The new policies quickly produced a gratifying expansion. Between 1895 and 1899 membership doubled (reaching 1,400), and attendance at meetings increased from 50 to more than 200.[17]

The same group that broke the Washington axis of the AHA simultaneously launched a strictly professional historical journal. Several Ivy League professors, headed by George Burton Adams and Hart, met in New York in April 1895 and founded the *American Historical Review* (*AHR*) independently of the American Historical Association. Since they wished to have an American publication with the highest technical standards, they created an entirely professional editorial board. J. Franklin Jameson, a young professor at Brown

[17] AHA, *Annual Reports* (1895-99); Jameson, *op. cit.*, *AHR*, XV (1909), 15-19.

University, was installed as managing editor. Three years later the Association began to subsidize the *Review* and elect new members of its editorial board. In 1915 an amateur member of the AHA, Frederic Bancroft, backed by some disgruntled southerners, made ugly charges of fraud and favoritism against the editors; whereupon the Association formalized its control of the *Review* by acquiring legal ownership.[18] The independence of the *Review* during its early years, however, insured its uncompromising professionalism at a time when the Association was still in transition.

Finally, the new leadership that emerged in 1895 recognized that history could not depend on the federal government for any considerable support or initiative. In the absence of congressional action, the AHA appointed its own Historical Manuscripts Commission "to edit, index, or collect information in regard to unprinted documents relating to American history." Over the succeeding years the Commission swelled the annual reports of the AHA with a variety of useful documentary and bibliographical publications. Then, to prompt some improvement in the disorderly archives of American governments, a Public Archives Commission, formed in 1899, turned its attention to the states. Methodically, it surveyed the records of one state after another and published its findings each year. Within ten years the Commission's reports had stimulated twenty-four states to make formal provisions for the preservation and custody of their unpublished records. Here was a major achievement to be credited to the organized, systematic outlook of the professional historian.

For all of their increasing self-confidence, the professional historians were not so foolhardy as to ignore their amateur brethren. The myriad of state, local, and ethnic historical societies commanded immensely valuable resources. The AHA continued, therefore, to welcome into membership everyone seriously interested in history and to strengthen ties with the other historical societies. In 1896 the recently established American Society of Church History was absorbed into the American Historical Association as its Church History Section. In 1904 the Association organized, in conjunction with its annual meeting, a regular Conference of State and Local Historical Societies to

---

[18] The formal account in Jameson, *op. cit., AHR,* XXVI, (1920), 1-17, should be supplemented by "The Reminiscences of Frank Maloy Anderson" (Oral History Research Office, Columbia University, 1957) and the Frederic Bancroft Papers (Columbia University).

stimulate greater cooperation among them and with the national Association.

The degree of cooperation actually attained depended on the responsiveness of the amateur bodies to a professional spirit. By and large, the eastern societies, which were privately endowed, socially prestigious, and genealogically inclined, held to a prosy, traditional course. They continued to putter with muster rolls, the military records of colonial wars, and the obituaries of their own members; they took little interest in anything outside their particular local jurisdictions. Their leaders were likely to be club men with nothing to do, interested in small antiquarian objects. On the other hand, the western state historical societies, having less tradition behind them, were more vigorous, adaptable, and cooperative.[19] The major societies in the Midwest relied heavily on state support, as did the major universities. Their leaders were active men, close to public affairs, like J. Sterling Morton, Nebraska railroad promoter and Secretary of Agriculture in the second Cleveland administration, or Reuben G. Thwaites of Wisconsin, a former newspaperman with the mind of an entrepreneur. Eager to learn and to improve, the principal western societies participated willingly in the AHA's Conference of State and Local Historical Societies. Moreover, they associated themselves with the history faculties in their respective state universities. Thwaites, who ran the best subsidized of all of the societies, persuaded the state of Wisconsin in 1901 to locate the state historical society on the campus of the University in a single building together with the University library and the graduate seminars in American history. In other states, notably Alabama and Mississippi, the strongest historical work was done by the newly created official departments of archives and history, which the AHA's Public Archives Commission had inspired; and there too professional attitudes took hold.[20]

The formation of the Mississippi Valley Historical Association in 1907 was another evidence of the vigorous midwestern entente between professional historians and state-supported historical agencies.

19 Elizabeth Donnan and Leo F. Stock, eds., *An Historian's World: Selections from the Correspondence of John Franklin Jameson* (Memoirs of the American Philosophical Society, vol. 42, 1956), p. 284.
20 H. Hale Bellot, *American History and American Historians* (1952), pp. 26-34.

The initial impulse for a unifying organization to advance research and conserve historical materials throughout the Mississippi Valley came from the secretaries of several state societies. Instead of holding themselves aloof from academic men, however, the secretaries proposed at the outset to link their regional association with the AHA by meeting conjointly each December. On the urging of Clarence W. Alvord, a German-trained professor at the University of Illinois who organized the first program of the new association, it decided against any effort to popularize history and turned its attention to scholarly publication.[21]

By the time the Mississippi Valley Historical Association appeared, the formative era in the creation of the American historical profession was over. The patrician historians, with very few exceptions, had either retired from the scene or subsided into ineffectual antiquarianism; and all amateur scholars of any note were following the lead of the professionals. By now, the American graduate school had come fully of age. Some sixteen American universities were training doctoral candidates in history. Altogether, they had produced about 250 Ph.D.'s since 1882.[22] Young men no longer went to Europe in large numbers for a professional degree. The attraction of Germany had declined perceptibly in the 1890's and more sharply after the turn of the century, though some Americans still went to Paris and Oxford.[23]

By now, too, the American professoriat had imposed its authority on historical instruction below the collegiate level. The AHA's Committee of Seven, disturbed by the haphazard, routine character of history in the secondary schools, proposed a sweeping revision in 1899. It called for a four-year history requirement in the college preparatory program, encompassing ancient history, medieval and modern Europe, English history, and American history. The Committee also insisted on supplementing rote-learning in textbooks with collateral reading and other projects. Within eight years these recommenda-

[21] James L. Sellers, "Before We Were Members—The MVHA," *Mississippi Valley Historical Review*, XL (1953), 3-24.

[22] William B. Hesseltine and Louis Kaplan, "Doctors of Philosophy in History: A Statistical Study," *AHR*, XLVII (1942), 766, 771.

[23] Richard S. Barnes, "German Influence on American Historical Studies, 1884-1914" (Ph.D. dissertation, Yale University, 1953), p. 68; Jameson, *An Historian's World*, p. 254.

tions became the accepted standard, greatly improving the position of history in the secondary schools.[24]

We may consider the year 1907 as the end of an epoch in respect also to the actual accumulation of research. The twenty-six-volume "American Nation Series," published between 1904 and 1907 and edited by Albert Bushnell Hart, constituted the first great professional synthesis of American history. Planning for it had begun at meetings of the American Historical Association in the late 1890's as a consequence of dissatisfaction with an earlier cooperative work edited by Justin Winsor, *A Narrative and Critical History of America* (8 vols., 1884-89).[25] The latter was only quasi-professional. The contributors, with a few exceptions, were amateur scholars. Although each provided a careful, unadorned summary of existing knowledge, their chapters had no integrative principle, no analytical pattern. All but two of the authors of the "American Nation Series," on the other hand, had had graduate training in history. Each volume in the series undertook to explain a sequence of development. The work represented a triumphant appropriation of the whole span of American history by professional historians.

Finally, the spearhead of professional activity, the American Historical Association, had acquired by 1907 approximately the form in which it survives to this day. Meeting that year at Madison, Wisconsin, the Association installed for the first time a president who was purely and exclusively a professional historian. The custom of choosing influential patrons of history was decisively put aside. Occasionally during the next two decades the AHA might still honor an outstanding patrician historian like Theodore Roosevelt or Henry Osborn Taylor; otherwise the presidency was henceforth exclusively in the hands of university professors. Appropriately, the first of this largely unbroken line was John Franklin Jameson. He was then only forty-eight years old; three decades of single-minded dedication to scholarship lay ahead. His elevation to the presidency in 1907 was a tacit acknowledgment that the American historical profession had developed its own unique leader.

Jameson was the first notable professional historian who did not

[24] William MacDonald, "The Situation of History in Secondary Schools," *Nation*, LXXXV (1907), 225-26; AHA, *The Study of History in Secondary Schools: Report . . . by a Committee of Five* (1911).
[25] W. A. Dunning, "A Generation of American Historiography," AHA *Annual Report* (1917), pp. 350-54.

study in Europe. Son of an unsuccessful New England school teacher and postmaster, he attended Amherst College while living at home with his parents. Having no money to go abroad, he went to Johns Hopkins for graduate study. There, in 1882, he received the first Ph.D. it awarded in history; and there he was fired by a vision of the coming transformation of American scholarship by "the professorial class." Jameson absorbed Herbert Baxter Adams' zeal for the new Germanic methods, but he scorned his teacher's indiscriminate promotional activities, particularly his truckling to the "elderly swells who dabble in history." [26] Austere in manner and conscientious to a fault, Jameson resented deeply anything that smacked of pretentiousness, bias, or careless and hasty workmanship. In himself he cultivated a breadth of knowledge so wide and an accuracy so impeccable that—in the words of one of his oldest friends—"it was always an act of audacity to question the reliability of his statements." [27]

Jameson had many of the qualities of a great historical writer: massive learning, precision of expression, a penetrating understanding of motives, and a subtle sense of relationships. Why he abandoned historical writing when he was scarcely forty remains something of a mystery. Part of the explanation lies in the cautiousness and severity of his critical standards, which quarreled and contended with the constructive power of his ideas. He was, in this sense, our American Lord Acton. As a young man, Jameson wrote a great deal, including an impressive study of William Usselinx, for which he learned Dutch, some illuminating essays on historiography, and a brilliant series of lectures on the American Revolution, which with characteristic diffidence he left unpublished for thirty years. None of this satisfied him, and his confidence in his ability to do the big books he really valued failed before he could put it to a test.[28]

Whatever feelings of personal inadequacy prompted this surrender, his decision had the support of a historical rationale. Jameson believed that he lived in a period uncongenial to great individual

---

[26] Jameson, *An Historian's World*, p. 47. The best biographical sketches are in the introduction to this volume and in the *Dictionary of American Biography*, vol. XXII.

[27] Memo by Charles M. Andrews in AHA Files 1936-40, Box 23, Archives of American Historical Association (Library of Congress).

[28] Note the confessions of inadequacy in Jameson, *An Historian's World*, pp. 86, 125, and compare with the bibliography of his early publications in *Herbert B. Adams: Tributes of Friends*, pp. 80-82.

achievements in history. He compared his own era to the seventeenth century. Then as now, historical scholarship was advancing "more by extensive accumulation and critical sifting of the evidences than by new endeavors toward their interpretation." The time-spirit required historians to work within modest limits. Against the dryness of such an atmosphere, they might take comfort in recalling that when the earlier "Age of Erudition had done its work of accumulating and sifting evidence, there emerged upon the Europe of 1750 the coordinating and philosophical ideas of the *Aufklärung*."[29] So Jameson felt sustained by history as he turned away from creative effort and sought opportunities to guide and organize the work of Erudition.

In 1895, while teaching at Brown University, Jameson undertook both the editorship of the *American Historical Review* and the chairmanship of the Historical Manuscripts Commission. Thus he assumed central responsibility for mobilizing sources and for setting standards of publication. But how much could be accomplished in the vast documentary and bibliographical field without strong institutional support? Clearly, the voluntary efforts of men who stole a little time from their own teaching and writing would hardly suffice. Jameson was soon dreaming of a national center for historical research. The establishment of the Carnegie Institution of Washington in 1902 opened such a possibility; for the Institution was designed to promote research in the liberal arts and sciences, especially such fundamental projects as might lie beyond the scope of governmental support and beyond the strength of a particular university. Jameson headed the advisory committee that recommended a program for history.

Jameson's committee formulated a precise and extensive plan for coordinating professional scholarship in American history. The principal service of an endowed institution, Jameson always believed, should be to make unprinted sources accessible to others. The proposed center should therefore prepare reports and indexes of the manuscript materials in the federal archives in Washington. It should hire scholars to do the same for materials on American history in European archives. It should undertake a continuing program of editing and publishing important national documents, as the *Monumenta Germaniae Historica* had long done in Germany. Furthermore, the full-time director of the center should run a kind of

[29] Quoted in Barnes, *op. cit.*, p. 87.

clearinghouse for scholars throughout the country, advising them on research opportunities and keeping them informed of one another's work. The center should also include, on a rotating basis, professors on leave of absence from their universities, who would guide graduate students coming to Washington to work on theses.[30]

This last function never materialized. The trustees of the Carnegie Institution, intent on a purely research operation, vetoed any arrangement for the instruction of students. Otherwise, the committee's proposals were fully adopted. The trustees even permitted the director of their Department of Historical Research to edit the *American Historical Review* as one of his official duties; and in 1905, after Andrew McLaughlin had served for two years, Jameson came to Washington to assume both posts. From the outset he had about him a small group of young assistants, the chief of whom was Waldo G. Leland, one of his former students at Brown.

For twenty-five years the Carnegie Institution's Department of Historical Research pursued undeviatingly the goals set forth in the original plan. When funds permitted, the Department occasionally subsidized a professor's independent research; but the energies of the permanent staff and of most of its temporary appointees went exclusively into elaborating the apparatus for research. Before Jameson took over, the Department had already published a preliminary guide to the Washington archives of the federal government, had begun collecting the letters of the members of the Continental Congresses, and had sent Charles M. Andrews to England to survey the manuscript materials for early American history in the British Museum. The Department had also inaugurated in 1903 an indispensable annual bibliography of *Writings on American History.* Jameson carried these projects forward, adding others of a similar nature from time to time. Meanwhile, he gave time and advice freely to the many scholars who called at his office while visiting Washington, and maintained a prodigious correspondence with all who asked for counsel. In spite of his frosty exterior, Jameson incarnated the professional ethic of cooperation; and this, together with his meticulousness in detail, made him tireless in helping others less talented than himself.

Jameson's energies reached well beyond the official circle of his duties. As a service to graduate students and their advisers, he insti-

[30] Carnegie Institution of Washington, *Year Book* (1902).

tuted and maintained an annual list of historical dissertations in progress in American universities. Since the Carnegie Institution refused to continue the *Writings on American History,* Jameson each year scraped together private donations sufficient to pay for it.[31] In 1908 his right-hand man, Leland, became secretary of the American Historical Association, and thereafter the two offices functioned almost as one. As the chairman of successive AHA committees, Jameson kept a drum-fire of criticism on Congress for neglecting its historical responsibilities; and each incoming administration was confronted with his patient, courteous insistence on centralized management of the nation's archives.

No other foundation has ever given history the sustained support that the Carnegie Institution provided between 1903 and 1928; that it did so was largely due to Jameson's determination and prestige. The real interest of the president and trustees of the Institution lay in the natural sciences. The only humanistic disciplines that secured a regular place in its structure were history and economics, and the Department of Economics was virtually deprived of support within a decade. The president and trustees had doubts about Jameson's program too; yet they let it go ahead, with modest but regular increases in appropriations. This enabled Jameson to play a more central role in organizing historical research than anyone before or since. Libraries then lacked professional bibliographers, and governments lacked professional archivists. Encouraged by Jameson and others, the historical profession undertook the work of both. Soon professional historians were infiltrating state historical societies and spreading higher standards of documentary publication; as early as 1904 C. W. Alvord became editor of the *Illinois Historical Collections* published by the State Historical Library. Jameson's example and initiative must have counted for more than anyone now can measure.

Yet there were serious limitations in a program so largely devoted to the tools and materials of scholarship rather than its results. Jameson's Department never became, in the full sense, an institute of historical research. Its activities acquired, therefore, too routine a character. Jameson perceived some of the new problems and needs of scholarship that were developing in the years after 1907. But he was a modest man of settled habits and convictions, and so maintained the unchanging tenor of his ways. "I struggle on," he told

31 Jameson, *An Historian's World,* p. 314.

Henry Adams in 1910, "making bricks without much idea of how the architects will use them, but believing that the best architect that ever was cannot get along without bricks, and therefore trying to make good ones." [32] Many of the bricks produced in his kiln came forth with painful slowness. Leland, who began work in 1907 on a guide to materials for American history located in Paris, published the first volume in 1932. Completion of a historical atlas of the United States took even longer. One member of Jameson's staff, Edmund C. Burnett, spent almost thirty years editing the letters of the members of the Continental Congress. Another, Elizabeth Donnan, worked fifteen years before publishing the first volume of her *Documents Illustrative of the History of the Slave Trade*.[33] These were valuable, painstaking aids to American historiography. But long before they were completed other agencies, including the federal government, were doing work of similar kind and calibre; Jameson's Department of Historical Research no longer played an innovating role.

At last, in 1928, this sedate and dignified operation was brusquely terminated. Jameson retired at the request of the president of the Carnegie Institution. Projects still outstanding were put on a terminal basis, and the appropriation for history was transferred to the support of archaeology.[34] Jameson, now approaching seventy, moved to the Manuscripts Division of the Library of Congress, where he remained the wise and honored elder statesman of the historical profession. But the world of the American historian had now grown too various, complex, and disjoined to allow any one person to exercise the institutional leadership that Jameson provided in the early years of the century.

---

[32] *Ibid.*, p. 136.

[33] Waldo G. Leland and J. J. Meng, eds., *Guide to Materials for American History in the Libraries and Archives of Paris* (2 vols., 1932 and 1943); C. O. Paullin, *Atlas of the Historical Geography of the United States* (1932); Edmund C. Burnett, ed., *Letters of Members of the Continental Congress* (8 vols., 1921-38); Elizabeth Donnan, ed., *Documents Illustrative of the History of the Slave Trade to America* (4 vols., 1930-35).

[34] For much further detail see the annual *Year Books* of the Carnegie Institution.

GROWTH SINCE 1907

In the first decade of the twentieth century, when Jameson emerged as the administrative genius of the historical profession, it was relatively small and uncomplicated. Total membership in the American Historical Association came to something more than 2,000, of whom about 300 attended the annual meetings. No participant could miss the Association's still heavy involvement in the organization of historical work. The program regularly featured a conference of state and local historical societies, a session on the teaching of history, and reports of the Public Archives Commission and the Historical Manuscripts Commission. The sessions devoted to scholarly papers were neither numerous nor very diverse. A typical program might have one session on European history, two sessions on American history, and perhaps a session of a general topical nature cosponsored by another scholarly society meeting at the same place.[1]

A comparison with the present situation gives a measure of the altered scale of professional activity. Between 1907 and 1962 membership in the American Historical Association increased fivefold; and since distances have shrunk, the annual meeting attracted ten times as many registrants in 1962 as it had in 1907. Instead of one joint session, in 1962 nineteen cooperating societies participated. Instead of two sessions on American history, there were thirteen. Instead of one session on European history, about seventeen took place. Some fourteen additional sessions were given to ancient, Russian, Latin American, African, and Asian history. In this vast concourse of subject-matter specialists, some attention still went to curricular problems (two sessions) and to the reproduction of research materials (one session).[2] But these obviously occupied a minor place in the total program. While the range and variety of historical research had grown enormously, much of the responsibility for surveying and indexing historical documents had devolved into other hands. Profes-

[1] See, for example, AHA *Annual Reports* (1906-1908). ,
[2] "The Chicago Meeting, 1962," *AHR*, LXVIII (1963), 880-83.

sional librarians, archivists, and curators, through their own societies and journals, were now doing a large part of the job.

The growth of historical activity, except for interludes during the two world wars, had been steady. It had also, for a long while, been slow. The very rapid expansion of the historical profession that occurred at the turn of the century did not resume until after World War II. For many years membership in the American Historical Association, for example, remained relatively static. Having reached 2,700 in 1909, it never climbed above 3,000 until 1926, or above 3,500 until 1939. During a span of three decades, in other words, AHA membership increased only 30 per cent, although the total number of college teachers in the United States rose almost 500 per cent in the same period.[3] The big boom came in the late 1940's and 1950's. AHA membership spurted from 3,800 in 1945 to 9,400 in 1960. The Mississippi Valley Historical Association grew at a comparable rate. The number of students receiving doctoral degrees in history reached a prewar high of 162 in 1938; in 1960 it climbed to 375.[4] Scholarly books and articles poured from the presses in greater volume and in more fields than ever before.

The major shifts in the growth rate—its decline in the early twentieth century and its spectacular upswing in recent years—correlate with important changes in the historians' milieu. Subsequent chapters will take up those cultural changes, which may account for a loss of momentum in some sectors of the profession after 1907 and for a new vitality after 1945. Before entering into such hazardous questions, however, it is necessary to notice an underlying, cumulative improvement in the capabilities of the American historical profession. Beneath all fluctuations of talent, status, and outlook, the total research effort has steadily expanded throughout the twentieth century. This expansion has resulted from a continuous proliferation of the institutional support for professional historical work.

To that support many agencies contribute: universities, libraries, private historical societies, governments, and foundations. In fact,

[3] Bureau of the Census, *Historical Statistics of the United States: Colonial Times to 1957* (1960), p. 75. All membership figures come from AHA *Annual Reports*.
[4] Figures compiled from various volumes of *Doctoral Dissertations Accepted by American Universities* and from *Index to American Doctoral Dissertations, 1959-1960*.

variety of sponsorship and diversity of output have strikingly characterized historical research in the United States. The sprawling, multitudinous nature of the whole institutional complex is evident in both of its major components. One of these is an intricate communications network, which has widened access to sources and multiplied channels for scholarly publication. The other is the system of higher education, which has given more and more people livelihoods as teachers of history and incentives for research in the area of their teaching. Although the two spheres of activity have developed simultaneously and in close relation to one another, each deserves separate consideration.

Since the past cannot be invented, all historical inquiry depends on the sources that a scholar is willing and able to consult. These may be physical remains, oral testimony, or written records. Relatively few historians in America have paid serious attention to nonverbal sources—to pictures, monuments, and other physical marks of the past. Perhaps because ours has been so largely a culture of the word, our historians have generally been librarybound, and their first concern in research has been access to adequate libraries.

In the nineteenth century most historians in the United States necessarily studied local history, since only local collections were within reach. An occasional wealthy gentleman like Francis Parkman and Henry C. Lea might employ copyists in foreign capitals to supply him with material. Others like George Bancroft might make effective use of diplomatic appointments. One pioneering scholar, Jared Sparks, America's first full-time professor of history, secured from the U.S. Department of State the financial backing that enabled him in 1818 to visit archives in London, Brussels, and Paris.[5] But these were men with very special advantages. The transformation of American scholarship began in the late nineteenth century with the creation of great research libraries of wide scope, which admitted any properly qualified student.

The pacemaker was the Library of Congress under the leadership of Herbert Putnam. The son of a distinguished New York publisher,

[5] Herbert Baxter Adams, *The Life and Writings of Jared Sparks,* vol. II (1893), pp. 5-8, 42-51. On the further significance of this trip see C. K. Webster, "Some Early Applications from American Historians to Use the British Archives," *Journal of Modern History,* I (1929), 416 ff., and Galen Broeker, "Jared Sparks, Robert Peel, and the State Paper Office," *American Quarterly,* XIII (1961), 140-152.

Putnam illustrates again the fruitful impulse that an aristocracy of culture gave to the institutionalization of scholarship. Partly through chance and partly through a love of books, he became a director of public libraries, first in Minneapolis and then in Boston. In 1899, yielding to a sense of duty, he accepted a call to the Library of Congress. Putnam found it a cluttered, dingy, understaffed institution, concerned principally with serving Congress. He made it the national library, undergirding research everywhere in the country and standing—in his own words—"foremost as a model and example in assisting forward the work of scholarship in the United States." [6]

Two years after Putnam took charge, the Library of Congress inaugurated three path-breaking policies. It started distributing its printed catalog cards to other libraries, thereby creating a uniform system of cataloging. It built up, adjacent to its own card catalog, a national union catalog of books located in other major American libraries. And, most remarkably, Putnam announced the willingness of the Library of Congress to lend books to other libraries for the use of scholars at a distance from Washington. In all these ways the Library of Congress prompted the consolidation of scholarly activity on a national scale.

Simultaneously Putnam was helping the Library of Congress to become the great American repository of historical manuscripts. In 1902 he brought from Boston another distinguished patrician scholar, Worthington C. Ford, to head the recently created Division of Manuscripts. Ford soon launched a historical publications program with the first volume of the *Journals of the Continental Congress* (34 vols., 1904-37). With the aid of Jameson's Bureau of the Carnegie Institution, Putnam also amassed vast quantities of transcripts of manuscripts in foreign archives pertaining to early American history.

Elsewhere research libraries grew prodigiously under the auspices of the leading universities, some of the states, and many wealthy individuals. If independent gentlemen ceased to write the most important historical books, they compensated generously by providing the materials for others to use. The Harvard University Library, which

[6] David C. Mearns, *The Story Up to Now* (Librarian of Congress *Annual Report, 1945-46*), pp. 184-94. See also *National Cyclopedia of American Biography*, vol. IX, p. 249, and Herbert Putnam, "Relation of the National Library to Historical Research in the United States," *Educational Review*, XXIII (1902), 217-32.

had 577,000 books in 1900, contained 882,000 in 1910 and continued to receive outstanding collections. The New York Public Library, whose vast research holdings were acquired and sustained by private endowment, was organized in 1895. The Newberry Library, launched in Chicago in 1887, amassed great resources for British and American history and literature. The John Carter Brown Library of early American history opened as a semiautonomous institution at Brown University in 1904. The old private historical societies gradually extended a warmer welcome to outsiders who wished to use their specialized holdings.[7]

During the 1920's many special libraries were founded: the Pierpont Morgan Library in New York, strong in medieval manuscripts and incunabula; the William L. Clements Library in Ann Arbor, concentrating on early American history; the Folger Shakespeare Library in Washington, D.C.; the Henry E. Huntington Library in southern California, emphasizing Tudor and Stuart England; and the Hoover Library at Palo Alto, California, specializing in modern international relations. A more recent creation, the Dumbarton Oaks Research Library in Washington, D.C., which Mr. and Mrs. Robert Woods Bliss gave to Harvard University in 1940, has made possible a tremendous upswing in Byzantine studies. All of these institutions take pains to serve visiting researchers. Some of them even attract foreign scholars who gladly come to the New World to study the Old.

Increasingly, the research libraries were staffed by professional librarians trained in library schools that excelled those in any other country. The new librarians, following in the footsteps of bookmen and amateur bibliophiles like Richard Rogers Bowker, developed the elaborate bibliographical guides and indexes that have become so indispensable to recent scholarly work. Before the 1920's, for example, there were virtually no general lists of the location of newspapers, periodicals, and manuscripts. Today, at any considerable library, a scholar can learn a great deal about the special resources of any other. In the last decade, as a consequence of foundation support

[7] Arthur E. Bestor Jr., "The Transformation of American Scholarship, 1875-1917," *Library Quarterly*, XXIII (1953), 164-79; Walter Muir Whitehill, *Independent Historical Societies* (1962), especially pp. 20-22. The Harvard statistics are taken from the Harvard University *Reports of the Librarian,* 1900, p. 217, and 1910, p. 7.

and increased cooperation among research libraries, progress toward national bibliographical control has been more rapid than ever before.[8] The Council on Library Resources, a subsidiary of the Ford Foundation created in 1956, has made possible such splendid projects as the *National Union Catalog of Manuscript Collections* (1962-   ). The American Historical Association, under the energetic secretaryship (1953-63) of Boyd Shafer, has recovered an active role in such projects. Shafer secured over a million dollars in grants for special aids to research and teaching.[9]

Together with these improvements in bibliographical armament, historians have acquired in recent years the means to conquer distance. The movement of the historian to his sources, and of the sources to the historian, proceeds on a scale and with an ease scarcely imaginable forty years ago. Although a handful of universities provided sabbatical leaves in the 1890's, before World War I very few academic scholars had both the time and the money to travel to distant archives; most of their research rested entirely on printed sources.[10]

In the prosperous 1920's, sabbaticals became widely available and research grants also materialized in more than exceptional cases. The John Simon Guggenheim Foundation, uniquely and exclusively devoted to the support of talented individuals, began its distinguished career in 1925, and over the next decade made more grants in history than in any other field.[11] The new Social Science Research Council, financed with Rockefeller money, inaugurated a program of research fellowships in the same year. It too subsidized at least as many historians as scholars in other disciplines. In 1930 the American Council of Learned Societies, a federation of national societies representing many disciplines, acquired sufficient foundation funds to

---

[8] Robert B. Downs, *American Library Resources, A Bibliographical Guide: Supplement, 1950-1961* (1962), p. vii.

[9] Boyd C. Shafer, "Partial List of Expanded, Renewed or New Activities Since 1953" (mimeographed report).

[10] C. W. Alvord, "The New History," *Nation*, XCIV (1912), 458; T. F. Tout, "History and Historians in America," *Transactions of the Royal Historical Society*, fourth series, XII (1929), 1-17.

[11] Lewis B. Cooper, *Sabbatical Leave for College Teachers* ("University of Florida Education Series," vol. I, 1932), p. 9; Bernard Peach, "John Simon Guggenheim Memorial Foundation: Investment in Free Individuals," *South Atlantic Quarterly*, LX (1961), 151, 202.

award its first postdoctoral fellowships, usually for travel abroad.[12] After World War II these and other opportunities, notably the Fulbright awards that sent American students and scholars to many foreign lands, increased prodigiously. Sixty Americans attended the International Congress of Historical Sciences at Paris in 1950; ten years later 170 Americans went to the Congress at Stockholm,[13] and it is doubtful that any large number of these paid their own way across the Atlantic. The American historian had become a global traveller.

Thanks to technology, historical records acquired a still more remarkable mobility. New machines enabled the historian to bring exact copies of many of his sources to his own study instead of going to them. The photocopying of historical records originated sometime before World War I, but it remained too costly to have any considerable application in individual research. The most ambitious of the early undertakings was carried out between 1927 and 1932, when John D. Rockefeller Jr. gave the Library of Congress $450,000 to acquire from various European archives nearly two million photostats of documents bearing on early American history.[14] Then, in the late 1930's, far cheaper techniques of photoreproduction—microfilm and microcard—became available. With the generous support of foundations, vast programs of microfilming materials in foreign archives began during World War II and continued with the aid of Fulbright scholars in subsequent years.[15] American libraries, learned societies, and commercial enterprises such as University Microfilms, published and sold photocopied editions of large categories of sources. By 1960 a revolution in the distribution of research materials had occurred, though its end was not yet in sight.

The more sources historians had at their command, the more out-

---

[12] Roy F. Nichols, "History and the Social Science Research Council," *AHR*, L (1945), 493; Waldo G. Leland, "The American Council of Learned Societies and Its Relation to Humanistic Studies," *Proceedings of the American Philosophical Society*, LXXI (1932), 179-89.

[13] *AHR*, LVI (1951), 746; LXVI (1961), 891.

[14] Elizabeth Donnan and Leo F. Stock, eds., *An Historian's World: Selections from the Correspondence of John Franklin Jameson* (Memoirs of the American Philosophical Society, vol. 42, 1956), pp. 335, 351-52.

[15] George L. Anderson, "Mechanical Aids in Historical Research," in *In Support of Clio: Essays in Memory of Herbert A. Kellar*, ed. William B. Hesseltine and Donald R. McNeil (1958), pp. 80-91; Homer C. Hockett, *The Critical Method in Historical Research and Writing* (1955), pp. 261-63.

lets they needed for publishing their researches. In the early years of the historical profession, such facilities were meager. Commercial publishers printed the best scholarly books, and one of them, G. P. Putnam, rendered a signal service between 1885 and 1910 by publishing reasonably accurate editions of the writings of the Founding Fathers. Four or five universities instituted presses in the 1890's for the benefit of their own faculty and graduate students.[16] Otherwise, professional historians had virtually no vehicle, except the annual reports of the American Historical Association and its *Review,* capable of reaching a nationwide scholarly audience.

The effective development of university presses as agencies of the whole academic community dates from the founding of the Yale University Press in 1908 by a New York broker, George Parmly Day. He welcomed manuscripts from all scholars, regardless of their institutional connections; and he published serious books of general intellectual interest in addition to research studies. In the 1920's a dozen universities organized presses; the output of university presses more than doubled; and the best of them, following Yale's example, advertised widely and served not merely as organs but as ornaments of their respective institutions. By 1960 there were about fifty university presses, and they accounted for about 10 per cent of the new titles published annually in the United States.[17]

Meanwhile, a phenomenal multiplication of the number of periodicals publishing professional historical research was under way. For professors of American history the long-established organs of the state and private historical societies furnished outlets once their editors became receptive to professional work. Before World War I the amateur societies confined themselves almost entirely to printing documents and the writings and addresses of their own members. The rising influence and insatiable needs of professional scholars have since turned these journals to an ever-growing diet of scholarly articles. In 1925 one-sixth of the contributors to five leading state historical journals were academic people. Thirty years later two-thirds of the contributors to the same journals had academic connections.[18]

[16] George H. Putnam, *Memories of a Publisher, 1865-1915* (1915), pp. 67-71; Chester Kerr, *A Report on American University Presses* (1949), pp. 17-19.

[17] Nelson A. Crawford, "American University Presses," *American Mercury,* XVIII (1929), 210-14; Helen L. Sears, *American University Presses Come of Age* (1959), p. 12.

[18] Based on a tabulation of the contributors to the following journals at ten-year

Meanwhile the professionals were also creating their own specialized organs. Some of these spoke for new scholarly societies; others came from the initiative and dedication of a single man. All of them arose from a desire to foster some previously neglected domain of historical knowledge. Among the earlier additions, the *Catholic Historical Review* (1916) reflected the incipient professionalization of Catholic historiography under the auspices of The Catholic University of America. The *Hispanic-American Historical Review* (1918) was founded by Professor Charles E. Chapman with funds supplied by a wealthy San Franciscan of Mexican descent. *Isis* (transplanted to the United States in 1922) was part of George Sarton's heroic labors in behalf of a professional history of science. The Twenties saw the launching of *Speculum* by the new Mediaeval Academy of America, *Agricultural History* by the Agricultural History Society, the *Journal of Economic and Business History* by the Business History Society, the *New England Quarterly* by a group of Harvard professors with aid from the Colonial Society of Massachusetts, and the *Journal of Modern History* by the University of Chicago Press. The Institute of the History of Medicine, created at Johns Hopkins University in 1929 with funds from the Rockefeller Foundation, established the *Bulletin of the History of Medicine*. The list of scholarly journals has since lengthened steadily, particularly under the influence of the interdisciplinary activities represented by such publications as the *Journal of the History of Ideas* (1940), the *Far Eastern Quarterly* (1941), the *American Quarterly* (1949), *Comparative Studies in Society and History* (1958), and *History and Theory* (1960). Today, instead of lacking outlets, a historian writing on almost any subject can choose among several.

What stands out in this extraordinary proliferation of the institutions of scholarship is the diversity of initiative and the relative weakness of centralized direction. Virtually every new development has democratized the opportunities for research achievement. In recent years, it is true, the American Historical Association and other agencies have striven to improve coordination of scholarly activity. But

---

intervals from 1925 to 1955: *Ohio Archaeological and Historical Quarterly, North Carolina Historical Review, Pennsylvania Magazine of History and Biography, Wisconsin Magazine of History,* and *Proceedings of the Massachusetts Historical Society.*

nowhere, since Jameson's heyday, has a single focus of authority and leadership materialized. Instead of a national center of historical research, Americans have created their own peculiar welter of voluntary associations, special projects, and particular agencies. Characteristically, the federal government has been exceedingly slow and hesitant in sponsoring historical inquiry. When Congress in 1958 finally provided some "National Defense" fellowships for graduate students in the social sciences, it acted on the quixotically democratic assumption that too few universities were producing the scientists and scholars of the future.[19] The National Defense fellowships have served therefore to decentralize still more the pattern of scholarly activity.

The reluctance of the federal government to assume historical responsibilities dogged Jameson at every step in his lifelong campaign for federal expenditures in behalf of history. As early as 1891 he pointed out that the United States gave less official care to the publication of historical documents, and to the preservation of unpublished records, than did even the smaller countries of western Europe. Yet his repeated insistence on centralized management of the nation's archives did not bear fruit until 1934, three years before his death, when the great National Archives Building on Pennsylvania Avenue was at last completed, and the principal records of all branches of the federal government became available to scholars in one efficient establishment.[20]

Jameson's desire for a systematic, governmental program of publishing historical documents proved even more difficult to realize. A few specialized projects, notably the long-established series "Foreign Relations of the United States" (1861-   ), did enjoy official sponsorship, though even "Foreign Relations" was not edited by a trained historian until 1921. Four years later, on Jameson's recommendation, Congress authorized publication of the *Territorial Papers of the United States* (25 vols., 1934-60), a task to which Clarence E. Carter devoted a lifetime of meticulous care. Another

[19] U.S. Office of Education, *Guide to the National Defense Education Act of 1958* (1959), pp. 11-12.
[20] J. F. Jameson, "Expenditures of Foreign Governments in Behalf of History," AHA *Annual Report* (1891), pp. 33-61; J. F. Jameson and Edward Channing, *The Present State of Historical Writing in America* (1910), pp. 5-10; G. Philip Bauer, "Public Archives in the United States," in *In Support of Clio*, pp. 65-67.

suggestion from Jameson prompted publication by Congress of *The Writings of George Washington*, edited by John C. Fitzpatrick (39 vols., 1931-44).[21]

Beyond these piecemeal ventures, Jameson strove to interest the United States in maintaining a permanent commission on national historical publications. His plan fell on deaf ears when a committee of leading historians recommended it in 1908, and made little headway when the American Historical Association urged it again in the 1920's.[22] The idea finally came alive in the 1950's—not because the federal government was prepared to assume real responsibility but because a number of private sponsors for grand documentary publications were appearing.

The precipitating factor was issuance in 1950 of the first volume of Julian Boyd's masterly *Writings of Thomas Jefferson*, underwritten by the *New York Times* in conjunction with the Princeton University Press. On this occasion, Wayne C. Grover, head of the National Archives, interested President Truman in making a call for a broad national program of works such as Boyd's. As a result, a National Historical Publications Commission, which had been quietly authorized in the National Archives Act of 1934, was reorganized and brought to life. The Commission, composed of public dignitaries as well as historians, was charged with laying plans for important documentary publications. After a general survey of needs and opportunities, it has initiated and sought sponsors for a large number of projects, chiefly critical editions of the papers of American statesmen.[23] Universities, foundations, and business enterprises are providing most of the funds. Not until 1964 did Congress make federal money available to the Commission for grants in aid of these important works. The success of the whole campaign is another indication of the dependence of American historical scholarship on dispersed and disparate auspices.

[21] Jameson, *An Historian's World*, pp. 308, 364-65; Richard W. Leopold, "A Centennial Estimate," summarized in *AHR*, LXVII (1962), 860.
[22] Clarence E. Carter, "The United States and Documentary Historical Publication," *Mississippi Valley Historical Review*, XXV (1938), 3-24.
[23] "Historical Activities," *Mississippi Valley Historical Review*, XLVIII (1961), 176-77; John Tebbel, "Safeguarding U.S. History," *Saturday Review*, XLV (June 23, 1962), 24-25, 52; "The Reminiscences of Guy Stanton Ford" (Oral History Research Office, Columbia University, 1956), pp. 892-94; "The Reminiscences of Solon J. Buck" (Oral History Research Office, Columbia University, 1957), pp. 16-19.

Since the 1930's the federal government has employed substantial numbers of historians, particularly in the Defense Department and the National Park Service. Nevertheless, seven out of eight Ph.D.'s in history make their careers in colleges and universities.[24] So the fundamental economic basis for the growth of the historical profession has been a massive spread of college education. Without the jobs and the research incentives thereby provided, the demand for sources and publication outlets would have been far weaker. Consequently it is useful, in following the expanding content of historical scholarship in the twentieth century, to keep always in mind the flexible and expanding character of the educational setting.

By the beginning of the twentieth century American universities conventionally taught ancient, European, and American history; and the first task of research was to establish a sound basis of scholarship within those fields. The earliest efforts of professional scholars were concentrated overwhelmingly in American history, for which original sources were most accessible and patriotic motives strong. Almost nine-tenths of the historical dissertations written in American universities in the Eighties and Nineties dealt with native subjects. Herbert Baxter Adams insisted on the title Professor of Institutional History rather than Professor of American History, but he assigned American thesis topics even to students like Charles Homer Haskins and Charles D. Hazen, who became distinguished European historians.[25] Jameson deliberately limited the work of his Department of Historical Research at the Carnegie Institution to American history, although his own knowledge and interests ranged far beyond. In the early years most of the contributors to the *American Historical Review* wrote about American history, which still received as late as the 1920's slightly more space than European history. The period from 1900 to World War I, however, marked the emergence of outstanding professional scholars in the principal non-American fields.

At first ancient history was taught chiefly in classics departments,

[24] *Report and Recommendations of the Committee of the American Historical Association on the Historian and the Federal Government* (mimeographed report, n.d. [1952?]); Dexter Perkins and John L. Snell, *The Education of Historians in the United States* (1961), p. 21.

[25] *Ibid.*, p. 30; W. Stull Holt, ed., *Historical Scholarship in the United States, 1876-1901* (1938), pp. 145-46. Other men who became prominent European historians after writing dissertations on American subjects included James Harvey Robinson, Robert L. Schuyler, William Shepherd, E. R. Turner, and E. P. Cheyney.

for it grew out of philological and archaeological studies already transplanted from Germany during the nineteenth century. The gentleman-classicist Charles Eliot Norton inspired the American School of Classical Studies at Athens (1881), which supplied graduate fellowships and a base for excavations.[26] Another American School of Classical Studies followed in Rome in 1895. Of America's pioneer ancient historians, both Tenney Frank and William Lynn Westermann got their training in Latin literature in the late Nineties and later shifted to history. In a series of magnificent books, Frank combined literature, history, and archaeology to interpret Roman civilization as a whole. On the other hand, America's first outstanding authority on Greek history, William Scott Ferguson, was from the outset a political historian. In three major books published between 1899 and 1913, he added significantly to the history of Athens and Greek imperialism.

The greatest of America's ancient historians, James Henry Breasted, developed from a background in biblical rather than classical philology. As a student in a midwestern theological seminary, he became fascinated with Hebrew and doubtful of Christianity. He transferred to Yale, whence his Hebrew professor sent him to Berlin for training in Egyptology; this resulted in a Ph.D. thesis (1894) on the solar hymns of Ikhnaton. Like Tenney Frank, Breasted mastered archaeological, literary, and official documentary sources. His *History of Egypt* (1905), the first scholarly, well-balanced history of the ancient Nile, was still the standard work at the time of his death thirty years later. His *Development of Religion and Thought in Ancient Egypt* (1912) expounded an exciting interpretation of the evolution of moral ideas. After World War I he developed the great Oriental Institute at the University of Chicago and gave most of his attention to its archaeological excavations in the Near East.[27]

Important professional scholarship in medieval history also began around the turn of the century. Although the American medievalists did not write on the scale that Breasted, Frank, and later Michael Rostovtzeff achieved in ancient history, they did distinguished work

[26] Louis E. Lord, *A History of the American School of Classical Studies at Athens, 1882-1942* (1947), pp. 1-48.
[27] W. F. Albright, "James Henry Breasted, Humanist," *American Scholar*, V (1936), 287-99. On Frank see *Dictionary of American Biography*, vol. XXII, pp. 203-205; on Westermann, American Philosophical Society *Year Book* (1955), pp. 509-12.

at an equally early date. Perhaps the first significant monographs were Charles Gross's dissertation on *The Gild Merchant* (1890), done at Göttingen, and Charles M. Andrews' *Old English Manors* (1892). Gross, the first Harvard historian to contribute to the literature of European history, inaugurated a great bibliographical enterprise with the publication in 1900 of *The Sources and Literature of English History to About 1485*. (Cooperation between the Royal Historical Society and the American Historical Association has carried this forward to the nineteenth century, but the series is only today approaching completion.) Other American medieval historians, notably L. J. Paetow, have also helped to confirm the prophetic remark that Jameson made back in 1891: "No nation in the world is so addicted to bibliography and indexing." [28]

Like Gross and Andrews, most of the early American medievalists concentrated on English history. England was the most accessible country with a medieval past, and its history before 1600 seemed peculiarly our own. As the principal source of American liberty and the incarnation of tradition, stability, and conservative social evolution, English institutions made a powerful appeal to the American aristocracy of culture. In 1900, George Burton Adams, who built Yale's Department of History practically from scratch, announced in the *American Historical Review* an impressive interpretation of the evolution of limited monarchy from the feudal principles preserved in Magna Carta. To Adams, the survival of feudal restraints upon power saved England from absolutism. Ultimately Adams synthesized this and many other contributions in his *Constitutional History of England* (1921), the first full-scale treatment after Maitland. Charles H. McIlwain's Harvard dissertation, *The High Court of Parliament* (1910), was perhaps an even more seminal book. Meanwhile, Charles Homer Haskins, surely the most learned and energetic of American medievalists, a full professor at Wisconsin at the age of twenty-two, was also studying Norman institutions; but Haskins ransacked archives across Europe and pursued the Normans wherever they had gone. His *Norman Institutions* (1918) remains the standard treatise on the subject.[29]

[28] J. F. Jameson, *The History of Historical Writing in America* (1891), p. 151. A good summary of Gross's career is in *Proceedings of the Massachusetts Historical Society,* XLIX (1916), 161-66.
[29] Reginald E. Rabb, "George Burton Adams," in *Some Modern Historians of*

Haskins' work illustrates another striking characteristic of American medieval scholarship. In contrast to the insularity of English historians leading Americans had, even in the Anglophile atmosphere of the early twentieth century, an unusual freedom from national or local parochialism. American scholars studied trans-European movements, and sought to grasp medieval civilization as a whole. Institutionalists moved in an increasingly comparative direction, which led to McIlwain's brilliant analysis of the medieval estates in the *Cambridge Medieval History* (vol. VII, 1932). Dana C. Munro awakened—first at Wisconsin where he taught from 1902 to 1915, then at Princeton—a strong American interest in the Crusades. Munro thought of the Crusading movement as a frontier of European expansion and in that sense analogous to American experience. Until very recently his students and disciples have maintained Crusading history as a feature of American medieval scholarship. After World War I the rise of intellectual history turned attention to another kind of contact between Eastern and Western civilizations. Haskins, deserting the Normans, became the principal authority on the transmission of Greek and Arabic learning to western Europe, while Columbia's Lynn Thorndike launched a massive *History of Magic and Experimental Science* (8 vols., 1923-58).[30]

Modern European studies have their own place later in this book. It is sufficient here to say that they too were established on a professional basis around the beginning of the century, but progress was slower than in the medieval field. Modern European history, especially since the Reformation, did not attract much interest and ability until after World War I. Of nearly four hundred articles printed in the *American Historical Review* before 1915, only eight related to nineteenth century Europe. As late as the 1920's Harvard turned out more Ph.D.'s in medieval history than in modern European.[31]

Beyond the standard subjects, the only history that took hold at a

Britain, ed. Herman Ausubel (1951), pp. 177-91; F. M. Powicke, *Modern Historians and the Study of History* (London, 1955), pp. 109-17.
30 This discussion owes much to an illuminating conversation with Professor J. R. Strayer on medieval historiography.
31 W. Stull Holt, "Historical Scholarship," in *American Scholarship in the Twentieth Century*, ed. Merle Curti (1953), p. 102; Samuel Eliot Morison, ed., *The Development of Harvard University Since the Inauguration of President Eliot, 1869-1929* (1930), p. 164; Charles H. Haskins, "European History and American Scholarship," *AHR*, XXVIII (1923), 215-27.

number of universities in the early twentieth century was Latin American. This was partly because of the contemporary interest in empire and the rapid extension of U.S. power. Moreover, Latin American history abutted directly on European as well as American history; it lay in a sense between them. Just as medievalists worked into continental Europe from a background in English history, so the early Latin Americanists worked into their field from a starting point either in American or in European history. Like the Europeanists, the first generation of Latin American scholars was preoccupied with the early (or colonial) period at the expense of the modern (or national) period. Their attention centered on the origin of institutions and on the theme of expansion into frontier areas. The first important book was Edward G. Bourne's contribution to the American Nation series, *Spain in America, 1450-1580* (1904), a book that reflected the American historians' interest in the transmission and modification of European institutions.[32]

At the University of California, whose three specialists in Latin American history made it the leading center of study, Herbert E. Bolton developed after 1911 the dominant school in the United States. He attracted many students into research on Spanish soldiers and missionaries in the borderlands, where Spanish settlement impinged on that of other empires. These studies gave Bolton the idea that all of the Americas had a unitary history shaped by common experiences. Every year he preached this pan-American doctrine to a thousand students in his course on the History of the Americas, and his numerous disciples took up the refrain.[33] Bolton lacked the analytical ability to make his concept fruitful; he gave a specious appearance of significance to a program of fragmentary research. Latin American historiography attained less intellectual maturity than European. The only truly outstanding book was Roger B. Merriman's *The Rise of the Spanish Empire* (3 vols., 1918-27), and this derived from an interest in Europe. As a student of early modern Europe, Merriman saw the Spanish Empire as a natural continuation of medieval institutions, not as a product of New World conditions.

While original scholarship was developing in ancient, European,

[32] Charles Gibson and Benjamin Keen, "Trends of United States Studies in Latin American History," *AHR*, LXII (1957), 856-59.
[33] Philip C. Brooks, "Do the Americas Share a Common History?" *Revista de historia de America*, XXXIII (1952), 75-83; Arthur P. Whitaker, *The Western Hemisphere Idea: Its Rise and Decline* (1954).

and Latin American history, the content of American higher education was steadily widening in all directions, most especially toward the present. An increasingly pragmatic attention to current problems and to the experience of the contemporary world was apparent before World War I. Thereafter this trend spread through the whole educational system. The expansion of historical scholarship proceeded mainly along similar lines. The most striking increase of effort after 1917 occurred in recent history, in the penetration of areas outside of western Europe and America, and in the numerous interdisciplinary interests an exploding curriculum produced.

A new course that embodied these objectives, a course usually entitled History of Western Civilization, became the staple of historical instruction between the two world wars. At Columbia College, where it originated in 1919, the course was named Contemporary Civilization.[34] Everywhere it emphasized recent history and the spread of European influences throughout the world. Everywhere it endeavored to bring the multiplicity of modern knowledge within a unifying historical perspective. Thus "Western Civ" renewed the function of the historian as a generalist in a present-minded culture. It did much to save history from the pedagogical decline that philosophy—another generalizing discipline—was undergoing. Although it did not arrest specialization in research, the teaching of Western Civilization surely encouraged the newer areas of research into which historians were moving.

A dramatic increase of activity in modern European history after World War I was only one manifestation of the shift of historical and educational interests toward the present. The balance of effort also shifted within the better established fields. The study of American colonial history suffered while modern American history boomed. In English history, through the work of Wallace Notestein and Conyers Read, the most distinguished American scholarship now concerned the Tudor and Stuart rather than the medieval period. In Latin American history a virtually exclusive preoccupation with the colonial period gave way to a new attention to the nineteenth and twentieth centuries.

As recent times came to the fore, the spectrum of historical scholarship widened to embrace the whole non-Western and semi-Western

[34] Arthur M. Schlesinger, "The History Situation in Colleges and Universities," *Historical Outlook*, XI (1920), 103-106.

world that was pressing in upon the United States. Slowly between the wars, and then with pell-mell speed since 1945, Russian history, east Asian history, and Islamic history have crowded upon the American academic scene.

The entry of professional scholarship into these areas followed the pattern we have glimpsed in the development of Latin American history. Historians gradually reached outward from established academic interests and appropriated the related or similar aspects of a new area. Thus the few American historians before World War II who wrote on Russian and Asian history stressed the Western aspects of the former and the Westernization of the latter, with special attention to diplomatic relations with the West. As in medieval and Latin American history, the theme of expansion appealed to Americans. Apparently the first American monograph on Russian history was Frank Golder's *Russian Expansion on the Pacific, 1641-1850* (1914), and possibly the most important American contribution to Chinese history before World War II was Owen Lattimore's *The Inner Asian Frontiers of China* (1940).[35]

In the 1920's and 1930's European dictatorships drove into exile many scholars trained outside the American historiographical tradition and capable therefore of widening its scope and enriching its substance. The emigré professors brought with them a more intimate understanding of cultures that American scholars had viewed from the perspective of the outsider, who can observe external forms more readily than their inner spirit. Not only Russia and the Far East, but also many other neglected fields of knowledge benefited. One of the early arrivals, Alexander Vasiliev, imported Byzantine history to America. Fleeing from Hitler, Ernst Kantorowicz brought an unprecedented grasp of medieval intellectual history. Stephan Kuttner's Institute of Canon Law at The Catholic University of America raised medieval church history to an importance it had lacked due to native preoccupation with American church history. In Spanish history a scholar uprooted by Franco, Americo Castro, revealed an endogenous pattern of development that Americans surely would not themselves have perceived. In the Russian field, Michael Karpovich at Harvard trained a new generation of American scholars, and

[35] John S. Curtiss, "History," in *American Research on Russia,* ed. Harold H. Fisher (1959), p. 23; Charles O. Hucker, *Chinese History: A Bibliographic Review* (1958), *passim.*

George Vernadsky at Yale wrote a monumental *History of Russia* (vols. 1-4, 1943-59) from the point of view of its internal dynamics. For the Far East, perhaps the most remarkable contribution came from Karl A. Wittfogel and Feng Chia-sheng. Their *History of Chinese Society: Liao* (1949) disproved conclusively the hoary idea that the Chinese had always assimilated their conquerors. Wittfogel went on to make a daring comparative analysis of *Oriental Despotism* (1957).

In the 1930's a second impetus quickened the expansion of historical scholarship into areas beyond America and western Europe. Foundations and scholarly organizations became concerned about the allegedly narrow scope of humanistic scholarship in the United States. The American Council of Learned Societies exercised decisive leadership. Sparked by Mortimer Graves, who later became its executive secretary, the ACLS in the early Thirties created "development committees" to promote underdeveloped fields of knowledge—Chinese, Japanese, Indic-Iranian, Byzantine, and Latin American among them.[36] The ACLS, a loose federation of learned bodies dominated by the humanities, had struggled along with scant support from the large foundations, whose humanistic interests rarely extended beyond the photogenic glamor of archaeology. Now the prospect of awakening America to an understanding of far-away peoples touched a responsive chord, particularly at the Rockefeller Foundation where international cooperation was an article of faith. Persuaded that humanistic studies were too largely snobbish and antiquarian, the Rockefeller Foundation decided to help culture become more "democratic and inclusive." [37] Its support made possible special conferences on non-Western areas, intensive language courses, traveling fellowships, and annual bibliographies (e.g., *Handbook of Latin American Studies,* 1936-). Initially, the dominant concern was with language training; very few of the American professors who wrote about the Far East knew any Far Eastern language. By the

[36] Kenneth Scott Latourette, "Far Eastern Studies in the United States," *Far Eastern Quarterly,* XV (1955), 6; American Council of Learned Societies, Committee on the Promotion of Chinese Studies, *Progress of Chinese Studies in the U.S.A.* (1931); Lewis Hanke, "The Development of Latin American Studies in the U.S., 1939-1945," *Americas,* IV (1947), 33.
[37] Raymond B. Fosdick, *The Story of the Rockefeller Foundation* (1952), pp. 239-42.

end of the Thirties the intriguing term *area programs* was beginning to circulate.

World War II dramatically forced the pace and altered the character of area studies. As in no previous war, American forces were deployed everywhere in the world. Suddenly the need for access to non-European societies became enormous. The federal government intervened in the history of scholarship on a massive scale. Army and Navy training programs and subsequent overseas experience gave a vocation to many of the young men who now—no longer young— are assuming leadership in area studies. The State Department promoted an exchange of professors with various countries and attached cultural officers to many embassies. The Library of Congress vastly augmented its resources in Asian, Russian, and Latin American fields. Many professors served in Washington agencies, where the need to answer immediate questions about a particular area convinced them of the value of pooling information controlled by several disciplines.[38] Ever since, historical scholarship in the "underdeveloped" fields has had a markedly interdisciplinary character.

In this respect the underdeveloped fields were not entirely unique. The urge to combine several disciplines for the understanding of a civilization as a whole goes back a long way. Ancient historians had always thought of themselves primarily as classical scholars or as Orientalists, as the case might be; and since the establishment of the Mediaeval Academy of America in 1925 medieval historians have increasingly identified themselves as medievalists. The distinctive feature of the area studies stimulated by World War II, however, was the utilitarian and contemporary stamp that the war put upon them. Programs initiated in the Thirties under literary, linguistic, and historical auspices passed, as a result of the war, chiefly into the hands of social scientists. This has created an educational pattern that now attracts to the study of Russian, Asian, and Latin American history students interested in analytical relationships and comparative generalizations. They try to understand the indigenous society in its own terms instead of seeing it merely in the perspective of Western expansion; but their social-science training has also given them a strong interest in testing general social theories.

[38] Philip E. Mosely, "The Growth of Russian Studies," in *American Research on Russia,* pp. 1-22; Hanke, *op. cit.,* pp. 32-35.

By the 1960's Persian history, African history, and comparative tropical history had found a place in the repertoire of American scholarship; its global embrace was virtually complete. Meanwhile, the range of human activities included in historiography had expanded as phenomenally as its geographical scope. At first, professional historians confined themselves in practice to certain kinds of political and economic subjects. Eventually, they learned to write about child-rearing habits, mass hysterias, and events in the laboratory. Like the movement into new geographical areas, the topical expansion of history has proceeded more or less consciously along interdisciplinary lines; and it too has reached a point at which further enlargement of the realm of history seems hardly possible.

Topically as well as geographically, historical scholarship expanded by reaching out from a familiar subject to the contiguous fringes of the unfamiliar. Thus political historians, on turning to economic history, initially concentrated on the economic operations of government; institutional historians, attracted to educational history, first studied educational organizations rather than the content of instruction; social historians drawn to the history of science could understand its social context more readily than its theoretical structure. In time, professional historians found their way closer to the center of these topics; and scholars inside the relevant disciplines assisted them, much as foreign-born historians helped Americans to penetrate unfamiliar areas.

The spread of professional history into new types of human activity is not so clearly visible a process as its chronological and geographical extension. New area-histories almost automatically crystallized into coherent divisions of historical knowledge; for each area possessed a culture and a tradition that needed to be understood in its own terms before it could be related satisfactorily to the history of other areas. But the addition of new topics to any single area-history produced in most cases a much more fluid situation. Most of the neglected strands of social and cultural activity that twentieth century historians uncovered were so interwoven with other strands of the same area-history that clear-cut specialization has been arbitrary and artificial. Certain labels, like *social history* or *intellectual history,* proved necessary, of course. Since no historian could be equally receptive to all phases of human activity, we needed convenient indicators of the wavelengths to which individual historians

46

were most attuned. But the labels seldom designated a coherent sphere of reality, and they have sometimes confined the historian instead of clarifying history. In practice, historians have widened their coverage of an area in response to changing interpretations of it; and have embraced whatever range of data their own sensitivity permitted or their interpretive pattern suggested.

Sometimes, however, a topical strand virtually requires a more distinct specialization, involving the whole career of many scholars. This is the case when professional historians become interested in the development of an organized body of skills and knowledge. Like constitutional law or the practice of medicine, an appropriate subject must, of course, affect powerfully many other strands of history and thus need the attention of the professional historian, not just the subject specialist; yet the topic must also present such technical difficulties that general historical syntheses cannot do it justice. These conditions are most apparent, and most conducive to historical specialization, when a body of skills and knowledge has had a continuous internal development, transcending the histories of individual countries and belonging therefore to no one of them. Two examples of such specialties will serve the present discussion: military history and the history of science.

The history of warfare and of science deserve to rank as important branches of professional historical scholarship. Both war and science exert a major impact on civilization; and both depend on an elaborate development of theory and technique on the part of a dedicated elite over many centuries. Although international in character, each takes a coloration from the society that contains it. Americans have written military history at least since Increase Mather's *Brief History of the War with the Indians in New England* (1676), and the history of science since Samuel Miller's *Brief Retrospect of the Eighteenth Century* (1803). In the twentieth century each has become a branch of professional history. Of the two, military history is the less recondite; yet the history of science, for all of its difficulty, has established itself more easily in the American historical profession.

Until the twentieth century the history of science suffered from polemical enthusiasm and from fragmentation. Those who treated the theme broadly celebrated the progressive triumph of science over religious superstition; specialists confined themselves to histories of the separate sciences. At one extreme stood such hagiographic works

47

as Andrew Dickson White's *History of the Warfare of Science with Theology* (1896); at the other were monumental compendia like Florian Cajori's *History of Mathematical Notations* (2 vols., 1928-29).

Twentieth century historians have had the task of working out a general history of science that would be more than a one-sided story of progress, and more too than the sum of the histories of the separate disciplines. Although the foundations of such a history were laid in Europe, since World War I some of the major advances have been made in the United States. The principal achievement—not wholly American—has been to show the continuity between modern and premodern science. Lynn Thorndike elaborately demonstrated the interlocking of magical and scientific thinking, while George Sarton, who emigrated to the United States from Belgium during World War I, produced a practically boundless encyclopedia, *Introduction to the History of Science* (5 vols., 1927-48), covering the subject to the end of the thirteenth century.[39] With Sarton's aid, Harvard University established a doctoral program in the history of science in 1935, and since World War II many other universities have competed feverishly for the few well-equipped scholars in the field. The study of medieval science continues to flourish. For the modern period the social history of science has received most attention, but Charles Gillispie's important book, *The Edge of Objectivity* (1960), offers a unifying view of modern science as a structure of knowledge.

In contrast, the study of military history has remained on a much lower level of generalization. The only American work of outstanding importance was done in the 1880's by a captain assigned to prepare a course of lectures on naval history at the new naval War College at Newport. Alfred T. Mahan's *The Influence of Sea Power Upon History, 1660-1783* (1890), followed by similar surveys of the French Revolution and the War of 1812, brilliantly demon-

---

[39] Herbert Butterfield, "History in the Twentieth Century," *The Historical Association, 1906-1956* (London, 1957), 71; C. Doris Hellman, "George Sarton, Historian of Science and New Humanist," *Science*, CXXVIII (1958), 641-44. A helpful review essay is I. Bernard Cohen's "Some Recent Books on the History of Science," *Journal of the History of Ideas*, XV (1954), 163-92. On the present organization of the field see Richard H. Shryock's "The History of Science in American Universities," *Proceedings of the American Philosophical Society*, CV (1961), 512.

strated how control of the seas affected the outcome of these conflicts. Subsequent Army and Navy scholars have rarely rivaled Mahan's grasp of the geographical, technological, and strategic aspects of military history. The American military establishment has hardly ever produced historians equal to Generals Sir Frederick Maurice and J. F. C. Fuller in England, and American soldiers have continued to read of their great commanders in the works of Maurice, Fuller, G. F. R. Henderson, and Liddell Hart.

World War II aroused much popular interest in America's own military history and some stirrings among professional historians also. Samuel Eliot Morison, nautical scholar par excellence, persuaded a nautical President to make him the Navy's historian. After seeing all the naval action one man could reach, Morison wrote from the vantage point of participant as well as scholar. Through fifteen volumes, which appeared on an average of one per year, his *History of United States Naval Operations in World War II* (1947-62) maintains an unflagging vigor and acumen. At the Pentagon, Kent Roberts Greenfield assembled a staff of young scholars who are telling the story of ground operations. Their individual volumes, detailed, learned, and sometimes very penetrating, will someday comprise a vast eighty-volume history of the *United States Army in World War II* (53 vols., 1947-61).

Some of this activity has spread backward into the study of earlier wars and military systems. As yet, however, scholars in the universities have studied little more than the politics of military groups and the details of particular military campaigns. The general history of war as an institution remains only a dimly perceived ideal. Academically speaking, military history is still a sideline.[40]

Why does the historical profession treat the history of science as a broader, more important domain than the history of war? The question opens an instructive view of the influences that have shaped the topical spread of research. Most obviously, the dominant intellectual interests of the profession play a part. The strong movement of inquiry in recent decades into areas of life beyond the scope of governmental affairs has aided the history of science while working against

---

[40] John Bowditch, "War and the Historian," in *Teachers of History: Essays in Honor of Laurence B. Packard,* ed. H. Stuart Hughes (1954), pp. 322-27. See also Richard Glover, "War and Civilian Historians," *Journal of the History of Ideas,* XVIII (1957), 84-100.

the grain of military studies. The quest for breadth in historical writing proceeded on the assumption that social and intellectual subjects are intrinsically "broad," whereas interest in the theory and practice of war smacked of the bad old "drum-and-trumpet" school, which, never having existed among professional historians, was all the more easily discredited. Thus the vast study of World War I sponsored in the 1920's by the Carnegie Endowment for International Peace was explicitly an economic and social history that excluded military and diplomatic policy. Even so, only half of the volumes originally projected were published; only three of these dealt with the United States; and none of the three was written by an academic historian.[41]

The antimilitarist bias inherent in the thrust of professional historical interests has received wider support from an old American predisposition to keep military and civil affairs separate. Viewing war as abnormal and episodic, American intellectuals have generally wished to leave military questions to military technicians. The new international situation after 1945, charged with persistent military danger and feverish scientific competition, greatly emphasized the continuous importance of both; but scholars have responded more readily to the scientific challenge. Doubtless the organization of academic life confirms this preference by denying to the military the prestige enjoyed by scientists. Historians venturing upon the terrain of the natural sciences enter willingly and profitably into interdisciplinary relations with fellow scholars in the disciplines most concerned; but the professors of "military science," assigned to campuses to indoctrinate students in reserve training programs, lack the scholarly attainments or intellectual prestige requisite to real participation in the academic community.[42]

Conceivably it might be possible to demonstrate how every extension of the subject matter of professional history has come from the intrinsic logic of historical study, from the general cultural milieu, and from the organization of academic life. But then we should miss much else. In general, we may conclude that the remarkable diversity of American historical scholarship today betrays the flexibility of

41 The genesis of this project, which Harry Elmer Barnes called "the most stupendous example of historical cooperation yet known to man," is reported in James T. Shotwell's *Autobiography* (1961), pp. 134-55.
42 Louis Morton, "The Historian and the Study of War," *Mississippi Valley Historical Review*, XLVIII (1962), 605.

these conditioning factors, the relative permissiveness of the whole setting. In spite of fashions and prejudices, no large topic has been entirely neglected. For this we may thank especially the eclecticism of the modern American university. By making a place for everything from home economics to African languages, it has encouraged academic historians to take seriously every dimension of human experience.

DISTRIBUTION AND RECRUITMENT OF TALENT

Thus far our story has been one of almost uninterrupted expansion, diversification, and increase of capacity. In a span of three generations, America developed the biggest and most comprehensive historical profession of any country. Yet any process of growth creates new problems, and the American historical profession has had its share. Internally, these have to do with the distribution of effort among fields of specialization and with the level of ability in the profession as a whole. In the twentieth century too rapid expansion in some fields occurred at the expense of others; one may even speak of a decline in certain areas of historical scholarship. More generally, the quality of professional historiography probably did not keep pace with the impressive growth of effort and spread of coverage. Evaluation of these differentials is not easily made; yet some tentative estimate seems essential to a balanced view.

On the question of "neglected" fields, it is hard to speak impartially, since all enthusiastic historians tend to believe that their own fields, or at least the most important aspects of them, suffer sad neglect. Historians in America, perhaps because they are so numerous and so loosely organized, have a propensity to make constant appeals to their brethren in behalf of neglected subjects, hoping thereby to win recruits in the everlasting competition for talent and effort. What stands out, however, above the clamor of so many voices, is the quiet fact that a few large areas of research have experienced a marked decline of attention and support during the last generation. The most notable of these losses have resulted from the passion for contemporaneity that has so stimulated interest in modern history at the expense of the remoter past.

Before World War I, freshmen in American colleges very commonly had a choice between ancient history, medieval and modern European history, and English history. By 1919—the year in which Columbia College launched the famous course significantly entitled "Contemporary Civilization"—ancient history had lost its time-honored place as a freshman elective in the great majority of leading universities and colleges.[1] A significant decline in scholarly activity did not become evident, however, until World War II. Many of the major historians of antiquity remained active through the 1930's, when Tenney Frank was supervising a five-volume *Economic Survey of Ancient Rome* (1933-40) and Michael Rostovtzeff was writing his great three-volume *Social and Economic History of the Hellenistic World* (1941). After World War II Americans continued to make notable archaeological discoveries, such as those of William F. Albright in Palestine and B. D. Meritt in Greece, and to publish an occasional major work like John A. Wilson's *The Burden of Egypt* (1951);[2] but ancient historiography dwindled to a very small fraction of the total historical effort. An attrition in graduate enrollments reduced the number of American graduate students working on doctoral dissertations in ancient history from a high of 36 in 1938 to as few as 15 in 1961.[3] Perhaps not coincidentally, this shrinkage closely followed the reallocation of foundation support in favor of more recent times and more exotic areas. In contrast to the handsome support the Rockefeller Foundation gave James Henry Breasted in the Twenties and Tenney Frank in the Thirties, it has given nothing in recent years for classical or for medieval studies.

As one might expect, the Middle Ages have attracted more students than antiquity, though not nearly a fair share. Over the decades the number of Ph.D.'s slowly increased. In the 1950's it rose somewhat above the level reached in the late 1930's; the loss has been relative rather than absolute. In recent years many more universities than ever before have had doctoral candidates in medieval history, but none any longer has more than a handful. The seventeen doctoral dissertations on medieval history completed in 1960 were done at fifteen different universities, a fact that illustrates both the general decentralization of American scholarship and the lack of a predom-

---

[1] Arthur M. Schlesinger, "The History Situation in Colleges and Universities," *Historical Outlook*, XI (1920), 103-106.

[2] Mortimer Chambers, *Greek and Roman History* (1958), pp. 11-13; Miriam Lichtheim, "Ancient Egypt: A Survey of Current Historiography," *AHR*, LXIX (1963), 37-39. Albright has sketched his autobiography and credo in *History, Archaeology, and Christian Humanism* (1964), pp. 287-327, but see also G. Ernest Wright, ed., *The Bible and the Ancient Near East* (1961), and Herbert F. Hahn, *Old Testament in Modern Research* (1954).

[3] I have counted the number of dissertations listed in successive editions of the AHA's *List of Doctoral Dissertations in History Now in Progress at Universities in the United States.*

inating leader or school.[4] As in other non-American fields, the arrival in recent decades of continental European scholars has helped to widen American academic horizons. A slow emergence of interest in social and economic themes and the penetration of American scholarship into geographical areas untouched before the 1930's—notably Byzantium, medieval Islam, and medieval Russia—have brought diversity in place of the concentration of an earlier day. It is no longer possible to accuse American medieval historians, as one of their number did in 1934, of regarding the Middle Ages almost exclusively from a classical, Western Christian standpoint.[5]

While ancient and medieval history have clearly not received the attention they deserve as the matrix of our civilization, it is less certain that the quality of scholarship in those fields has suffered to a pronounced and special degree. Wherever the technical difficulties of research are unusually formidable and the interested segment of the intellectual community is small, the general dangers of academicism increase. A preoccupation with minutiae is encouraged, the larger action of the intellect clogged. Nevertheless, all the major divisions of history have continued to recruit lively, talented minds. And if, as seems true, Americans trained since World War I have produced very few major books on premodern history that break new ground in a large way, a similar judgment may also be made of the far larger company of modern historians. For all of its growth, the American historical profession in the twentieth century has not wholly lived up to the high expectations of its early leaders.

Although the discovery of new fields and techniques of investigation has never ceased to excite professional historians, many of the best of them grew disappointed with the general state of their discipline after its formative era ended. In the Eighties and Nineties enthusiasm for the new movement of historical research was unqualified. "It was a time of exhilaration and almost religious fervor among the younger scholars," Andrews remembered.[6] The humblest young

---

[4] S. H. Thomson, "A Note on American Doctoral Disertations," *Progress of Medieval Studies in the United States,* Bulletin 20 (1949); *Index to American Doctoral Dissertations,* 1959-1960, p. xvii, and preceding annual editions. See also Loren MacKinney, "Medieval History and Historians during World War II," *Medievalia et humanistica,* no. 5 (1948), pp. 24-35.

[5] Charles W. David, "American Historiography of the Middle Ages, 1884-1934," *Speculum,* X (1935), 125-37.

[6] Charles M. Andrews, "These Forty Years," *AHR,* XXX (1925), 233.

teacher, going out from one of the new seminars to a torpid southern or western college, could feel himself anointed for a pioneering role. A conviction that they were laying the intellectual foundations for great historical work gave the early professional historians a wonderful zest; they confidently expected to produce successors greater than themselves. In 1904 Woodrow Wilson, one of the early Hopkins Ph.D.'s, opened the historical sessions of the Congress of Arts and Sciences at the St. Louis Exposition with the happy announcement, "We have seen the dawn and the early morning hours of a new age in the writing of history, and the morning is now broadening about us into day."[7] After 1907, when the pioneering was over and the modest record and limited accomplishments of the second generation of professional scholars became gradually evident, disappointment set in.

"Time and the vast hordes of youths eager to acquire collegiate education have somewhat undeceived us," confessed Jameson in 1910, while Edward Channing challenged anyone to "see if he cannot count the really first class works of American historical writers within the last twenty-five years on his fingers; and yet conceive of the number of persons engaged in historical pursuits and the number of books constantly published under the guise of history!" Jameson continued to hope for better things. After World War I he predicted that it would—like the Napoleonic wars—usher in "an age of generalization, of synthesis, of history more largely governed and informed by general ideas."[8] The new era did not arrive on schedule, and leading academic historians continued to remark sadly on the amiable mediocrity that their movement, now become a settled institution, seemed to produce. In the late Twenties a committee of the American Historical Association deplored the waning of the historian's influence. One of the judges of the Guggenheim fellowships commented privately in 1946 on the surprisingly small number and poor quality of the applicants in history. On retiring from the executive secretaryship of the American Historical Association in 1953, Guy Stanton Ford made much the same observation on "the poor

[7] *Congress of Arts and Sciences, Universal Exposition, St. Louis,* 1904, vol. II (1906), p. 3.
[8] J. F. Jameson and Edward Channing, *The Present State of Historical Writing in America* (1910), pp. 12, 29; J. F. Jameson, *The American Historian's Raw Materials* (1923), p. 41.

status of history," which he attributed to overspecialization and lax standards in the schools.[9]

In 1948 the American Historical Association asked the members of its Council to rank the six greatest American historians no longer living The only trained, academic scholar who received first place on anyone's list was Frederick Jackson Turner. The other front-runners were gentlemen-historians: Henry C. Lea, Henry Adams, George Bancroft, William H. Prescott, and above all Francis Parkman. In general, the rulers of the AHA, despite the bias one might expect them to have shown in favor of professionalism, cast slightly more votes for amateur historians, whose chief work was done in the sixty-year period from 1840 to 1900, than for professional scholars who wrote in the fifty-year period from 1890 to 1940. The results might have been a bit different if Charles A. Beard had not still been alive, but it is interesting that Beard's own list of six included only two professionally trained historians, Jameson and Andrews, whom he ranked toward the bottom.[10]

All of this suggests a surprisingly persistent, long-standing dissatisfaction among the senior statesmen of the historical profession. Obviously, some of their melancholy should be discounted. Even if the complaints were otherwise entirely accurate, they would tell us nothing about the accomplishments of recent years or about the present trend of scholarship, which is in many respects encouraging. Also, as an appraisal of past performance, such retrospective judgments are open to the charge of nostalgia. Encouraged by the self-critical habits of scholarship, historians in their later years may yield as easily as anyone else to an undervaluation of the present in comparison with the remembered promise of an earlier day. There is always a special temptation to underrate the young men coming forward by magnifying the titans of the past.

[9] Jean Jules Jusserand et al., The Writing of History (1926), pp. v-vii; Edwin F. Gay to Arthur H. Cole, January 28, 1946, in "Economic History: Memoranda and Reports," Files of the Social Science Research Council; "The Reminiscences of Guy Stanton Ford" (Oral History Research Office, Columbia University, 1956), pp. 145-47.
[10] "Council Business 1948," Archives of the American Historical Association (Division of Manuscripts, Library of Congress). For another prestige rating made about the same time by the chairmen of about 130 history departments and confined to "the distinguished professors of American history since 1875," see Gladys A. Wiggin, "Selecting and Appraising Personnel," in Democracy in the Administration of Higher Education, ed. Harold Benjamin (1950), p. 133.

The very character of historical research may lend a certain objective credibility to this sense of declining greatness. After the first broad surveys of a topic or a period are worked out, historical study necessarily becomes more demanding and complex, making the execution of ambitious books progressively more difficult. Only if advances in historical thought keep pace with the growing burdens of research can scholarship avoid an appearance of narrowing scope and diminishing effectiveness.

Allowing for the difficulties of such comparisons, one may still suspect a modicum of truth behind the feeling of declension that haunted many leading scholars. Although the number of good historians has steadily increased with the growth of the profession, the generation that came of age after the formative era was perhaps not so rich in outstanding talent as the one preceding. Of the men who secured graduate training between 1880 and 1905, one may nominate at least seven who became scholars of enduring distinction. To the field of American history belonged Frederick Jackson Turner, Edward Channing, Charles Maclean Andrews, and—the youngest of the lot—Charles A. Beard. In European history their peer and contemporary was Charles Homer Haskins, in ancient history James Henry Breasted, and doubtless we should also include, as a thinker and essayist, Carl Becker.[11] Did as many Americans of equivalent stature emerge from the graduate schools during the next quarter century? In European history William Langer may be ranked with Haskins. In American history Arthur M. Schlesinger Sr. has probably in his own way had an importance comparable to that of Andrews, and either Allan Nevins or Samuel Eliot Morison may deserve a place beside Channing. But how many of the doctoral graduates of 1905 to 1930 can we put in the company of Turner, Beard, Breasted, and Becker? Judgments about individuals will differ, and such ratings easily become invidious; the likelihood remains that few present-day scholars would wish to challenge the pre-eminence of the best historians educated in the late nineteenth century over the best of the succeeding generation.

The complaints about a shrinkage of outstanding talent have generally been coupled with a broader criticism of the recruitment and motivation of professional historians generally. It has often been

[11] Becker actually received the Ph.D. degree in 1907, but his days as a graduate student ended in 1899 when he started college teaching.

said, for example, that too few graduate students have a genuine research drive, and that the average historian therefore does not produce *enough*. As early as 1909 Jameson lamented that the *American Historical Review* was not getting an increasing number of articles and that at least half of the professors of history published nothing at all. The American Historical Association in 1926 appointed a committee to investigate why graduate study was leading to so little productive research. The committee estimated that no more than 150 of the 600 men and women with Ph.D.'s in history engaged persistently in research and publication.[12]

These figures tell us little about the vitality of the profession, and less about the trend of excellence. From the outset, teaching has been the primary obligation of a Ph.D. in history, and a large proportion of our professors have devoted themselves, by choice or necessity, exclusively to that. In all likelihood there has never been a time when much more than half of the profession has done any effective postgraduate research. A careful study has shown that Jameson's estimate of the proportion of nonproducers in 1909 held true in the late nineteenth century as well. Fifty per cent of those who received Ph.D.'s in history from American universities before 1892 published nothing at all in the next decade.[13]

Productivity apparently reached a peak during the decade of the Great Depression, when competition for academic posts was at its keenest. By 1939 more than 60 per cent of the historians who received doctoral degrees in the late 1920's had publications to their credit. Since World War II the percentage of productive scholars among younger members of the profession has declined, probably because the immense demand for college teachers has enabled throngs of students to secure degrees and to settle comfortably into teaching careers. In a recent study that seems closely comparable to the earlier report on the 1930's, a social scientist has found that only 34 per cent of those who secured doctorates in history in 1947-48

[12] Elizabeth Donnan and Leo F. Stock, eds., *An Historian's World: Selections from the Correspondence of John Franklin Jameson* (Memoirs of the American Philosophical Society, vol. 42, 1956), p. 125; Jameson and Channing, *The Present State of Historical Writing*, p. 12; Marcus W. Jernegan, "Productivity of Doctors of Philosophy in History," *AHR*, XXXIII (1927), 1-22.
[13] William B. Hesseltine and Louis Kaplan, "Doctors of Philosophy in History, A Statistical Study," *AHR*, XLVII (1942), 795.

published anything during the next eight or nine years.[14] Historians produced more under the spur of hardship than they do with all of the affluent opportunities and soft inducements of today.

We should not conclude that either the average quality or the total quantity of scholarship has fallen off. Because of the enormous postwar expansion of the profession, American historians collectively publish far more than ever before. In some fields, notably American history, the deluge of print has become an intellectual menace, threatening the capacity of scholars to keep abreast of research while maintaining a large and coherent view. Yet this outpouring has not depressed the average quality of historical publication. Anyone who looks back at the frequently stiff and pedestrian articles in the leading historical journals during the Twenties and Thirties may feel reassured about the general level of contemporary work: it is more deft, often more perceptive, and usually more substantial. We have, then, no reason to suppose that the American historical profession has ever lost ground as a result of a slackening of the drive and skill for research. Indeed, European scholars have often been amazed by our sheer assiduity.[15]

On the other hand, the relative paucity of major historians who have come out of the graduate schools during a good part of the twentieth century does point to some limitations in the composition or training of the American professoriat.

The easiest explanation of talent shortages has always been the Ph.D. system. Allegedly, it forces graduate research into tight little subjects unsuited to significant generalization, deprives students of a ranging and reflective education, stifles creativity and rewards conformity. The criticisms have been made for decades, although always by a relatively small minority in the profession. At the 1904 meeting of the American Historical Association George Burton Adams proposed that the doctoral dissertation be abandoned, and from time to time other leading historians have recommended a relaxation of the requirement. The difficulties that such critics stress have surely existed; but there is reason to suspect that the recurrent complaints have generally served a ritualistic rather than a constructive purpose.

---

[14] *Ibid.;* Bernard Berelson, *Graduate Education in the United States* (1960), p. 55.
[15] For a recent instance see the *Economist,* March 17, 1962, p. 1030.

By blaming "the system," which in fact could be as flexible as individual departments and professors might desire, critics have attributed to Germanic techniques the deficiencies in American performance.

The curious thing about the American Ph.D. program is its concern over technique. As American students discovered the doctoral dissertation in Germany in the nineteenth century, it was simply an exercise demonstrating one's capacity to do original research and to defend publicly an argument based thereon. Historical theses ran to about seventy pages; they occupied only a few months of a student's time. At first, American universities simply copied these procedures. Consequently, the dissertations their students executed in the 1880's were clearly works of apprenticeship, which did not involve so heavy a commitment of time and energy as to determine a man's subsequent career. Fears that America—with all of its heterogeneity—would permit the high standards of a European degree to deteriorate encouraged a progressive raising of the formal requirements. What had originally been a two-year graduate program lengthened in the Nineties to three years, and the student was expected to devote a full year to his thesis.[16] While the concept of defending an argument became perfunctory, the object of making a substantial display of newly discovered information was more and more insisted upon. By the 1920's it was generally reckoned that getting a Ph.D. meant four or five full years of graduate study, and the average candidate, in the words of Wilbur C. Abbott, was "almost always in a state of nervous hurry from at least the beginning of his second year."[17]

Although the stultifying effects of such extended labors were apparent, academic folkways proved exceedingly inflexible. Ironically, the swollen size of theses and the inflation of printing costs after World War I gradually forced universities to suspend the traditional rule that theses must be published, thereby permitting a further sacrifice of quality. A conference on graduate study called by the American Historical Association in 1932 urged a shortening of dissertations and an improvement in literary standards. The same recommendations, sternly repeated twenty-five years later by a committee of grad-

[16] Association of American Universities, *The First and Second Annual Conferences* (1901), pp. 23-24, 39; Ephraim Emerton, "The Requirements for the Historical Doctorate in America," AHA *Annual Report* (1893), pp. 79-90.
[17] Jusserand, *op. cit.*, pp. 43, 134.

uate deans, remain to date largely unrealized.[18] In spite of the deans' recommendation in 1957 that dissertations ought not to exceed 250 pages, the average length of doctoral theses in history accepted in six major universities actually increased from 351 pages in 1950-52 to 357 pages in 1959-61.[19] Evidently the problem did not inhere in the formal requirements of the system but rather in the people who operated it and the students whom it recruited.

A second shortcoming that leaders in the profession have repeatedly emphasized over the last forty or fifty years takes us closer to the human factor and may have more to do with the dip in scholarly distinction that seems to have occurred after 1905. At least from the early twentieth century until fairly recently, history and the social sciences—to judge from the complaints of their elder statesmen—failed to attract at the graduate level the brightest and most enterprising of their undergraduate majors. Instead, the ablest students usually entered business or such professions as law or medicine. "What we have then," declared W. E. Dodd stonily, "is to take in the main the poorest material and make of it the thinking element of the country." Evarts B. Greene added the depressing reflection in 1933 that the low level of intellectual interest prevailing among graduate students deprived the few promising novices of valuable stimulus.[20]

Two interconnected explanations have customarily been advanced for the diversion of talent into other careers: American society is excessively materialistic, and professors' salaries are accordingly too low to attract the most vigorous people. Men such as Turner and Jameson, who remembered the more spacious life of the late nineteenth century, thought that a "steady diminution of the salaries of professors" accounted for the supposedly poorer quality of the students of 1920 as compared with those of the 1890's. Actually, college professors had always felt aggrieved by their modest remuneration; and average salaries at the better institutions, except briefly after World War I, kept pace quite well with the rising cost of living

[18] "Conference on Graduate Study," AHA Files 1933, Box 6, Archives of American Historical Association; *New York Times,* November 13, 1957, p. 28.

[19] Figures compiled largely from *Dissertation Abstracts* and based on theses presented at Columbia, Princeton, Pennsylvania, Illinois, Michigan, and North Carolina.

[20] Jernegan, *op. cit.,* p. 19; *AHR,* XXXVIII (1933), 303. See also Jameson, *An Historian's World,* pp. 190, 255; "Research," *Encyclopedia of the Social Sciences,* vol. XIII, p. 333; Thomas C. Cochran, "A Decade of American Histories," *Pennsylvania Magazine of History and Biography,* LXXIII (1949), 179.

during the long inflationary era that began in 1897. The great prizes of academic life—the chairs that paid four or five thousand dollars in the 1890's—did become relatively less rewarding as time went on. Moreover, the great multiplication of Ph.D.'s forced an increasing proportion of them into those innumerable respectable but struggling colleges where a professor's income allowed no margin at all for buying books, for travel, or for major illnesses.[21] This was not a prospect to attract a highly select student body.

Nevertheless, the problem of recruiting outstanding students after the early years of the twentieth century surely arose from less tangible difficulties, which bad pay served mainly to objectify. The basic hindrances the profession encountered were social and cultural rather than economic. The social status of the humanistic professor and the cultural status of history deteriorated in the early twentieth century. They have only recently begun to revive. Although these trends were interconnected and concurrent, it will be useful first to trace the social question, which relates more directly to recruitment. Essentially, the life of scholarship was being democratized and therefore detached in greater degree from patrician associations. As that happened, history became less attractive to young men of inherited culture, excellently qualified by background for scholarly pursuits.

This is not to say that the historical profession ever drew its talent preponderantly from any one stratum of society. The persistent, nostalgic myth that our foremost professors of history used to come predominantly from elite families needs serious qualification. Of the many Adamses who played so large a part in historical scholarship before World War I, for example, none who made history a professional career had prominent parents or notable family connections. Charles Kendall Adams was a poor farm boy; Herbert Baxter's father was a local lumber merchant; George Burton and Ephraim D. sprang from plain Congregational ministers. Academic life has always offered an avenue of social mobility to young men of modest means and unpretentious background.

By examining the social origins of professional historians suffi-

[21] Reliable figures translated into real purchasing power are given in Beardsley Ruml and Sidney G. Tickton, *Teaching Salaries Then and Now* (Fund for the Advancement of Education, Bulletin No. 1, 1955), pp. 46, 54, 65. For further data see Claude C. Bowman, *The College Professor in America* (1938), and—for the darker parts of the picture—"The Small College and Its President," *Popular Science Monthly*, LXXXIV (1914), 450.

ciently eminent to be included in the *Dictionary of American Biography* and similar compendiums, it is possible to understand more precisely how changes in American society in the early twentieth century influenced the recruitment of talent. Attribution of family status on the basis of such sources must often be approximate. Nevertheless, a rough classification of ninety-seven prominent, native-born historians who completed their graduate training between 1882 and 1946 throws some light on their geographical and social origins.[22]

These origins have always been diverse. Leading historians hailed from almost every part of the country, although New England was somewhat overrepresented before World War I, and the states west of Kansas produced only two members of the entire group. At least half of those who took their degrees during the 1920's and earlier grew up in communities of less than 10,000 population. Over the years a consistently large proportion of the historians in my sample— 23 per cent before World War I, 26 per cent after—were sons of unpretentious men engaged in quasi-intellectual pursuits: school teachers, clergymen, and journalists. This suggests that intellectual incentives in the family have always counted for academic success more heavily than any particular social rank.

Still, it is noteworthy that the proportion of distinguished historians recruited from wealthy or otherwise prominent families declined substantially after the early years of the twentieth century. Of the leading historians trained before 1918, 26 per cent originated in this high status category. Only 13 per cent of the notable historians trained in the 1930's and early 1940's sprang from families of comparable standing. Moreover, the dwindling elite group no longer included, as it did at the beginning of the century, a good many sons of highly successful businessmen. The offspring of bankers and man-

[22] In order to avoid any criteria other than reputation, I included in this analysis every professional historian for whom I could find a fairly adequate biographical sketch. Since my interest was specifically in the most eminent historians, I did not undertake to determine the composition of the rank and file of the profession, and some of my results may not be representative of the whole group. (For data on the whole body of history graduate students in 1958, see Dexter Perkins and John L. Snell's *The Education of Historians in the United States,* 1961, pp. 42-46.) A limitation of my method is the inevitable decline in the number of usable biographies as one approaches the present. I felt able to tabulate both the geographical and social origins of 47 historians who completed their training before 1907, 19 who did so from 1907 to 1918, 16 from 1919 to 1930, and 15 from 1931 to 1946. I included only historians born in the United States or Canada or of American parentage.

ufacturers now fled from the Groves of Academe. "Men of means," Frederick Jackson Turner noted in 1922, "like the type of Coolidge and Merriman in their younger period, seem to prefer to carry on in their own environment." [23] As the representation of elite groups fell, my statistics show a corresponding increase in the proportion of leading historians recruited from the children of shopkeepers, salesmen, and urban immigrants.

This shift was undoubtedly not in itself unfavorable to first-class historical work, for we know such work can be done by men of many sorts and conditions. The diminished appeal of academic pursuits to sons of illustrious families was symptomatic, however, of a more general status problem. Here we must return to a very large subject already touched upon in another connection: the breakup of the aristocracy of culture.

Although the old-time college professor of the mid-nineteenth century was a man of uncertain repute, commonly considered an ineffectual refugee from active life, the enrichment of the leading colleges and universities after the Civil War lifted their faculties to a position of some eminence. Men of dignity and sober rectitude, these professors enjoyed an intimate connection with the local social elite while participating increasingly in the culture of a wider world. They had, therefore, a status not inappropriate to sons of the "best families"—young men like Archibald Coolidge, Edwin F. Gay, Roger Merriman, William A. Dunning, Allen Johnson, James Harvey Robinson, and Conyers Read—whose fathers were distinguished merchants and manufacturers and whose mothers might read Greek as well as charm a drawingroom.

In the twentieth century matters changed. The absorption of scholarship within a nationwide professional system separated the life of the professor from that of the cultivated layman. Typically, a professor now derived prestige from a display of expert knowledge within his academic discipline or in practical affairs, not from his social standing in the community. We have already observed a separation of professional from patrician at the turn of the century in the transformation of the American Historical Association. Another

[23] Turner to Jameson, November 14, 1922, J. F. Jameson Papers, Box 85 (Division of Manuscripts, Library of Congress). In the group I studied, 12 per cent of those trained before World War I were sons of very substantial businessmen. Only one such historian appeared after World War I, and he became a college president.

gulf opened between college trustees and college faculties: they ceased to move in the same sphere.

To many, the change signified a loss of status. Some observers spoke hopefully of the public approval that a new type of professor was winning, "practical, hustling fellows, live wires," who knew all about public utilities and industrial efficiency and tainted meat. The humanistic scholar more often felt elbowed aside. When thoroughly professionalized, he counted for less in local society, received less respect as a model of character and culture, and accepted perforce the plain title of *Mr.*[24] By World War I, a new literary genre, the academic novel, was dramatizing his self-denigration. As an absent-minded fellow, he was a prime butt of popular jokes.

Thus, an academic career separated from patrician association lost attractiveness to the social class possessed of the fullest cultural advantages. This seems plain enough. More important is the likelihood that the lower status of the professorial office put it at a disadvantage in the competition for the ablest young men of middle- as well as upper-class origins.

Few today will wish to return to the social distinctions of the late nineteenth century. Nor need we, in the interest of the historical profession, want to do so. The depressing sense of a loss of status, which was so widespread in the first quarter of the twentieth century, has been dramatically reversed since World War II. Instead of looking backward to the esteem attached to "character" and "culture" among the genteel classes of the late nineteenth century, college professors have become conscious of their rising importance as a relatively autonomous group on the national scene. The jibes that cultural critics of the 1920's leveled at the ineffectuality of academic men have all but vanished; and the stock figure of the absentminded professor is gone from our folk humor. Fears of his dangerously growing influence, so pronounced in the 1930's and 1940's, have also subsided into acceptance and respect. "Intellect," declared Lionel Trilling in 1952,

---

[24] Robert Morss Lovett, *All Our Years* (1948), p. 62; George Trumbull Ladd, "The Degradation of the Professorial Office," *Forum*, XXXIII (1902), 270-77; John James Stevenson, "The Status of American College Professors," *Popular Science Monthly*, LXVI (1904), 122-30; Carl Becker, "On Being a Professor," in *Detachment and the Writing of History: Essays and Letters of Carl L. Becker*, ed. Phil L. Snyder (1958), pp. 91-113. A different and I think too simple picture is presented in Richard Hofstadter's *Anti-intellectualism in American Life* (1963), pp. 204-206.

"has associated itself with power, perhaps as never before in history, and is now conceded to be in itself a kind of power." More recently, the 1960 Republican candidate for president wrote a book about himself partly—he tells us—because his successful opponent had advised him that authorship "tends to elevate [the politician] in popular esteem to the respected status of an 'intellectual.' " [25]

Certainly the university has never before played so large a part in American intellectual activity as it does today, nor has it ever before so completely controlled access to social and economic opportunity. The increasing services of university men to governments, businesses, and civic organizations have dramatized for all to see the power of specialized knowledge in contemporary life. The enormous expansion of college enrollments, and now the frantic clamor for admission, reveal a general acceptance of higher education as essential to nearly every position of responsibility. The professor has emerged, therefore, not only as the visible possessor of intellectual authority but also as the gatekeeper at the citadel of all of the elites, whom every aspirant for honor must pass. In place of the reputation once derived from association with a social class, the professor has acquired a new, occupational prestige from his entrenchment in a mighty institution.

Salaries too have risen substantially. After a painful decline in the 1940's, the purchasing power of faculty salaries moved upward in the 1950's, aided by increasing national concern over education. By 1953 professors in large state universities had almost regained the purchasing power they had fifty years before. In the next decade, salaries soared, to say nothing of unprecedented fringe benefits. [26] The change was swift enough to loose talk about "the affluent professors," and an influential columnist in the *New York Times* expressed some concern that too many, rather than too few, of the ablest young people might be choosing academic careers.

[25] Lionel Trilling, *A Gathering of Fugitives* (1956), p. 66; Richard Nixon, *Six Crises* (1962), p. xi. See also *Detroit Free Press*, March 14, 1963, p. A-11. An early and still useful discussion of status trends is in Richard H. Shryock's "The Academic Profession in the United States," American Association of University Professors *Bulletin*, XXXVIII (1952), 50-54.

[26] Ruml and Tickton, *op. cit.*, pp. 54, 65. By applying to 1962-63 statistics on average salaries of professors the same arithmetical procedures Ruml and Tickton used, one reaches the conclusion that the average professor's purchasing power (not including fringe benefits) was 40 per cent greater in that year than it had been in 1904. Based on AAUP *Bulletin*, XLIX (1963), 142.

Since historians mature slowly, it is probably too early to appraise the consequences for historical scholarship of this striking improvement in professorial status. Whether great historians are developing today, we do not yet know. Nor is it yet clear how large a share history is receiving of the new talent that is going into graduate study. We have, however, some reason to be optimistic. Historians have pretty much ceased to complain that their brightest undergraduate majors are spurning the graduate schools. An extensive survey of college seniors in 1957-58 showed that 55 per cent of the history majors with A averages were planning to undertake graduate study.[27] If, as seems likely, the proportion is higher today, the trend in academic recruitment augurs well for historical scholarship in the years ahead.

It would be wrong to suppose that social incentives fully explain the trend of recruitment or that those incentives are really separable from other considerations. Genuine distinction in historical work depends at least as much on how Americans value history. We turn, therefore, from changes in the status of the professor to concurrent changes in the status of history in American culture.

---

[27] Perkins and Snell, *op. cit.*, p. 38. By contrast, in the late 1920's only 20 per cent of the undergraduates in "selected institutions" who took honors in the social sciences (including history) became graduate students in those subjects. "Conference on Graduate Study," *loc. cit.*

✣ 4 ✥

THE HISTORIAN AND HIS AUDIENCE

Looking back to the dazzling success of the great literary historians of the mid-nineteenth century, the professionals and their critics have often deplored the existence of a wide gulf between modern academic historians and the general public. Usually responsibility is laid at the door of the ivory tower in which professional historians supposedly dwell. "They have abdicated their whole position in our culture," said a disgruntled Alfred Knopf recently.[1] The complaint is an old and chronic one, going back at least to the early years of the twentieth century. Always, it charges the professional historian with failing a waiting public by making history dull, jejune, and overly specialized.

That there is constant tension between the built-in objectives of a profession and the changing demands that society makes upon it cannot be denied. But the nature of the demand is a critical factor in this relationship. We shall examine the objectives of the professional historian at length in the next chapter. Meanwhile, it is reasonable to assume that a country gets, for the most part, the sort of history that it wants. A survey of the demand for history since the late nineteenth century should help to correct an oversimplified, unhistorical view of relations between historians and the general culture.

These relations involve other kinds of historians as well as professionals. In spite of the relative decline of the gentlemen-historians after the turn of the century, America has never lacked good amateur scholars. Ordinarily we expect that the best of them will reach a wider public than will their professional peers, who for their part will have more interest in basic problems of methodology and interpretation. The difference is never absolute, and the best amateur history has never been mere popularization. History, because of its fluidity and openness, is not an arcane discipline. Although its critical operations are exacting, its fundamental tasks of organizing data into a design and thereby recreating the life of the past does not depend on

[1] Interview with author, March 1961.

68

any systematic methodology. Nor has history a special language of its own. Consequently, professional historians are unable to immure themselves completely within a specialized sphere, and writers un-blessed with special training are often capable of doing important historical work. Then the professional faces stiff competition. To understand the situation of the professional historian requires, therefore, an understanding of the changing nature and appeal of the amateur.

All historians in America were amateurs when the famous historical spirit of the nineteenth century was at its height. In the 1830's —forty or fifty years before the era of the professional began—history became the most remunerative of all literary genres. Its popularity and prestige diverted Washington Irving from light belles-lettres and for several decades supplied an immense market for cheap reprint editions of the historical works of Jared Sparks, Joel T. Headley, Irving, and others. A taste for solid historical instruction, aided in America by the moral and intellectual earnestness of the Puritan tradition, extended far beyond the limits of any single class. Prescott's weighty and expensive *Conquest of Mexico* (1843) appealed so widely that seventy or more American newspapers reviewed it within a month of publication. When the first half of Macaulay's *History of England* appeared in 1849, four American publishers seized upon it instantly, and the first year's sale in the United States was estimated at no less than two hundred thousand copies. This would amount to one copy for every fifteen white families. The publishers could not recall another work of any kind that had ever so completely taken the whole country by storm.[2]

By the end of the nineteenth century, when professional historians were appearing on the scene, serious historical interests were still considerable but apparently less widespread. Prestigious, dignified monthly magazines such as the *Atlantic* and the *Century* teemed with historical essays in the Eighties and Nineties. The *Century* serialized Nicolay and Hay's monumental biography of Abraham Lincoln month by month for two and a half years. The bustling popular journals, on the other hand, paid virtually no heed to the past. In the

[2] William Charvat, *Literary Publishing in America, 1790-1850* (1959), pp. 74-77; Harry Hayden Clark, "The Vogue of Macaulay in America," *Transactions of the Wisconsin Academy of Sciences, Arts, and Letters,* XXXIV (1942), 238.

casual view of *Harper's Weekly,* the disappearance of "links that still connect us with the past . . . is one of the inevitable consequences of progress and improvement."[3]

The works of leading historians accumulated on the shelves of gentlemen's libraries. John Fiske, the best-selling American historian of the period, wrote as vividly as most of his more popular predecessors; yet few of his books sold as many as fifteen thousand copies in their year of issue. Perhaps the most brilliant of all American historical works, Henry Adams' profound and scintillating *History of the United States during the Administrations of Jefferson and Madison* (1889-91), sold a mere three thousand sets during the entire decade of the Nineties.[4] Expecting no better, Adams took a compensatory pride in the class character of the whole historical enterprise. In dismissing the possibility of a businesslike return on his literary property, Adams told his publisher:

> In truth the historian gives his work to the public and publisher; he means to give it; and he wishes to give it. History has always been, for this reason, the most aristocratic of all literary pursuits, because it obliges the historian to be rich as well as educated. I should be very sorry to think that you could give me eight thousand a year for my investment, because I should feel sure that whenever such a rate of profit could be realised on history, history would soon become as popular a pursuit as magazine-writing, and the luxury of its social distinction would vanish.[5]

The luxury of its social distinction! This, much more than sales, sustained the chief nonacademic historians who carried on after the turn of the century. A number of men of independent means who had taken up historical pursuits in the late nineteenth century continued active in the early twentieth, and all of them addressed a still smaller audience than Fiske in the 1890's. The most renowned was James Ford Rhodes, a retired Cleveland industrialist who moved to Boston to write his muscular *History of the United States from the Compromise of 1850* (1892-1906). Each volume sold about two or three thousand copies in its first year in print. Henry Osborn Taylor,

---

[3] *Harper's Weekly*, XV (1871), 1022.
[4] Milton Berman, *John Fiske, the Evolution of a Popularizer* (1961), pp. 258-59; Harvey Wish, *The American Historian* (1960), p. 172.
[5] Quoted in Roger Burlingame, *Of Making Many Books: A Hundred Years of Reading, Writing, and Publishing* (1946), pp. 157-58.

author of *The Classical Heritage of the Middle Ages* (1901), *The Medieval Mind* (1914), and many other books designed to show what men throughout the past had deemed best and highest, made nothing from his distinguished books.[6] Of lesser note were William Roscoe Thayer, member of the Harvard Board of Overseers and biographer of Cavour; the Virginia gentleman Philip Alexander Bruce, who made himself the leading authority on the early history of his state; Ellis P. Oberholtzer, a proper Philadelphian who devoted his life to continuing the work of his teacher, John Bach McMaster; Frederic Bancroft, witty and sometimes venomous Washington bachelor and student of the slavery controversy; and Hiram Martin Chittenden, who spent his leisure as an Army officer in the Missouri River Valley writing *The American Fur Trade of the Far West* (1902).[7] The occasional journalist, like Ida Tarbell, who found time and incentive for historical biography was distinctly rare.

None of these authors appeared on any best-seller list during the first two decades of the century; nor did any other historical book except a biography of Mark Twain.[8] After the turn of the century even the upper-class interest in history declined. The excitement of reform in the Progressive Era caught up many of the "best people," and the elite magazines held their readers to the extent that they dropped a leisurely retrospective view in favor of a critical examination of the contemporary scene. Ida Tarbell shifted from the grandeur of Lincoln to the reality of Rockefeller; Brooks Adams turned from the laws of history to the principles of business administration; Winston Churchill abandoned historical romance for political fiction. During the Eighties and Nineties Theodore Roosevelt, Woodrow Wilson, and Henry Cabot Lodge had written much history; neither they nor any

[6] Robert Cruden, *James Ford Rhodes* (1961), pp. 90-91; H. O. Taylor to James Truslow Adams, April 30, 1929, James Truslow Adams Papers (Columbia University).

[7] Thayer, *The Life and Times of Cavour* (1911), and *Life and Letters of John Hay* (2 vols., 1915); Bruce, *Institutional History of Virginia in the Seventeenth Century* (2 vols., 1910), and *History of the University of Virginia* (5 vols., 1920-22); Oberholtzer, *History of the United States Since the Civil War* (5 vols., 1917-37); Bancroft, *Life of William H. Seward* (2 vols., 1900); Jacob E. Cooke, *Frederic Bancroft, Historian* (1957); Gordon B. Dodds, "Hiram Martin Chittenden, Historian," *Pacific Historical Review*, XXX (1961), 257-69.

[8] Alice Payne Hackett's *Sixty Years of Best Sellers, 1895-1955* (1956), p. 29, summarizes data from *Publisher's Weekly*. The *Bookman* published monthly lists throughout the period; these too are barren of history.

other politically active patrician continued historical work amid the whirlwind of reform after the turn of the century.

Beneath the obvious ferment of progressivism, a deeper change in the intellectual temper—less specific, less easy to define—worked in the same antihistorical direction. The genteel and conservative cultural standards with which history had long associated itself were breaking down. A passion for intense life, for the vitality of immediate experience, was challenging the dignified, elevated attitudes that history had always suggested. The impetuous modern temper did not become fully evident until the 1920's, whereupon a reaction against it appeared; but the historical spirit was already reaching a low point as early as 1905, when even the costume novel went clearly out of fashion.[9]

In view of this unreceptive atmosphere, criticism of the professional historians for failing to speak to a general audience misses the mark. There was no general audience. It dissolved in the excitements of contemporaneity and scattered in the winds of democracy. Even a scholarly work so controversial and contemporary in interest as Charles A. Beard's *An Economic Interpretation of the Constitution* (1913) sold fewer than eight thousand copies over a span of four decades, and then only with the aid of a second edition published during the Constitutional crisis of the 1930's. Academic historians had good reason to feel thrown upon their own resources: the decline of their status as professors coincided with a vast indifference to their work as authors. One can sympathize with the complaint made by the secretary of the American Historical Association in 1917 about the public image of his guild. It is customary, he said, to regard historical scholarship as "a harmless, though amiable pursuit, but one of little if any 'practical' use, and to look upon the student of history as a person who, having too few red corpuscles in his blood, is content to bury his head in the dust of the past, oblivious to the interests and exigencies of the present." [10]

As if to confirm the diminished status of their craft, historians found their control over secondary school curriculums waning. The four-year pattern of history courses the AHA persuaded the schools

---

[9] Ernest E. Leisy, *The American Historical Novel* (1950), pp. 16-17.
[10] Waldo G. Leland, "Concerning Catholic Historical Societies," *Catholic Historical Review*, II (1917), 387. Beard's sales are given in *Charles A. Beard: An Appraisal,* ed. Howard K. Beale (1954), p. 310.

to adopt at the beginning of the century began to break down before World War I. First civics, then other contemporary "social studies," demanded recognition for contributing directly to "social efficiency." [11] History had patriotic uses; otherwise it was something of a bore.

Under such circumstances the professional historian who desired to be heard beyond the circle of his colleagues addressed himself to the one audience that was growing visibly before his very eyes: his students. Historians of the highest caliber lent their talents to the writing of textbooks, both for college and for high school. These had been dull and lifeless compendiums, the products of second-rate minds. Scholars like Becker, Breasted, Beard, and James Harvey Robinson made history textbooks in the United States outstanding. But the profession paid a price for this achievement. Habituated to writing blandly for their students, as the natural and profitable alternative to writing technically for their colleagues, historians fell captive to an artificial and immature audience. The requirements of such an audience may have lessened their desire to find, and their ability to satisfy, a genuine historical public.

After World War I a new audience for the serious writer emerged in America, and it has been gaining maturity ever since. It has neither the homogeneity nor the assurance of position and tradition that belonged to the aristocracy of culture. That older audience was unified by its consciousness of itself as a social class with certain well-defined responsibilities, and it also shared common intellectual interests shaped by the standard educational curriculum that prevailed through most of the nineteenth century. The new audience, much more fluid and diversified, rests on a broader basis. It has grown from the extraordinary expansion of higher education in recent decades, from the multiplication of specialized white-collar occupations, and from a concomitant increase in leisure time. Its intellectual interests reflect the multifarious content of modern higher education and the immense variety of opinion-making agencies. It seeks knowledge, not out of a moral imperative but out of a need to integrate and understand its discordant experience. The current "cultural explosion" is only the most recent manifestation of the rising level of taste and activity on the part of this hungry and restless audience.

[11] E. Dawson, "For Recognition of the Social Studies" and "History and the Social Studies," *Educational Review*, LXVIII (1924), 22-25 and 67-70.

Early manifestations of the new American "middlebrow" appeared in the 1920's, when nonfiction books and major novels sprang into prominence on the best-seller lists. For decades the best sellers had consisted almost exclusively of sentimental fiction. Now Sinclair Lewis, F. Scott Fitzgerald, Thornton Wilder, and Theodore Dreiser ranked among the top novelists. More surprisingly, sales of books on history, popularizations of science, and analyses of current events often equaled or surpassed the sales of novels. For one example, H. G. Wells's *Outline of History,* issued by a hesitant publisher at an exorbitant price in 1920, sold one and a half million copies—one copy for every twenty homes in the country—within twelve years. Circulation data from public libraries show a tremendous rate of increase in book reading under way in the 1920's and continuing since that time. Moreover the underlying trend toward nonfiction, strongest among college graduates, has steadily advanced with the spread of higher education.[12]

The surprisingly avid interest of this new public in history was twofold. First, it wanted a framework to provide some sense of order and stability behind a world in tumult; it wanted some ground on which to stand. The very emancipation and turbulence of the modern temper bred a compensatory demand for large-scale, panoramic history. This accounts for the spectacular success of such universal history as Wells's *Outline,* Hendrik Van Loon's *The Story of Mankind* (1921), James Harvey Robinson's *The Mind in the Making* (1921), and, after World War II, the abridgment of Arnold Toynbee's *A Study of History* (1947). The same need, expressed in nationalistic terms, explains the huge popularity of the sagas of American experience written between the wars by James Truslow Adams, Mark Sullivan, Claude G. Bowers, and Van Wyck Brooks.[13]

Second, the new audience wanted biography—not formal, discreet, the life heavily overlaid with the objective circumstances of the

---

[12] William S. Gray and Ruth Munroe, *The Reading Interests and Habits of Adults: A Preliminary Report* (1929), p. 48; Henry C. Link and Harry Arthur Hopf, *People and Books: A Study of Reading and Book-Buying Habits* (1946), pp. 71, 158, 163; *Wilson Library Bulletin,* XXXVI (1962), 402-404. On Wells see his *Experiment in Autobiography* (London, 1934), p. 719, and W. Warren Wagar's *H. G. Wells and the World State* (1961), p. 40.

[13] Adams' *The Epic of America* (1931) was the top nonfiction bestseller in 1932. Sullivan's *Our Times* (6 vols., 1926-35), Bowers' *Jefferson and Hamilton* (1925), and Brooks's *The Flowering of New England* (1936) were also among the most popular books of their day.

times, but rather vividly personal biography in which portraiture and the interpretation of subjective experience play a large part. The boom in biography doubtless catered to a desire for familiar contact with dominant personalities, thereby offsetting the anonymity and impersonal standardization of modern urban life. The rise of humanized biography coincided with the emergence of the newspaper columnist and radio commentator and with an extreme exploitation of personality in the entertainment world. All served the same function. The biographies might be as shallow and romanticized as Emil Ludwig's *Napoleon* (1927) or as flippant and precious as Lytton Strachey's *Queen Victoria* (1921); they might also rise to the commanding historical stature of Douglas Southall Freeman's *Robert E. Lee* (1935).

The cultural revolution that called forth the popular demand for history and biography also produced its suppliers. The new historical writers of the Twenties and Thirties came chiefly from the world of journalism and literature. Never before had so many journalists and free-lance writers possessed the ability and incentive to undertake serious historical research. Their movement into this kind of nonfiction reflected the same broadening of intellectual interests, and the same desire for a stable background, that was creating their audience. Occasionally these amateur scholars had connections with the old aristocracy of culture. Such was the case, for example, with James Truslow Adams and Van Wyck Brooks. But Brooks had rebelled partially against his patrician background; and Adams, who deserted a career in Wall Street to pursue historical studies, became partially dependent on selling his literary wares. Literary ambitions, sometimes linked with political interests, inspired the postwar amateur historians. Unlike their late nineteenth century predecessors, they felt toward history little sense of the luxury of its social distinction.

Two great Lincoln biographers in the 1920's gave an example and impetus to amateur scholarship. Albert J. Beveridge, a former United States senator and an accomplished writer on current events, had done an astonishingly successful four-volume biography of John Marshall (1919) before he retired completely from politics and surpassed all previous biographers of Lincoln in breadth of research and in critical acumen. During the first six months of publication, Beveridge's *Lincoln* (2 vols., 1928) earned $51,000 in royalties. Carl Sandburg was no less successful. The first two volumes of his

Whitmanesque biography (*The Prairie Years,* 1926), written while he was a Chicago newspaperman, enabled him to quit his job. He spent the next decade as a wandering troubador, reading folk songs and collecting material for a four-volume continuation of the work (*The War Years,* 1939).[14]

A few others, by inheriting or marrying money or by frugal living, managed to dispense with a steady job and put their energy primarily into history. Van Wyck Brooks, forsaking a distinguished career as literary critic and editor, spent all of his time for nineteen years on a finely wrought, deeply informed, and highly personal history of American literary culture (5 vols., 1936-52). Matthew Josephson, who was schooled in the 1920's to the insecurity of the literary life, developed in the 1930's—partly under the influence of his Connecticut neighbor Charles A. Beard—into a vivid portraitist of the leaders of the Gilded Age. George Dangerfield, an English immigrant, left the literary editorship of *Vanity Fair* in 1935 and devoted himself to an increasingly disciplined fusion of art and scholarship.[15] At the age of sixty Irving Brant forsook a newspaper career and by frugal living devoted himself intensively to the life and times of James Madison (6 vols., 1941-61).

Such men were relatively uncommon. Most journalist-historians pursued research in time bought by much routine work. Bernard De-Voto edited magazines while lavishing on a three-volume history of the American West (1943-52) "an effort whose intensity and cost no one but me will ever appreciate." [16] *Harper's* editor, Frederick Lewis Allen, wrote deft and often perceptive history on the side. Douglas Southall Freeman, editor of the *Richmond News Leader,* gave half of his very long working day between 1915 and 1934 to *Robert E. Lee.* George Fort Milton produced major books on the politics of the Civil War era while editing the *Chattanooga News.*

---

[14] James Truslow Adams to Mark Howe, March 18, 1929, Adams Papers; Alfred Harcourt, "Forty Years of Friendship," *Illinois State Historical Journal,* XLV (1952), 396.

[15] Brooks describes the writing of his *Makers and Finders* in *From the Shadow of the Mountain* (1961); Josephson's memoir, *Life Among the Surrealists* (1962), stops in 1930. His principal books on American history are *The Robber Barons* (1935), *The Politicos, 1865-1896* (1938), and *Edison: A Biography* (1959). Dangerfield's main contributions are *The Era of Good Feelings* (1952) and *Chancellor Robert R. Livingston of New York, 1746-1813* (1960).

[16] Bernard DeVoto, "On the Writing of History," *Chicago History,* II (1951), 314.

Henry F. Pringle was associate editor of *The Outlook* during the writing of his impressive and scholarly *Theodore Roosevelt* (1931); thereafter he taught journalism at Columbia. Wilbur J. Cash composed a solitary masterpiece, *The Mind of the South* (1941), at his desk as associate editor of the *Charlotte News*. Walter Millis found time, amid editorial duties at the *New York Herald-Tribune,* to write influential books on military and diplomatic history.

Although the rewards of historical writing could be substantial, the struggle to attain financial independence was grueling and usually unsuccessful. Marquis James, who did a vivid biography of Sam Houston (1929) while supporting himself as a staff writer for the *American Legion Monthly,* lost that job in the Depression. He holed up in an attic to complete the first volume of an excellent life of Andrew Jackson (2 vols., 1933-37). The second volume was written with money paid by Bernard Baruch for ghostwriting his memoirs. After that James became entangled in a succession of subsidized undertakings and never got free until it was too late. Allan Nevins, on the other hand, found time and security to do his best work in an academic chair. During the 1920's he produced six substantial historical books at night after spending a full day on a New York newspaper. Like his friend Claude G. Bowers, a more popular but more partisan historian who also worked for the *New York World,* Nevins often left his downtown office at four in the afternoon, raced to 42nd Street, and squeezed in a half hour of research in the Reserve Room of the New York Public Library before it closed at five.[17] At the end of that herculean decade he settled into a professorship at Columbia University.

These writers, all scholars addressing a general audience, answered a demand that professionally trained historians were not filling. The only professionals who reached a large, adult public in the Twenties and Thirties were two who had cut loose from an academic environment: Charles A. Beard and James Harvey Robinson. Both wrote runaway best sellers in the 1920's after resigning from Columbia University in disgust with its policies; and if Robinson's *The Mind in the Making* (1921) was no more than a polemic, Beard's *The Rise of American Civilization* (1927) was an intellectual as well as a popular triumph. Many other professional historians would have liked to have the public's ear. Some of the younger ones, overcoming

[17] Bessie R. James to author, May 18, 1964; Nevins to author, June 1, 1961.

the profession's earlier disinterest, responded in the 1930's to the vogue of biography. None equaled the popular success of amateurs in this genre, and most professional scholars either ignored or positively distrusted the new public.

Their aloofness was partly a function of their social and institutional situation. It has already been suggested that the academic environment subjected the relatively few gifted writers in the profession to the tempting and devitalizing burden of textbook writing. Other scholars found their environment inhibitive to any communication with unspecialized readers. The security the professional historian enjoyed in a university sheltered him from the daily necessity that disciplined the free-lance writer to the utmost clarity and pungency of expression. The increasing number of seminars and professorships in each of the major universities encouraged more and more division of labor and specialization, the reverse of what the layman wanted. Then too, every form of resistance to a general audience was perhaps stiffened by the academic man's general feeling of being unwanted and unappreciated outside his own realm. The wound to his self-esteem inflicted in the early twentieth century remained unhealed. To the academic scholar in the Twenties, Thirties and Forties, no improvement of status was apparent. Rather the public success of the amateur historians suggested the reverse. The failure of the public to appreciate the professional historical expert—as it appreciated both the popular historian and the scientific expert—rankled deeply.[18] This aggravated the professionals' defensiveness.

At the same time, professional historians had strong reasons of principle to shrink from catering to popular taste. The reigning theory of history in the universities, which will concern us more extensively at a later point, distinguished sharply and invidiously between science and art. It is perhaps equally important that general readers of history in the interwar period rarely cared for any complex formulation of man's experience. The pursuit of an audience therefore en-

---

[18] Charles M. Andrews, "These Forty Years," *AHR*, XXX (1925), 226-27; Raymond J. Sontag, "On the Study of Diplomatic History," *Pacific Historical Review*, XV (1946), 212-13. Some of the professionals felt outclassed: "One day up at Columbia [Dixon Ryan] Fox and some others were talking on that very point and the general opinion was that at present more and better historical writing was being done by men with no academic connection than by those who had such." James Truslow Adams to Allan Nevins, September 20, 1925, Adams Papers.

tailed grave intellectual risks from which professional historians wished to guard their discipline. The public's hunger for "human interest" fed upon an episodic display of personality rather than an integrated analysis of process, which was history's more fundamental concern. In 1935 Henry Steele Commager, one of the most vivid and popular of professional scholars and an excellent biographer withal, complained that the rage for biography had become "so extreme that history as such has all but disappeared." [19]

In overpersonalizing history, the popular writer was tempted to strain for effect. The desire for excitement and color easily degraded history into melodrama, a tendency that subtly corrupts both the detachment of the historian and the integrity of his art. No one put the case against melodrama better than the great Dutch historian Johan Huizinga. In the late 1920's, he said of the kind of historical writing then fashionable:

> Overestimating the emotional content of everything it touches upon, it interprets the taut figures of history according to an unkempt generation's need for edification. It gluts itself on poorly understood and poorly understandable -isms. It knows the riddles of the soul of every saint, every wise man, every hero. It concocts tragic psychological conflicts for artists who created their greatest work while whistling a tune. . . . Soberness, restraint, a certain skeptical reserve in investigating the deepest emotions of the heart—all of which are the duty of true historical writing—do not please the contemporary reader.[20]

As an accurate description of the history that sold well in the Twenties and Thirties, Huizinga's statement went too far, doing less than justice to Beveridge, Beard, and Freeman and their countless readers. But as a general characterization of popular taste, the judgment struck home; and as a warning of the vulgarity that a would-be popular historian courts, it made a valid point.

In addition to the risks of simplified causation and cheap histrionics, popularization raised another hazard, which many professional historians felt keenly. Preoccupation with dissemination might undermine the cherished value of discovery. The scholar's great com-

[19] Henry Steele Commager, "The Literature of American History, 1935," *Social Studies*, XXVII (1936), 252.
[20] Johan Huizinga, *Men and Ideas: History, the Middle Ages, the Renaissance* (1959), pp. 45-47.

mitment to the acquisition of new knowledge might suffer from too eager a quest for an audience, as the experience of some historical museums and societies indicated. In contrast to the universities, most of the historical societies and museums welcomed the boom in American history. Timidly in the Twenties, then with mounting gusto in the Thirties and since, societies that had given all of their attention to scholarly endeavors criticized themselves for having been too pedantic and aloof. They inaugurated radio programs, traveling exhibits, lavish historical reconstructions, and many other forms of salesmanship. Although some societies gained new resources for scholarship from their public activity, others allowed scholarly functions to wither.[21] Might that not happen in the universities and professional organizations too?

The issue was posed acutely at the end of the 1930's by an incident in the American Historical Association that revealed how wide the gulf between professor and public remained. By then a number of members of the AHA had become restive. Critical of the stodginess of the organization and respectful of the achievements of some of the amateur scholars, they wished to cooperate with the latter in promoting public interest in history. One such man was Conyers Read, executive secretary of the Association, who had managed a textile firm during a long interval (1920-33) between professorships at Chicago and at Pennsylvania. Another was Allan Nevins. Although many professionals adopted a clubby, disparaging attitude toward Nevins's phenomenal productivity, he tried more than anyone else to unite the values of the free-lance historian with those of the academic scholar. In 1938 he published *The Gateway to History,* a book at once learned and inspirational, which sought to communicate to the general reader Nevins's own vivid and eclectic sense of the meaning and excitement of history.

In the preface to the book, Nevins urged the establishment of a popular magazine of history. Conyers Read fell in with the idea enthusiastically, as did William L. Langer of Harvard, who saw an op-

[21] David D. Van Tassel, "Historical Organizations," in *In Support of Clio: Essays in Memory of Herbert A. Kellar,* ed. William B. Hesseltine and Donald R. McNeil (1958), pp. 145-46. See also *Proceedings of the Conference of State and Local Historical Societies* (1937, 1938). The trend is severely criticized in Walter Muir Whitehill's *Independent Historical Societies* (1962) and Wilcomb E. Washburn's "Scholarship and the Museum," *Museum News,* XL (October 1961), 16-19.

portunity to "revitalize" the profession. Nevins, who had hitherto
avoided historical conventions, joined the American Historical Association, and his allies quickly arranged his election to the Council
of the Association. At the annual meeting that December, Read and
Nevins put forward a plan for a popular historical magazine to be
sponsored by the AHA and published by Condé Nast. The Council
approved the scheme by a narrow margin, but the Association itself,
after an impassioned debate, rejected it. The opponents detected a
commercial taint to the enterprise. They wanted the AHA to stick to
pure scholarship.[22]

The rebuff so enraged Nevins that he lost his customary urbanity.
A few weeks later he published in the *Saturday Review of Literature*
a blistering attack on academic pedantry, entitled "What's the Matter
with History?"

> The pedant . . . has found means in our university system and our
> learned societies to fasten himself with an Old Man of the Sea grip
> upon history. . . . Though the touch of this school benumbs and
> paralyzes all interest in history, it is supported by university chairs,
> special foundations and funds, research fellowships, and learned
> bodies. It is against this entrenched pedantry that the war of true
> history will have to be most determined and implacable.

Most of our best historical writers, Nevins concluded, are still outside academic life, and a body uniting them with the best of the university writers should be formed to promote history as literature.[23]

This blast, with its dire implications of dual unionism, created an
uproar. One leading department of history was reportedly shaken to
its foundations. Nevins and Read went ahead with the organization
of a new society to back the proposed magazine; but they failed for
many years to raise adequate funds. Meanwhile the dominant forces
in the profession turned coldly against them. Read, whose imperious
ways had offended in other matters also, was eased out of the executive secretaryship of the AHA. His successor, Guy Stanton Ford, followed an extremely conservative policy throughout a twelve-year

[22] AHA *Annual Report* (1938), pp. 6, 10-11, 32, 58; Robert L. Schuyler to
Charles A. Beard, February 14, 1939, AHA Files 1936-40, Box 24, Archives
of American Historical Association (Division of Manuscripts, Library of Congress). See also Professor Langer's review of *The Gateway to History* in *New
York Herald-Tribune, Books,* XV (September 18, 1938), 4.
[23] "What's the Matter with History?" *Saturday Review of Literature,* XIX
(February 4, 1939), 4, 16.

tenure. Twenty years passed before the Association called Nevins to the honor of its presidential office; whereupon he returned to its meetings and, in his presidential address, renewed with gentleness and dignity his old plea for union of academic and lay historians: "We are all amateurs, we are all professionals." [24]

It seems clear in retrospect that no amount of tact and goodwill could have bridged the distance between the two groups in the 1930's. Too few individuals had, like Nevins, a foot planted in both camps, and each side had too much cause for distrust and resentment of the other. On the whole, the historical profession *was* stuffy, defensive, pedantic. The lay public on the other hand, was inchoate, undisciplined, unselective. Gratifying its emotional demands, writers dependent on the public—in spite of often admirable scholarship— cared too much about dramatic effects and too little about intellectual problems. Only a few of the widely read, free-lance historians dealt seriously and critically with relations between past and present; very few raised speculative or interpretive questions of any substance. The great middle-class audience for history was too new and unformed to relish genuine intellectual encounters.

Since World War II the relations between professional historians and the reading public have moved gradually into a new and more hopeful phase. The sharp intellectual cleavage of the Twenties and Thirties has diminished, just as the social grievances of the academic man have lessened. Considerable public interest in the past persists. What is more important, much of that interest operates now on a higher plane. The spectacular and florid types of historical literature that flourished in the 1930's, the historical novel and the romantic biography, have greatly declined. Nor do sweeping surveys, like *The Outline of History* or *The Epic of America,* any longer answer our cultural needs. Instead, a better educated public is, with more self-assurance, buying substantial histories of a war, an age, or a single episode.

This advance in sophistication has brought part of the reading public within reach of professional historians. Many of them, in turn, are welcoming the chance to be heard without demeaning themselves. For the first time since the days of Motley and Macaulay, an intensive study in European history, such as Garrett Mattingly's *The Armada* (1959), can win a great company of readers. For the first

[24] Allan Nevins, "Not Capulets, Not Montagus," *AHR,* LXV (1960), 253-70.

time since the days of George Bancroft, a scholarly, multivolume narrative of a whole period in American history, notably Arthur M. Schlesinger Jr.'s *The Age of Roosevelt* (3 vols., 1956-60), has received immense acclaim.

In the study of history, as in other disciplines, communication between the academic and the extra-academic world has become more continuous and diversified than ever before. Father Walter J. Ong has remarked upon the interaction that is occurring as the academic study of literature and the writing of literature grow together.[25] A like trend seems to be under way in the historical field. We do not have today so many highly talented amateur historians as flourished between the wars. The emergence of Bruce Catton and George Kennan hardly balances the passing or retirement of Freeman, Beveridge, Sandburg, Brooks, Cash, and others. Today, more completely than ever before, serious historical writing is done under the auspices of academic institutions. This near monopoly creates public responsibilities that academic life as presently organized does not adequately fulfill. Still, the public standing of the professional scholar has surely benefited from his clear possession of the field. It is no longer possible to say that most of our best historical writers are outside academic life.

Nor is it now possible to say, as Jameson gloomily did forty years ago, that no American magazine of the first class ever prints a historical article. Late in 1962 the *Nation* devoted an entire issue to historical thought and activity in America today, while the *New Yorker* simultaneously made an unprecedented foray into similar territory, printing a book-length report on the intellectual doings of professional historians in Britain.[26] The *New Yorker* has not yet found American historians so interesting, doubtless with good reason. America has a less developed historical consciousness, and our historians do not belong to so well defined an intellectual community. We seem to be moving, however, in that direction.

One milestone was passed in 1954. The fruition of Nevins's long-held dream of a popular magazine of history marked both the substantial progress and the peculiar problems of connecting profes-

[25] W. J. Ong, "Synchronic Present: The Academic Future of Modern Literature in America," *American Quarterly*, XIV (1962), 256-57.
[26] "The Uses of History," *Nation*, CXCV (November 24, 1962); Ved Mehta, "The Flight of Crook-Taloned Birds," *New Yorker*, XXXVIII (December 8 and 15, 1962), 59-147 and 47-129.

sors with an American lay public. A skillful promoter, James Parton, a former editor of *Time,* organized an impressive coalition of sponsors for a magazine designed to meet the standards and enlist the talents of academic scholars as well as journalists. Parton combined the group that Nevins had organized in 1939, the Society of American Historians, with an association of state and local historians that was publishing a magazine for teachers on how to use local history in the schools. This magazine, *American Heritage,* was transformed under the sponsorship of both groups into a slick, elegant monthly for the general, upper middle-class reader. The distinguished free-lance historian Bruce Catton became editor. Within a couple of years circulation reached two hundred thousand.[27]

The realization of Nevins's dream has revealed its limitations. *American Heritage* proved to have great appeal, high technical finish, and no intellectual challenge at all. The sharpness, freshness, and variety of its historical vignettes could not conceal its studied avoidance of controversial issues. Evading analysis, desiring always to please and never to dare or to disturb, *American Heritage* has maintained a nice compromise between nostalgia and realism.

Its blandness was the inevitable result of a successful penetration of the adult historical audience as an undifferentiated whole. The basic defect lay in the terms in which the problem had always been conceived: professor *versus* public, technical specialization *versus* a democratic culture. The search for a "mass" audience necessarily homogenizes it, reducing the actual diversity of tastes and interests to the most common denominator of "human interest." The historian, encouraged to write for everyone who will take some instruction along with entertainment, addresses no one in particular. The readers, encouraged to accept a passive role, discover what they have in common with one another (i.e., their "heritage"), instead of exercising their capacity to discriminate.

As a reflection of the old ideal of one unified democratic culture, *American Heritage* may not be representative of current trends. Today the pursuit of excellence and the intense concern over the quality of American life are working against intellectual homogeneity. As the upper strata of the reading public come into greater prominence and significance, we are becoming conscious of many publics, at

27 "The Reminiscences of James Parton" (Oral History Research Office, Columbia University, 1959), *passim.*

varying levels of sophistication. The fading of a simple antithesis between professor and public has also made these differentiations within the supposedly amorphous, unspecialized popular audience more visible. Consequently, a professional historian can feel the possibility of communicating with a special, though not an exclusively technical, audience that is eager for the kind of history that makes an argument, offers a new idea, or reveals a fresh dimension of experience. Today's professor, if he has something to say and knows how to say it, need not choose between writing for his professional colleagues on the one hand or "popularization" on the other, with the radical change of pace and method that implies. He may speak to a selective public, confident at least of its growing size and importance.

The selective publics—there must be many of them—do not put books at the top of the best-seller lists. They take their pick of the quality paperbacks and the special-interest book clubs that have appeared within the last fifteen years. History enjoys no special status with the elite audiences, as it once did with the aristocracy of culture. It competes and blends with other intellectual interests. To do so successfully, it must meet critical standards that are neither exclusively literary nor exclusively professional; it must engage the modern mind.

Bemused by the seductive clamor of textbook publishers on one side and intimidated on the other by the production schedule of his dean or department, the academic historian may not easily discern the waiting presence of an intellectual audience. If only because of such obstacles, he needs that audience almost as much as it needs him. Most historical work, of course, will—and should—continue to have more special aims. The vast majority of research studies necessarily treat subjects of purely professional concern; and a legitimate place remains for popularization. But great history speaks to cultivated, unspecialized minds, and surely it will speak most strongly and clearly in a culture that listens. Whatever advances the present trend in listening strengthens the capacity of the historian to speak.

Thus the sanctions of the cultural milieu, along with the distribution of institutional support and social prestige, have played a part in the ebb and flow of excellence. All of these conditions, as they impinge on the professional historian, interact with his own conception of his task. This too has altered over the years. Having appraised the

❧ II ❧

THEORY

American historians in recent years have shown a special predilection for writing about historical writing. Although still uncomfortable in the rarefied regions of philosophy of history, they have become addicted to the more tangible sort of commentary we call historiography. The sheer quantity is astonishing: historians ordinarily know that their own history is too small and provincial a part of their whole jurisdiction to deserve a large share of their attention.

A practical problem of communication accounts in part for the change. In an age of multitudinous specialization, few specialists can keep their bearings unaided. The historiographer has stepped in as a middleman in scholarly discourse, taking over where the book reviewer leaves off. He conserves the scholarship of the past that seems currently relevant. He directs attention to convergent aspects of current scholarship, helping individual historians discover the relation of their own interests to larger currents of thought.

Historiography has also a less routine but more dangerous appeal: it is a critical weapon. Since it blends historical explanation with critical appraisal, it provides a vehicle of emancipation from ideas and interpretations one wishes to supersede. Accordingly, it flourishes in response to conflict and revision in historical thought. In its polemical function historiography has ratified many a rebellion. Unfortunately, it usually loses thereby some of its historical integrity. Historiography is ordinarily written by the winning side, which tends to present the losers' intentions and presuppositions in a partisan light. Over the course of time the criticisms that successive generations make of their predecessors may accumulate in the historiographical record.

This is so much the case in American scholarship that the course of historical theory in this country appears on the surface quite desultory and confusing. One gets the general impression of a seemingly circular debate over objectivity. We call the early professional historians the Scientific School; for they disparaged preceding historians like Bancroft and Parkman as men of letters lacking in the scientific spirit essential to a proper objectivity. The Scientific School, in turn, came under attack in the twentieth century from a group of scholars who ultimately called themselves Objective Relativists. They charged the Scientific School with failing to understand the limits of objectivity and with stultifying history in the pursuit of an impossible goal. Since World War II most historians have tended to accept all of these criticisms, while adding that the relativists went too far in denying objectivity and thereby made history too "present-minded."

A dimension very much lacking from this composite picture is that of agreement and continuity. Throughout the long and sometimes bitter argument, differences of principle were actually less sharp than they seemed. No one, including the "literary" historians, rejected the ideal of objectivity in the ordinary sense of unbiased truth; no one gave up the effort to attain it; and no one thought it wholly unapproachable. Consequently, we must go behind the distorted picture that each generation has left of its predecessor in order to tell what all the shouting was about. A more coherent pattern begins to emerge once we ask each group—the early professionals, their critics, and their critics' critics—about itself instead of taking the word of its successor. How did historians in each group perceive their own situation and their own tasks?

In asking this question, the social history of the profession sketched in the preceding chapters offers a point of departure. The views that scholars have had of themselves as participants in American life evolved hand in hand with their ideas about history. Academic historians in the 1880's and 1890's, we have seen, marked out a role for themselves in American culture with splendid confidence. At the same time, they put a high estimate on their capacity to grasp objectively the patterns of history. In the twentieth century they lost much of this confidence, becoming simultaneously doubtful of their status, dissatisfied with their achievement, and skeptical about the character of historical knowledge. In recent years their self-esteem has significantly revived; and as it has gone up, their faith in history as a form of knowledge has also risen. Historians have taken the self-sufficiency of their principles and of themselves for granted at one time, and have fallen into doubt and self-criticism on both scores at another. Their theoretical premises have changed as they have altered their image of themselves.

Accordingly, historical theory in America has moved within a circle of confidence and doubt. What the early professional historians overestimated was not the ideal of objectivity, but rather their own ability to take charge of history independently of its former connections with literature and philosophy. What the relativists discovered was not the limits of scientific objectivity (which their predecessors had recognized), but rather the limits of a discipline that was failing to live up to expectations. What the contemporary critics are reacting against is the deflation of historical consciousness that occurred when twentieth century scholars fell into an excessive skepticism about the possibilities of historical knowledge. At each of these stages Americans took from the ample storehouse of European precept and example what served their own purposes and mood.

SCIENTIFIC HISTORY:
THE AMERICAN ORTHODOXY

Scientific history—if we may so designate the formative orthodoxy of the early professional historians—came to America in the third quarter of the nineteenth century. It arose from no single source, and it materialized without programmatic announcement. By the beginning of the twentieth century the academic historians were convinced that they alone had established a "scientific" approach to history in America, and that they had transplanted it directly from the German universities where about half of them had studied.[1] Actually, what they called scientific history had already taken root in America outside of academic circles. It did not become fully self-conscious and systematic until sustained by a professional apparatus and professional training. But some of the principal attributes of scientific history first appeared in the work of a good many amateur historians, beginning perhaps with Richard Hildreth, whose six-volume *History of the United States* was published between 1849 and 1852. No one represented the ideals of scientific history more fully or more ably than the Philadelphia publisher, Henry C. Lea, whose first books on medieval history came out in 1866 and 1867. Neither Hildreth nor Lea nor many other amateur pioneers of scientific history studied abroad.[2]

In a large sense, the new historical movement was part of the turn in American culture from romanticism to realism. The contemporaneous novels of John W. De Forest and William Dean Howells, and the paintings of Winslow Homer and Thomas Eakins, came out of the same world view that shaped the writing of scientific history. In

[1] J. F. Jameson's "The American Historical Review, 1895-1920," *AHR*, XXVI (1920), 2, estimates that half of the academic historians of 1895 were trained in Germany.

[2] Donald E. Emerson, *Richard Hildreth* (1946); Edward Sculley Bradley, *Henry Charles Lea: A Biography* (1931); William M. Armstrong, "Henry C. Lea, Scientific Historian," *Pennsylvania Magazine of History and Biography*, LXXX (1956), 465-77. For a valuable account of other "critical historians" who emerged in the 1850's see David D. Van Tassel's *Recording America's Past, 1607-1884* (1960), pp. 121-34.

fact, one of the early literary realists, Edward Eggleston, was also a leading scientific historian. In every genre, realists distrusted imagination. The realistic artist, novelist, or scholar did not necessarily achieve a more truthful representation of human experience than the romanticist did, but he adopted a more impersonal tone. The realistic historian did not necessarily surpass the romanticist in factual accuracy, but he felt a special zeal to correct errors of subjective judgment. Unlike the romantic thinker, the realist avoided identifying himself with his subject. He stood apart from it, observing from the outside. He did not submerge himself in the mood and feelings that a situation suggested.

In all fields, realists were reacting against the romantic disposition to idealize and spiritualize life. Consequently, they shrank from exploring the mysterious depths of human character. They looked away from the uniqueness of personality in order to emphasize concrete, external relationships. Similarly—but less successfully—they refrained from elucidating timeless moral verities. In contrast to the intensive inwardness of romantic thought, realists cultivated an extensive view of the tangible and the multifarious. In these respects realism resembled photography, which was also coming into vogue during the third quarter of the nineteenth century. Justin Winsor in 1890 touched a major aspect of the whole cultural change in comparing the historian's task with that of the camera, which "catches everything, however trivial," and in assuming that "everything" registers on a photographic plate.[3]

Since the attention of the realist ranged across an extended surface, his transcription of life was open-ended rather than self-contained. Romantic artists and historians, endeavoring to concretize universal values, cast their work into a symbolic design; but realists presented theirs as a fragment of experience, which continued indefinitely beyond the somewhat arbitrary limits of the canvas or the narrative. For the romantic Francis Parkman, *The Discovery of the Great West* (1869) had a representative unity in the career of La Salle. But realists considered this sort of thing episodic; and for Frederick Jackson Turner *The Rise of the New West* (1906) was a segment cut from a seamless web.

All forms of realistic expression reflected, of course, the growing

[3] Justin Winsor, "The Perils of Historical Narrative," *Atlantic Monthly*, LXVI (1890), 296.

influence of the natural sciences in the latter half of the nineteenth century. This immense, diffuse influence spread through many channels: through the systematic organization of knowledge, through the replacement of traditional superstitions by matter-of-fact habits of mind, through the transforming impact of technology on practical life. Far from beginning in 1850, scientific influences had been gathering strength for a long time, and in American historical writing had made themselves felt since the early eighteenth century. In fact, romantic historians could never have achieved the effects they desired without already possessing the critical outlook associated with scientific inquiry. The change that occurred in the age of realism was not the introduction of scientific methods into humanistic studies but rather a sweeping displacement of the countervailing elements of romantic thought and feeling. What we call scientific history involved much more than a critical approach to evidence; it also subordinated romantic values to a scientific spirit. That spirit was impersonal, collaborative, secular, impatient of mystery, and relentlessly concerned with the relation of things to one another instead of their relation to a realm of ultimate meaning. Scientific history incorporated these attitudes.

It also incorporated, and put a new emphasis upon, evolutionary theories. The concept of cumulative, on-going change, operating through an endless chain of tangible causes and effects, became for scientific historians the very essence of historical wisdom. The meaning of every event, every form of experience, inheres in its location in the chain; and the historian's task is to make each link intelligible by discovering its genetic connection with what preceded and what followed. So applied to human affairs, the evolutionary hypothesis sealed the partnership between history and science; and history became Darwinian while biology became historical.

Actually, the idea of evolution—broadly defined as a continually unfolding process of development—entered historical thought long before Darwin. It was, as John B. Bury said, "the great transforming conception" that enabled history in the nineteenth century to take front rank among humanistic studies. Romantic historians, in spite of an emphasis on representative men and moments, had a deep feeling for the organic interconnectedness of human experience through time. A romantic historian like George Bancroft was more of an evolutionist than some of the early realists, such as Hildreth and

Winsor, who treated historical changes one by one with no concern for underlying continuity. Winsor confessed with positive pride that he made history "a thing of shreds and patches." [4]

From a realistic point of view, the weakness of the romantic idea of development was its idealistic character: it signified chiefly an emanation of spirit. By the 1870's, however, evolutionary ideas under the impact of Darwin and Spencer were losing their transcendental associations; evolution was becoming naturalized. A mechanistic and materialistic version of evolution thereupon completed the transition in America from romantic to scientific history.

As a doctrine of biophysical change, evolution strengthened the realistic approach to history immensely. It showed that history was not a thing of shreds and patches, and this made the revolt against romantic history coherent and intellectually exciting. The evolutionary sequence seemed self-explanatory, containing its dynamism wholly within itself. Consequently, it discredited the romantic emphasis on ideal, transcendental principles. Evolutionary science also justified abandonment of the romantic concentration on great, representative moments of human experience, for evolution reduced every moment to a link in the chain and imputed significance to the chain rather than the individual microcosm. Similarly, the unbroken continuity of evolution justified an open-ended narrative in place of the artistically contrived design of romantic history. To historians who saw the possibility of approximating in their work an all-embracing, objective pattern, the personal shape and flavor of romantic history became illusion.

In addition to its sheer intellectual appeal, scientific history suited the practical interests of a good part of the American aristocracy of culture in the late nineteenth century. To appreciate fully the dominion that "objectivity" won, and the enthusiasm it awakened, one must take its social relevance into account. As we have already observed, the patrician intelligentsia of the post-Civil War era was bent on establishing standards—on bringing discipline, stability, and solidity into what had been a chaotic, excessively individualistic intellectual life. The impersonality of scientific history met this demand exactly. Both in method and in content scientific history subordi-

---

[4] *Ibid.*, p. 297; John B. Bury, "The Science of History," in *The Varieties of History*, ed. Fritz Stern (1956), p. 214. On the romantic historians see David Levin's *History as Romantic Art* (1959).

nated individuals to institutions. It replaced the waywardness and subjectivity of romanticism with a sense of regular, uniform processes. It stressed cumulative scholarship and revealed a cumulative development in the organization of society. The scientific historian resembled, in his concern with impersonal standards, the civil service reformer of the same period. Both were subjecting passion and caprice to objective law.

While advancing the work of consolidation, scientific history was also congenial to the high-minded, cosmopolitan conservatism that the aristocracy of culture upheld. The lesson of continuous, unbroken development taught a sober respect for the dependence of the present on the past. From history so conceived, a nation prone to precipitate impulses might learn due caution; a people falsely convinced of its youthful exemption from the problems of older societies might learn responsibility. Charles Kendall Adams's *Manual of Historical Literature* pointed out:

> We see that the strongest and most lasting work is not that which is set up complete by act of independent creation, but that which has been framed little by little into the affairs of life as it has been needed. Perhaps, most important of all, we in America come to see that we are not under that exceptional protection which Von Holst has sneeringly said was long supposed to be vouchsafed by the kindness of a partial Providence to Americans as well as to women and children. On the contrary, we find that we are under the same rigorous laws that have shaped the destinies of nations on the other side of the Atlantic. We are awakened to the fact that our tendencies are essentially the same that have shown themselves in other republics.[5]

As a group the early professional historians not only shared the conservative evolutionism of their patrician associates; they had further reason of their own for zealous allegiance to the principles of scientific history. Scientific history was in fact their explicit raison d'être, and they embraced it with a special fervor because it constituted a declaration of independence for their academic discipline. For professional historians the scientific approach cut the fetters that had en-

[5] Charles Kendall Adams, *A Manual of Historical Literature*, 3rd ed. (1889), pp. 17-18. In this as in most respects Frederick Jackson Turner's youthful essay of 1891, "The Significance of History," was simply representative of current historical thought. See *Frontier and Section: Selected Essays of Frederick Jackson Turner*, ed. Ray Allen Billington (1961), pp. 11-27.

tangled history with older academic subjects and had subordinated it to literature and philosophy.

History had been a minor aspect of the classical education offered in American colleges. The new professional historians, therefore, were taking over functions formerly performed—or more often neglected—by teachers of languages and literature. Similarly, the professionals were pushing toward the leadership in historical writing that had formerly belonged to literary gentlemen. The criticism that scientific history made of the romantic school served the professional historians' need to dissociate themselves from literature.

Accordingly, the professional historian staked out a special claim to the ideal of objectivity and denied that the literary artist could faithfully serve so jealous a master. Distrusting the dramatic and the rhetorical, professionals insisted that "the appetite for literary effects requires constant curbing lest it betray the writer into distortion of the truth." History should not be regarded as an art. "The false assumption that history is a branch of literature, that an historical narrative must be a work of art, has seriously hampered the progress of scientific historical work," a methodologist sternly counseled. "It leaves the field open to a horde of amateurs." [6] An emphatic differentiation between history and literature fortified the professionals' sense of superiority toward a "horde of amateurs."

In making this differentiation, the professionals also registered their scorn for "mere narrative." [7] In practice, they arranged their facts according to patterns of narration inherited from their predecessors, but they considered themselves engaged in a very different kind of enterprise. Whereas literary amateurs dealt extensively in personalities, the professionals prided themselves on tracing the evolution of institutions. Institutional history exemplified their cult of objectivity by providing an impersonal, external framework for historical events. Moreover, institutional history expressed their own sense of organizational solidarity: it shaped history to the pattern of their own group consciousness, their own corporate spirit.

[6] Homer C. Hockett, "The Literary Motive in the Writing of History," *Mississippi Valley Historical Review*, XII (1926), 476; Fred Morrow Fling, *The Writing of History: An Introduction to Historical Method* (1920), p. 157. See also Frederic A. Ogg, "Literary Decline of History," *Dial*, XXXII (1902), 233-235.
[7] R. H. Dabney, "Is History a Science?" *The University Magazine*, X (January 1894), 3-9.

Next to literature, the early professional historians dreaded most an entangling alliance with philosophy. The connection of history with philosophy was almost as old as its connection with literature; history had long been defined as philosophy teaching by example. The rebellion against this tie had begun in Europe in the early nineteenth century, much before the professionalization of history in the United States. In a large sense, the whole historical movement of the nineteenth century was antiphilosophical. History was struggling to free itself from teleological assumptions, and historians who followed in the footsteps of Leopold von Ranke saw that philosophy imposed an arbitrary pattern on history, alien to reality. They tried to replace formal truths with particular, inductive relationships, and thus to make philosophy itself historical. Among American professional historians, however, the distrust of philosophy went to an almost paralyzing extreme.

The special bête noire of American academic historians was philosophy of history. They commonly equated it with "preconceived opinions" and with the introduction of moral judgments in historical writing. In recommending standard requirements for the Ph.D., Ephraim Emerton of Harvard conceded hesitantly that students might "venture upon a brief excursion" in philosophy of history; but he quickly added that it was a "dangerously speculative subject better reserved for later years in any deep way."[8]

A particular objection to philosophy of history was that it had usurped the name of science. Before the professional historians arrived on the scene, philosophy of history in the Anglo-American world had become positivistic. Following Auguste Comte, the positivists believed they could reduce history to a natural science by hypothesizing a system of unvarying evolutionary laws. The historical positivist most influential in America was the Englishman Henry T. Buckle, whose *History of Civilization in England* appeared in 1857. Throughout the rest of the century, certain amateur scholars in the United States, chiefly John W. Draper, Brooks Adams, and Henry Adams, carried on the effort to create a fullfledged science of history.[9]

[8] AHA *Annual Report* (1893), p. 87. See also Henry E. Bourne, *The Teaching of History* (1905), p. 15, and John Martin Vincent, *Historical Research: An Outline of Theory and Practice* (1911), pp. 8-9.
[9] Buckle's impact, although not yet adequately appraised, is attested in almost

Modestly construed as a search for specific, piecemeal laws of development, the science of history had a real fascination for the early professional historians. But even this became increasingly suspect; and systematic attempts to work out general laws of history they considered decidedly premature. They shrank from the apriorism of such undertakings, which seemed "dangerously speculative" rather than truly scientific. A systematic science of history threatened to subordinate history again to philosophy just when it was winning independence. In the face of this jurisdictional conflict, a fixation on the criticism of documents and the patient accumulation of facts hardened. The empirical outlook of the professional historian was, on one side, a reaction against positivistic theories, as it was at the other extreme a reaction against romantic subjectivity.

Scientific history tended toward a rigid factualism everywhere in the late nineteenth century, but perhaps nowhere more strongly than among American professionals. Unlike their contemporary colleagues in England, France, and Germany, the Americans made not a single, sustained effort to discuss the nature of historical knowledge. Even in the handbooks they wrote on historical method, American scholars dispensed with the theoretical sections of the European treatises—chiefly Ernst Bernheim's *Lehrbuch der historischen Methode* (1889)—on which they otherwise relied.

Americans consistently attributed to Ranke the happy severance of history from philosophy, and acclaimed the German historian as the founder of their own severely factual, realistic approach. Yet only a couple of Americans studied under Ranke, who retired in 1871; few read his work extensively; and no American translated any part of it. Ranke himself, as most German historians recognized by the end of the nineteenth century, was a romantic idealist, who always sought an intuitive apprehension of the universal within the particular. For Germans in the idealist tradition, history embraced and fulfilled the task of philosophy; for American empiricists the two were worlds apart.[10]

It is easy enough to say, in accounting for this curious difference be-

---

all the early manuals on history. See Winsor, *op. cit.; Autobiography of Andrew Dickson White,* vol. I (1905), p. 42; Charles Francis Adams Jr., *Massachusetts, Its Historians and Its History* (1893).

[10] Georg G. Iggers, "The Image of Ranke in American and German Historical Thought," *History and Theory,* II (1962), 17-33.

tween American scholars and the German academic world in which many of them were trained, that Americans are a practical people who do not respond congenially to speculative discourse. Consequently, science and scientific history had a down-to-earth, nontheoretical meaning for Americans. In German culture, on the other hand, the realm of spirit was never so sharply distinguished from the concrete realities of science; the German word for "science" (*Wissenschaft*) refers broadly to every kind of organized knowledge. Americans welcomed the practical techniques of German scholarship, but were more impervious to the German philosophical tradition, which in fact was at a low point in the 1880's when American professional history crystallized.[11]

Undoubtedly an American ethos did encourage hardheaded preoccupation with tangible facts, but not so decisively as to account for the tone of early American professional history. On the hypothesis of national character, one might have expected American academic philosophy in the late nineteenth century to exhibit the same practical-scientific bent that history displayed. Among American professors of philosophy, however, a highly abstract idealism reigned triumphant, and it was German idealism at that.[12]

The difference lay primarily in the contrasting situation of historian and philosopher. The academic historian confronted an essentially practical problem of establishing his own separate, autonomous status. He had to show what history was not: not literature, not philosophy. The academic philosopher, on the other hand, already belonged. His problem was to defend what philosophy was: the spokesman in American education for the "higher" truths of religion. Now the rising natural sciences threatened philosophy's traditional role. Meeting this intellectual challenge called for the profoundly theoretical resistance that German idealism supplied.

Unlike the philosopher, the historian faced no difficulty on the

[11] Richard S. Barnes, "German Influence on American Historical Studies, 1884-1914" (Ph.D. dissertation, Yale University, 1953), p. 112, points out that the peak influx of American students to Germany coincided with the brief flowering of positivism there. It should, however, be said that J. G. Droysen had a certain influence on some American historians. See especially John W. Burgess, "Political Science and History," AHA *Annual Report* (1896), vol. I, pp. 203-219.

[12] Herbert W. Schneider, *A History of American Philosophy* (1946), pp. 441-490.

level of basic principles. He already had, all unwittingly, a philoso-phy of history. He believed, serenely and implicitly, in progress; and his confidence in the general advance of wisdom and virtue enabled him to ignore theoretical problems in going about his practical busi-ness. If the historian took care of the facts, the values would take care of themselves. We may conclude, then, that the narrow con-ception of scientific history among American professional historians reflected their struggle against older rivals and their intellectual se-curity in waging it.

This self-confidence becomes still more impressive when we con-sider closely the attitude of the early academic historians toward their vaunted objectivity. They did not, as modern critics would have us believe, think themselves capable of complete objectivity. The early professional historians freely acknowledged the contingent, frag-mentary nature of historical evidence. Modestly, they denied that his-torians could attain the certainty possible in the "exact" sciences; for they appreciated the difficulties that chance and the unpredictable actions of individuals introduce into the problem of historical causa-tion. Moreover, they recognized that no historian can eliminate his own predilections from his work. Indeed, they conceded that the shift of attitudes and interests in each generation requires a constant re-writing of history. "New conditions give rise to new problems, and these to new conceptions; and when we turn again to examine the past, we put to it questions never before asked." [13]

But such admissions did not vex or dispirit the men who made them. Against skepticism, their faith in progress stood them in good stead. They taught the inexactness of history with the intention and expectation of attaining an ever-increasing precision. They wel-comed changes in historical perspective as cumulative, expecting that each partial truth would enrich the whole corpus of histori-cal knowledge. When Henry E. Bourne noted in *The Teaching of History* (1905) that every generation looks back on the past from a changed point of view, he added that it therefore discovers "fresh significance in many a fact that hitherto appeared commonplace.

[13] Quoted in Ogg, *op. cit.,* p. 235. See also Charles Kendall Adams, *op. cit.,* pp. 4-7; Vincent, *op. cit.,* pp. 300-302; Allen Johnson, *The Historian and His-torical Evidence* (1926), pp. 160, 172; and the influential work of the prom-inent English historian Edward A. Freeman, *The Methods of Historical Study* (London, 1886), pp. 122, 148-51.

The scope of history itself has by this means been several times enlarged."[14]

In sum, the founding fathers of professional history proudly capitalized on many a negation. In the name of history, they denied literature, philosophy, and even the certainties associated with the natural sciences. Yet they did not restrict themselves solely to the determination of facts, nor did they stand apart from the general intellectual advances of their age. They were, after all, enthusiastic evolutionists, eager to explore genetic relationships, to discover developmental patterns. The same kind of inquiry was flourishing in other fields of study, particularly in jurisprudence—where Oliver Wendell Holmes Jr.'s *The Common Law* (1881) left a powerful impress—in biblical scholarship, in philosophy, in political economy, and in anthropology. The historians felt themselves part of a great movement, in which the historical method was invigorating many disciplines simultaneously. They welcomed these allies gladly, doubtless thinking themselves at the head and front of the whole advance. To such collaborators the historians readily recognized their own indebtedness. They appreciated, sometimes in strikingly modern terms, the value of the comparative analysis that philologists and others were employing for an understanding of continuity and change. Jameson, for example, regarded the comparative study of religions and comparative jurisprudence as two of "the most potent causes of the recent expansion of historical work." The comparative method, in the eyes of Jameson, Charles M. Andrews, and many of their contemporaries, was broadening history, as the historical method was refining comparative study.[15] Here was no narrow academic isolationism, but rather large sympathies grounded in common objectives. Whatever the limitations of scientific history in American universities, it enjoyed the great advantage of growing up during what may be called the Historical Era in humanistic scholarship.

Little wonder, then, that the early professional historians, though

[14] Pp. 85-86.
[15] J. F. Jameson, "Development of Modern European Historiography," *Atlantic Monthly*, LXVI (1890), 332; Charles M. Andrews, "Some Recent Aspects of Institutional Study," *Yale Review*, I (1893), 381-410; Freeman, *op. cit.*, p. 66. On the impressive American contribution to historical jurisprudence during this period see W. S. Holdsworth's *The Historians of Anglo-American Law* (1928), pp. 99-117; on the "golden age" of biblical scholarship, George Ernest Wright's "The Study of the Old Testament," in *Protestant Thought in the Twentieth Century*, ed. Arnold S. Nash (1951), pp. 17-31.

they lacked the faith that writes epics, possessed the faith that moves mountains. Their cautiousness, austerity, and unimaginativeness have not been an entirely happy heritage. But their confidence in the progressive nature of historical knowledge must command a wistful respect. Unlike earlier historians from Thucydides to Parkman, they did not address posterity; they wrote for their immediate successors, fully expecting to be superseded. Without hope of achieving permanence, the best of them put an inexhaustible, harmonious energy into the creation of great multivolume works. Edward Channing labored ceaselessly on a single scholarly project for thirty years, and is supposed to have said that he would be satisfied if it were of some use for twenty-five. Men of this kind had the perseverance and zest to carry out grand designs with infinite patience in detail. It is characteristic that William A. Dunning, who wrote a dull, magisterial, three-volume history of political theories since antiquity, should have enjoyed one of the happiest days of his life when he discovered, by a comparison of handwritings, that Andrew Johnson's first message to Congress was actually drafted by George Bancroft. "I don't believe," he told his wife, "you can form any idea of the pleasure it gives me to have discovered this little historical fact." [16]

[16] Letter to Mrs. Dunning, April 23, 1905, William A. Dunning Papers (Columbia University). Channing's remark is mentioned in Crane Brinton's "The 'New History' and 'Past Everything,'" *American Scholar*, VIII (1939), 147.

2

THE NEW HISTORY

By 1910 a number of younger historians had launched a spirited attack on their elders. Gradually the assault gathered momentum, becoming more radical and enlisting increasing support, until it seemed finally in the 1930's to overthrow the reign of scientific history. Looking back on the quarrel today, we can see that the sharpness of the attack obscured its somewhat superficial character. The dissenters were so largely a product of the orthodoxy they wanted to change that they did not realize how much they accepted its basic principles. Only after a quarter of a century of dissatisfaction did a broad and basic challenge to scientific history take shape, and even then it was ambiguous. The hold that scientific history took on the mind of the American professional historian was extraordinarily tenacious. Nothing reveals this more than the confused struggle, from 1910 to 1945, for reform.

A running criticism of orthodox scientific history became apparent during the first decade of the twentieth century. One indictment came from laymen. A second and quite different arraignment came from social scientists. Together, these criticisms reflected—and brought home—the difficulties professional historians were beginning to face: the decline of historical consciousness in American culture, the isolation of the professional historian from a larger sphere of influence and activity. Most historians reacted defensively; a significant few accepted the challenge.

From laymen arose the accusation that the scientific school was making history unreadable. Assailing "German pedantry," leading amateur historians such as William Roscoe Thayer and Charles Francis Adams Jr. deplored the loss of literary quality that had accompanied a gain in scientific method. Between 1905 and 1909 the *Nation,* the *Independent,* the *Atlantic,* and *Putnam's Monthly* aired a number of such complaints, which Theodore Roosevelt summed up in a Presidential address, "History as Literature," to the American Historical Association in 1912. These critics argued that history must make "its final appeal not as a monument of erudition, but as a masterpiece of art." The same view was repeatedly expressed in the 1920's and 1930's in the pages of the *Saturday Review of Literature.*[1]

Ignored for the most part, the charge awoke an echo among historians whose scientific training had not obliterated a lingering attachment to the literary tradition. Contact with the English academic world, where a certain gentlemanly flourish survived, helped to keep that tradition alive. It persisted more than elsewhere at Harvard, nourished by the literary heritage that still flavored Cambridge and Boston society. At Harvard College a "field of concentration" in history and literature, established in 1906, kept open channels of communication that had elsewhere closed. Among the Harvard faculty before World War I both Edward Channing and Albert Bushnell Hart at least paid lip service to the art of history, and in the period between the wars its most accomplished and vigorous spokesman was their distinguished student, Samuel Eliot Morison.[2] In the profession at large, one gesture of concern came in 1920 from the Council of the American Historical Association. Taking cognizance of a "general public protest" against the stylistic faults of professional history, the Council appointed a committee that eventually published a small book, *The Writing of History* (1926), containing the standard laments and some ineffectual suggestions for improvement.

The terms in which these critics scolded their colleagues suggest why they accomplished so little. Invariably, they conceived of good writing as a technical embellishment, a matter of "style" and of knowing how to tell a story clearly and straightforwardly. They distinguished sharply between science as a method of investigation and art as a method of presentation. The content of historical scholarship, they assumed, is supplied by scientific method, while the form of historical scholarship should come from literary method. The content of existing scholarship they accepted as praiseworthy; the deficiency lay only in its form. This naïve distinction preserved the critics' respectability as scientific historians in good standing. It also permitted

---

[1] E.g., William Roscoe Thayer, "The Outlook in History," *Atlantic Monthly,* XCVI (1905), 65-78; William Garrott Brown, "Mr. Rhodes as a Historian," *Independent,* LXII (1907), 552-54; "Naturalistic History," *Nation,* LXXXIV (1907), 427-28; James Truslow Adams, "Is History Science?" *Saturday Review of Literature,* IV (1928), 497-99.

[2] A. B. Hart, "Imagination in History," *AHR,* XV (1910), 246-51; J. F. Jameson and Edward Channing, *The Present State of Historical Writing in America* (1910), p. 25; Samuel Eliot Morison, "History as a Literary Art," in *By Land and By Sea, Essays and Addresses* (1953), pp. 289-98.

them to simplify a basic problem into a practical question of technique. Since the critics asked merely that professional history wear a sprightlier dress, their colleagues naturally received the complaint as a matter of no great intellectual significance. No one in the historical profession suggested that art arises from an organic fusion of manner and matter, and that great history does also in a special way of its own.

The fundamental implications of the concept of history as art had been available since 1909, when Benedetto Croce's *Aesthetic* was translated into English. Occasional editorials in the *Nation* and the *New Republic* commented appreciatively on Croce's views,[3] but no professional historian who discussed this question before 1940 showed the slightest awareness of them. The professional historians who regretted the loss of literary qualities were very largely conservatives who looked back nostalgically to the condition of history in Macaulay's day, not forward to what history might become.

A far more influential line of criticism originated among the social scientists. Literary objections to academic history, having started among laymen, bore the taint of amateurism and could be regarded lightly. But the complaints of fellow scholars in allied disciplines carried the imprimatur of scientific authority. This criticism touched the very source of pride: it challenged the scientific status of scientific history. The ensuing controversy had all the intensity of a family quarrel. The lines between history and other social disciplines in nineteenth century universities had been very indefinite, partly because of the broad appeal of the historical and evolutionary approach, and partly because of the smallness of faculties. History did not possess separate departmental status, but rather belonged in a common department with political science and often with economics and sociology. Of these, only economics acquired its own professional organization before the twentieth century. The historically inclined American Economic Association had been formed in 1885 at the second meeting of the American Historical Association, and for many years the two societies frequently held their annual meetings together. The secession of these erstwhile allies after the turn of the century was symbolic of a deeper cultural schism.

On the surface, the trouble arose from the impatience of many so-

[3] "History as an Art," *Nation*, LXXXIX (1909), 643; "The Return of Clio," *New Republic*, XXXVI (1923), 117-18.

cial scientists with the orthodox historians' reluctance to specify regularities or laws in history. In 1902 Professor Edwin R. A. Seligman, a distinguished historical economist, commended a qualified, nonsocialistic version of the Marxian economic interpretation of history to a joint meeting of the American Economic and Historical Associations. The next year, at another joint meeting, a sociologist, Franklin H. Giddings, set forth a "Theory of Social Causation." About the same time geographers, notably Ellen C. Semple, were expounding the geographical determinants of history. These arguments carried the not unreasonable suggestion that history had better establish some general principles if it was going to fulfill the program of any bona fide science. Most historians recoiled from the suggestion, which seemed to them both officious and—in the present state of knowledge—unsound. To historians, the demand for systematic interpretation looked like a dangerous reversion to the discredited theories of positivism, in opposition to which their own notion of historical science had crystallized. Replying to Gidding's proposal in 1903, Emerton exclaimed, "Under the seductive name of sociology we are here meeting once more the ghost of our ancient enemy, the philosophy of history." [4]

The scornful attitude of social scientists, appearing at the same time that laymen were turning critical of professional history, threw many historians into a defensive posture. This was the first indication of the wider loss of confidence and vigor that overtook the historical profession in the early twentieth century. A new insularity of outlook became apparent. The earlier receptiveness of scientific historians to comparative analysis and to the larger vistas of the evolutionary process diminished. Many now retreated to a virtually exclusive concern with discrete facts and the conditions immediately surrounding them.

George Burton Adams' outraged rebuttal to the social scientists in 1908 revealed the stultifying effect of their criticism on the orthodox mind. Replying to the "attack upon our position, systematic and concerted," Adams in his presidential address to the American Historical Association defined history strictly as "a science of investigation," wholly independent of the theoretical activity of the rebellious disciplines that had invaded its domain. Adams, though he knew bet-

[4] AHA *Annual Report* (1903), pp. 34-37. Cf. the sharp controversy over Ellen Semple's paper, AHA *Annual Report* (1907), vol. I, pp. 21, 47-48.

ter, spoke as if history had no object except getting its facts straight. Thereafter, orthodox historians fell into the habit of distinguishing invidiously between interpretation and synthesis. The secretary of the American Historical Association explained to a group of amateurs in 1917 that some historians "coordinate the work of others and produce histories of more general range, and there are also those who interpret, but these are called philosophers." [5]

For their revulsion against large generalizations, American professional historians in the first years of the twentieth century found intellectual support and guidance in Germany. A revitalized discussion of historical theory sprang up there in the 1890's. Echoes of it soon reached America, partly through the revisions that Bernheim made after 1900 in his influential *Lehrbuch*. Heinrich Rickert and Wilhelm Windelband brought forward a sharp distinction between history on the one hand and the natural and social sciences on the other. The systematic sciences, they asserted, make generalizations by abstracting from experience its typical, its repetitive, its deterministic aspects; but history grasps every phenomenon as unique, individual, and concrete. The implication was that history, by adhering to its own individualizing logic, gets closer to the real thing. As in their understanding of Ranke, however, the Americans once again bit only half of the Teutonic apple. The German neo-Kantians were rehabilitating the subjective and qualitative insight by which the historian apprehends values. American historians seized upon the distinction between history and social science with the opposite intention of keeping subjective thought out of their ken. They wanted to vindicate their own scientific respectability.[6]

The real problem in early twentieth century America was not one of emancipating history from science, but rather the reverse: preventing science from repudiating history. The danger that history faced was the intellectual isolation into which orthodox professors were backing. In large measure, the quarrel between history and the

[5] G. B. Adams, "History and the Philosophy of History," *AHR*, XIV (1909), 223-29; Waldo G. Leland, "Concerning Catholic Historical Societies," *Catholic Historical Review*, II (1917), 388.
[6] The first considerable report of the new German wisdom was Fred M. Fling's "Historical Synthesis," *AHR*, IX (1903), 1-22. Note Fling's defensiveness about history and his delight that Rickert has supplied "a scientific basis for the methods of history."

social sciences broke out in the United States because social scientists were deserting history. The argument over the scientific status of scientific history is best understood as an overt expression of this deeper rift.

During the first two decades of the twentieth century, historical and evolutionary interests lost the commanding position they had formerly held in the academic social sciences. The Historical School of economists retreated before the doctrine of marginal productivity, leaving Thorstein Veblen an outcast and economic history a modest special field. It was symptomatic that Seligman, who began his career as a historical economist and who urged an economic interpretation of history in 1902, thereafter published almost exclusively on public finance. In political science empirical studies of contemporary problems and policies came to the fore.[7] Sociologists and anthropologists also put aside the broad evolutionary approach of the nineteenth century. The sociological study of change shrank to an examination of specific processes evident in the existing social order. American sociologists so cavalierly neglected historical sociology that many of them after a time confused it with the history of sociology. Only in the study of primitive cultures did a historical method flourish, and there it was used against history in a larger sense. Among anthropologists, as among orthodox historians, the historical method became a means of particularizing individual phenomena and thereby criticizing general developmental patterns.[8]

Across the entire range of social sciences, the fascination of the present tended to overshadow the long record of historical experience. In its own way, the academy was behaving much like the patrician intelligentsia and the reading public. The past was becoming

[7] Joseph Dorfman, *The Economic Mind in American Civilization*, vol. III (1959), pp. 243, 256-57, 349-51; Bernard Crick, *The American Science of Politics* (1959), pp. 92-93. There are striking indications of disdain for history in *Recent Developments in the Social Sciences*, ed. Edward C. Hayes (1927), pp. 248, 315-22, and Robert Hoxie, *Trade Unionism in the United States* (1917), pp. xxviii-xxix. A less common attitude of upholding the potential value of history while denouncing all historians informs the work of Frederick J. Teggart.

[8] Harry Elmer Barnes, *The New History and the Social Studies* (1925), pp. 315-16; L. L. Bernard, ed., *The Fields and Methods of Sociology* (1934), pp. 18-32; Frederica De Laguna, ed., *Selected Papers from the American Anthropologist, 1888-1920* (1960), pp. 871-74, 877-83; Murray Wax, "The Limitations of Boas' Anthropology," *American Anthropologist*, LVIII (1956), 63-74.

unfashionable. John Dewey, although one of the most historically minded intellectuals of the period, pronounced its characteristic judgment:

> It is a familiar saying that the great intellectual work of the nineteenth century was the discovery of history. . . . As we notice the shift of emphasis and interest which is now going on . . . would it not be nearer the truth to say that the nineteenth century discovered *past* history? Since what is characteristic of the present time is speculation about the future, perhaps it will be the task of the twentieth century to discover *future* history.[9]

Accordingly, the most urgent disadvantage of scientific history in the new climate of opinion was probably not that it failed to produce broad generalizations about the long ago, but rather that it paid little heed to the here and now. The social scientists, ironically enough, were plunging into a piecemeal empiricism of their own at the very time they were criticizing historians for neglecting general theories. But the social scientists' empiricism—their surveys of urban slums, their bureaus of municipal research, their statistics on commodities, transportation, and prices—was excitingly contemporary. *Their* facts concerned the practical problems that most of the American people after 1900 wanted solved. Such studies satisfied the mind, and often aided the reforms, of the Progressive Era.

The more vigorous, younger historians followed suit. Under the influence of progressivism, and particularly under the spur of criticism from social scientists, a liberal minority in the historical profession refused to accept the isolation of history from contemporary life and from the disciplines concerned with it. Instead of reacting defensively to the threat to history's status, they embarked on a campaign to reform history, to bring it into line with current interests, and to keep in step with the social sciences. Surely history too must become progressive. So, in the election year of 1912, when Theodore Roosevelt campaigned for the New Nationalism and Woodrow Wilson championed the New Freedom, Professor James Harvey Robinson

[9] John Dewey, "Instrument or Frankenstein," *Saturday Review of Literature,* VIII (1932), 581. For Dewey, as Hans Meyerhoff has observed (*History and Theory,* I [1960], 91), it was the analysis of science, not history, that was the key to philosophy. It is therefore hardly surprising that he gave so little attention to philosophy of history.

of Columbia University published the major manifesto of historical reform under the title *The New History.*

Others had already said, and practiced, most of the principles that Robinson asserted. His titular phrase and much of his argument had appeared in the *American Historical Review* in 1898 in a favorable appraisal of the unorthodox German historian Karl Lamprecht written by Earle Dow of the University of Michigan. Edward Eggleston touched on aspects of "the New History," as he too called it, in addressing the American Historical Association in 1900. Frederick Jackson Turner, replying in 1910 to George Burton Adams, had stated the essential case with temperateness and discrimination. Robinson's crusading fervor was newer than his doctrine, and a sympathetic reviewer in the *Nation,* disappointed in finding so little novelty, complained that the author had set up "whole armies of strawmen . . . for the purpose of exhibiting his delightful method of putting them to rout." [10] Nevertheless, Robinson baptized a movement and speeded its attainment of intellectual ascendancy in the historical profession.

Robinson might well have attacked the conservative historians of his day for retreating into a shell, since he sought in effect to reopen the congenial relations that had obtained between historians and other social scientists in the late nineteenth century. But Robinson, intensely progressive in outlook, saw himself in a more fully pioneering role. He presented the New History as the culmination of a hitherto slow struggle against antiquated traditions. Writing with a belligerence that raised the hackles of orthodox scholars, the Columbia professor united certain fresh perspectives with conventional ideas, which he advanced with the same air of *épatant les bourgeois.*

First among the innovations the New History proposed was a deliberate subordination of the past to the present by selecting and emphasizing the aspects of the past that are most relevant to present needs. History would thereby become, as never before, pragmatically useful. Scientific historians had, of course, always considered history

[10] C. W. Alvord, "The New History," *Nation,* XCIV (1912), 457-59; Earle Dow, "Features of the New History," *AHR,* III (1898), 431-48; Frederick Jackson Turner, *The Frontier in American History* (1920), pp. 311-34. As Arthur M. Schlesinger has pointed out in a graceful appreciation, Eggleston was merely reiterating the convictions that had long guided his historical work. See Schlesinger's introduction to Eggleston's *The Transit of Civilization* (1959), p. xix.

utilitarian; their belief in it as the essential medium of civic education and political responsibility had imposed a complete four-year sequence from ancient to American history on the nation's high schools. But traditional scientific historians had thought their subject so naturally useful that they felt no urge to make it so. Now that its utility was called into question, the New Historians wanted history to prove itself.

It could do that chiefly, they thought, by stressing the recent past, thereby explaining the origin and character of present conditions. Excursions into remoter times should reveal "the technique of progress" by showing how outworn ideas and institutions had been overthrown. This was Robinson's particular plea for intellectual history, of which he was the pioneer among American professional historians. In keeping with Veblen's theory of cultural lag and with Dewey's attack on absolute truth, Robinson acclaimed intellectual history as the best means of exposing the transient, relative nature of hallowed beliefs and so enabling us to keep our thinking abreast of changes in our environment.[11] The utility of history depended, therefore, on foreshortening it and emancipating men from it. Like the Enlightenment, the early twentieth century was an unhistorical age, and the New Historians were, in a sense its *philosophes*. Robinson's scintillating course at Columbia—the History of the Intellectual Classes of Europe—was appropriately known among the students as "The Downfall of Christianity." [12]

Second, while foreshortening the past, the New History proposed to widen immensely its scope. All aspects of human affairs belonged within its generous embrace. History, according to the New Historian, had too long scanted common, mundane experience. It had too long concentrated on political events apart from their social and economic environment. A more inclusive outlook would strengthen the alliance of history with progressivism. Attention to everyday life would, presumably, make history democratic. "The older History was essentially snobbish and exclusive," Arthur M. Schlesinger com-

---

[11] James Harvey Robinson, *The New History* (1912), pp. 101-31. On Robinson's relation to the earlier study of intellectual history and on some limitations of his approach see John Higham's "The Rise of American Intellectual History," *AHR*, LVI (1951), 454-59, and "American Intellectual History: A Critical Appraisal," *American Quarterly*, XIII (1961), 221-25.

[12] Arthur M. Schlesinger, *In Retrospect: The History of a Historian* (1963), pp. 34-35.

plained. Actually, the literary historians of the mid-nineteenth century—Carlyle, Macaulay, and J. R. Green—had already broadened the subject matter of history to take in the life of the common people; but they had also celebrated heroic leaders, whereas the New Historians (to quote Professor Schlesinger again) considered "the Great Man as merely the mechanism through which the Great Many have spoken." [13]

The particular restriction of scope against which the New History contended was the formal, institutional framework that ordinarily enclosed the more traditional kind of scientific history. Scientific historians had concentrated on the evolution of towns, states, and economic organizations, emphasizing in each case the internal development of policy and structure. The New History looked outward from institution to context, from structure to environment. It sought explanation of historical change in the "social forces" (to use one of Turner's favorite phrases) surging behind and beyond the visible form of the body politic. In their determination to break down supposedly artificial compartments, the New Historians were joining the general effort of progressive intellectuals to democratize American culture. A common "revolt against formalism," designed to put the intellectual in touch with everyday life, united the New History with muckraking journalism, the pragmatism of Mead and Dewey, and the shift in social science from doctrines and systems to immediate facts.

These sympathies also help to account for the third salient feature of the New History: its enthusiastic alliance with the social sciences. To turn toward the social sciences was, by 1910, to turn toward the present. To look to another discipline for aid in understanding history was to cross conventional boundaries and so to participate in the revolt against formalism. Robinson urged history to "surrender all individualistic aspirations," recognizing that the progress of knowledge depends on cooperation between overlapping disciplines. Moreover, if historians were going to be useful in the sense of discovering "the technique of progress," they would need to participate in the search for laws or regularities having some predictive value. The special contribution of history lay not so much in its distinctive interest in the past, but rather in its ability to synthesize the results of

[13] Arthur M. Schlesinger, "History," in *Research in the Social Sciences*, ed. Wilson Gee (1929), pp. 218-19.

more specialized sciences.[14] Thus the New History revived and perpetuated the nineteenth century quest for specific laws applicable to history. But it did so in a new milieu in which the historian was becoming quite modest about his own conceptual resources and was primarily bent on assimilating and somehow integrating the wisdom of other disciplines.

The great value that Robinson, Turner, and other progressive historians put on cooperation with the social sciences sounded novel in 1910 or 1912 because those sciences were no longer historically oriented. History could no longer take its primacy among them for granted. In order to cooperate, it would have to stretch. Nevertheless, the situation had changed much more than historical theory had. The *Nation's* reviewer caught more than half the truth in calling *The New History* "this restatement of the scientific position." We might better describe the outlook of the younger scholars as scientific history reformed; but their progressive version adhered devoutly to the basic premises laid down by the first American professional historians.

Once we discount the New Historians' view of their predecessors as old fogies, their own methodological orthodoxy becomes overwhelmingly evident. They too were evolutionists, equally hostile to an "episodic" treatment of the past and equally convinced that an appreciation of cumulative change had raised history to the dignity of a science. As evolutionists, the New Historians simply attached more importance to environment and less to heredity. Similarly, in substituting a fascination with "social forces" for the older historians' interest in institutions, the New Historians practiced an impersonal kind of history characteristic of professional scholarship from the beginning. American historiography remained unresponsive to individuals or subjective states of mind, betraying at times a touch of determinism.

A related hallmark of scientific history appears in the New Historians' distrust of literature and philosophy. Turner sometimes advised graduate students against taking a minor in literature, on the score that "the old union between history and literature is now broken." Before World War I Charles A. Beard professed a sovereign disdain for theory as unreal and mythical. As late as 1921, he dis-

[14] Robinson, *op. cit.*, pp. 67-74. On the general intellectual climate see Morton White's *Social Thought in America: The Revolt Against Formalism* (1949).

114

missed political philosophy as merely "a great deal of talk." Robinson rejoiced at the emancipation of history from "its long servitude" to literature and philosophy; and he took pains to distinguish social scientists also from "the now nearly extinct tribe of philosophers of history, who flattered themselves that their penetrating intellects had been able to discover the wherefore of man's past without the trouble of learning much about it." [15]

Finally, the New Historians accepted essentially the same concept of objectivity that scientific historians had upheld in the nineteenth century. They cherished it without expecting fully to attain it. History, Robinson thought, must always remain a highly inexact and fragmentary science because of the nature of its evidence. Moreover, its conclusions will change as each age exercises the right to select from the annals of the past those facts that bear on present problems. The older scientific historians had reluctantly admitted as much.

Neither they nor their present-minded successors supposed that the incompleteness and relativity of historical knowledge need compromise the pursuit of objective truth. Beard as well as Robinson explicitly disapproved the introduction of moral judgments into historical writing. The interests of the present should determine the aspects of the past that deserve attention; but the objective facts that the historian then discovers will, as science progresses, more and more determine his conclusions. An underlying faith in the progress of reason in human affairs enabled both New and old historians to assume that each generation's revision of the past would be an improvement. "We have learned to recognize," Robinson concluded, "that . . . relativity is conditioned by our constant increase in knowledge." [16]

The New History was not an exercise of contemplation, not a theory finely drawn in the interest of system or logical coherence. It was a diffuse stimulus to action, a kind of yeast that worked for thirty years or more in an otherwise sluggish profession. During this long fermentation, a question that Robinson and Turner had answered ambiguously forced its way gradually to the surface. How can history

---

[15] Robinson, *op. cit.*, p. 99, and "The Conception and Methods of History," *Congress of Arts and Sciences, Universal Exposition, St. Louis, 1904*, vol. II (1906), p. 50; Bernard C. Borning, *The Political and Social Thought of Charles A. Beard* (1962), p. 121. On Turner see Charlotte Watkins Smith's *Carl Becker* (1956), p. 15.

[16] Robinson, *The New History*, p. 130. See also Turner, *op. cit.*, p. 323; Edward P. Cheyney, *Law in History and Other Essays* (1927), pp. 142 ff.

best reveal the "technique of progress"? By joining the social sciences in the positivist program of constructing general laws? Or by deriving criteria of progress in history from the values that are uppermost in the changing present? In effect, the formulators of the New History had recommended both without distinguishing between them; for they considered present-mindedness and science-mindedness as complementary. In time, the two policies seemed less so. As the quest for reliable generalizations grew increasingly urgent, the struggle to absorb scientific uniformities into history became incompatible with the tendency to rely on relative and changing values. In trying to hold the two halves of their faith together, progressive historians stumbled into deepening perplexities and confusions. A movement that began before World War I with the intention of making history more objective ended, in the 1930's and 1940's, in making it more relativistic.

3

RELATIVISM

Throughout the 1920's and even into the 1930's the scientistic side of the New History remained in the forefront of professional attention. Getting in a right relation with the social sciences was the principal subject of theoretical discussion, and the New Historians continued to quarrel with their conservative, isolationist colleagues chiefly on this point. A student of Robinson's, Harry Elmer Barnes, emerged in the 1920's as the most rabid prophet of the coming victory of historical science over the "appalling inadequacy and narrowness" of traditional scholarship, which he identified with "pietism, obscurantism, and the political fetish." In more sober terms several presidents of the American Historical Association summoned the profession to search for laws of history, and one, Edward P. Cheyney, announced in 1923 the discovery of several tentative laws. These—including the necessity of elasticity and adaptiveness, the interdependence of the human race, the growth of democracy, and the march of progress—turned out to be the presuppositions of the New History writ large.[1]

Why did rapport with the social sciences loom so large in the interwar years? Primarily because of the importance those disciplines were acquiring in American academic life. During the 1920's the general public became for the first time conscious of at least some of the social sciences, especially economics and psychology. The secession of political scientists, economists, and others from departments dominated by historians had begun at the turn of the century and was now completed at all of the major universities. These new departments were expanding at a prodigious rate. They were also getting princely support from the great foundations. In 1921 one hundred foundations disbursed $181,471 for research and advanced education in the social sciences, including history; their outlay, rising

[1] Edward P. Cheyney, *Law in History and Other Essays* (1927), pp. 7-25; Edward C. Hayes, ed., *Recent Developments in the Social Sciences* (1927), pp. 340-41. Dana C. Munro's presidential address to the AHA in 1926 followed Cheyney in urging a search for historical laws in partnership with the social sciences.

steadily, reached $7,843,846 in 1927. But history captured a modest share of this bonanza only by associating itself with social science; the humanities were receiving relatively little.[2]

The rapid development of specialization within the social sciences and the prevailing antipathy to general theories let loose a flood of empirical research. Taking alarm, social scientists rallied around slogans of "cooperation" and "interdisciplinary research," the very gospel that the New History was preaching. In response to the cry for coordination, special research agencies sprang up. Beardsley Ruml, the dynamic young director of the Laura Spelman Rockefeller Memorial (later incorporated into the Rockefeller Foundation), supplied much of the initiative. Ruml's chief creation was the Social Science Research Council (SSRC), which from its founding in 1923 incarnated the idea of group work and "cross-fertilization." At first the American Historical Association backed off from an invitation to join the Council; but in 1925 all objections gave way to the desire to share in the Council's fellowship program.[3] The Association thereupon took care to choose as its representatives on the Council members who were in sympathy with SSRC objectives. Over the years these representatives, notably Arthur M. Schlesinger and Roy F. Nichols, played an always conciliatory and constructive role.

Yet historians had no part—until the late 1930's, and only in a small way then—in the interdisciplinary projects that the SSRC ambitiously launched. The New History was, to tell the truth, exceedingly vague in specifying how history could effectively cooperate with the social sciences and participate in their search for general laws. Robinson had suggested that the historian is better equipped than anyone else to deal with the interrelation between the various aspects of human affairs and that he performs therefore the special task of synthesis. But historians, New or old, studied the past; and toward historical synthesis most social scientists were indifferent. Moreover, the New Historians' concept of synthesis was unmanageably diffuse. They wanted so much to embrace everything, to in-

2 Eduard C. Lindeman, *Wealth and Culture: A Study of One Hundred Foundations* (1936), pp. 70-82.
3 Waldo G. Leland to J. S. Bassett, January 29, 1925, and February 6, 1925, Correspondence of W. G. Leland 1924-1926, Archives of American Historical Association (Library of Congress). On the origin of the SSRC see Herbert Heaton's *A Scholar in Action: Edwin F. Gay* (1952), pp. 206-209.

tegrate the whole of reality in their writing, that they could rarely analyze a single causal relationship intensively. In search of breadth and completeness, they widened the scope of history instead of isolating regularities within it.

By the mid-1930's the term *New History* had become discredited through association with an indiscriminate electicism.[4] The urge to remodel history along the lines of the social sciences was stronger than ever. Amid the national and international crises of the Thirties, the sluggishness of history in "catching up" with the supposedly more advanced sciences that treated current issues seemed intolerable.

Perhaps a more selective and intensive application to history of the concepts of particular social sciences would help. Some historians, inspired by the Lynds and their successors in sociology, thought that individual communities might provide a coherent matrix for research, and the Social Science Research Council gave its first historical committee, appointed in 1938, the job of preparing a guide for the study of local history. The anthropological concept of culture, which Ruth Benedict popularized in the early Thirties, exercised a special fascination. Culture, as the anthropologist conceived it, was an all-embracing pattern, which would satisfy the New Historians' desire to comprehend society as a whole; yet it might also reveal a unifying structure and provide a basis for selection.

With ideas such as these, some bold spirits set about shaking up the historical profession. Beard became president of the American Historical Association in 1933, just when it acquired a full-time executive secretary in the person of Conyers Read. Read's own work as a Tudor biographer was traditional; but he joined enthusiastically in Beard's determination to make history directly relevant to contemporary social thought and issues. Beginning that year, the annual meetings of the Association took on an increasingly experimental and contemporary air. In 1939 "The Cultural Approach to History" was the theme of the whole program. Scholars imported from other disciplines, to teach historians how to do it, dominated most of the sessions. "Not only the past but the historians themselves sometimes struggled for a place in the proceedings," a conservative professor

---

[4] Crane Brinton, "The New History: Twenty-five Years After," *Journal of Social Philosophy*, I (1936), 134-47; Esmond Wright, "History: The 'New' and the Newer," *Sewanee Review*, XLIX (1941), 479-91.

wryly commented.[5] Some of the best of the younger historians went seriously to work along the proposed lines. In the most striking instance Thomas C. Cochran embarked in the 1940's on a pioneering quantification of cultural trends and came to think of himself as an anthropological historian.[6] A good part of the profession, on the other hand, was antagonized by the obeisant attitude that most of the reformers evinced toward their sister disciplines.

Meanwhile, in the 1930's, the other side of the New History—its pragmatic concern with values—emerged belatedly as a more exciting issue. Robinson had invited historians to choose their facts according to canons of present relevance. So long as historians unquestioningly trusted in science to supply the canons, they did not closely examine the nature of the invitation. Only when faith in empiricism was shaken did some begin to consider their philosophical position.

Long before the relativistic implications of the New History touched other historians, they were troubling the agile mind of Carl Becker. This gentle man of irony and laconic wit—strangely sprung from rock-ribbed Iowa Methodist farmers—had gone to Wisconsin to study under Turner and then to Robinson at Columbia, and had absorbed everything that was progressive and challenging in their teaching. Yet he was a rara avis among the New Historians. No one else in the historical profession in 1910 could have written, as Becker did to Turner, "To me nothing can be duller than historical facts, and nothing more interesting than the service they can be made to render in the effort to solve the everlasting riddle of human existence."[7] Becker's suspicion of facts, in contrast to the usual desire of New Historians for the greatest possible variety of them, was one starting point of his particular heterodoxy. Closely connected was his preoccupation with "the everlasting riddle of human existence."

[5] AHA Files 1933, Box 6, Archives of American Historical Association; William C. Binkley, "Two World Wars and American Historical Scholarship," *Mississippi Valley Historical Review*, XXXIII (1946), 15; "Educating Clio," *AHR*, XLV (1940), 505; Caroline Ware, ed., *The Cultural Approach to History* (1940).

[6] Thomas C. Cochran, *Railroad Leaders, 1845-1890: The Business Mind in Action* (1953); *The Inner Revolution: Essays on the Social Sciences in American History* (1964). See also Oscar Handlin, *Boston's Immigrants, 1790-1865: A Study in Acculturation* (1941); Sylvia Thrupp, *The Merchant Class of Medieval London, 1300-1500* (1948).

[7] Burleigh Taylor Wilkins, *Carl Becker* (1961), p. 32. I am much indebted to this admirable book.

Other New Historians before World War I took the intelligibility of the universe for granted; they concentrated on the problems of society. Becker's mind delighted rather in philosophy and in literature, and was in that crucial way alien to the antiphilosophic empiricism of the New History. Yet he had little in common with the lingering literary tradition that Samuel Eliot Morison and later Allan Nevins represented. Skeptical rather than traditional, Becker was clearly on the side of the present against the past.

Virtually alone among professional historians in the early twentieth century, he was neither anchored in the security of a conservative culture nor swept confidently forward by the promise of reform. The loss in the 1890's of the trustful piety of his youth marked him permanently: he wore always a somewhat deracinated air. This ingrained sense of spiritual loss accounts for most of the attitudes that set the early Becker apart from his professional contemporaries: the distaste for hard, heavy facts, the ambivalent feelings about science, the metaphysical pathos, and the doubts of progress. All of these qualities, still bathed in personal experience, came together ultimately in his haunting view of the modern intellect:

> as the time and space world is expanded . . . the gods, withdrawing from the immediate affairs of men to the place where absolute being dwells, fade away into pale replicas of their former selves— into the Law of Nature, the Transcendent Idea, the dynamic principle of Dialectic, or whatever it may be. Philosophy in turn becomes Natural Philosophy, then Natural Science, then Science; and science, dispensing altogether with the assistance of the gods and their numerous philosophic progeny, presents for contemplation the bare record of how as a matter of fact the outer world behaves, of what as a matter of fact has occurred in past times, leaving man alone in an indifferent universe. . . .[8]

Becker began speculating about history at the point where Robinson left off. Robinson had learned from John Dewey to associate a pragmatic conception of truth with the forward march of science, and so to discredit conservative absolutes as rationalizations of transitory conditions. Becker read the pragmatists too; and like Robinson he was contemptuous of the dogmatic factualism in which conservative scientific historians were taking refuge. But Becker, as early as 1910, carried the pragmatic argument a long step beyond Robinson.

[8] Carl Becker, "What Is Historiography?" *AHR*, XLIV (1938), 28.

If history gets its point and force by selecting facts that are useful to the present, Becker asked, do not the interests of the present enter also into the very constitution of the facts? Are they not themselves merely mental images? Other New Historians distinguished between selection (or synthesis), which is the function of the present, and the facts as such, discrete and immutable. This distinction supported their expectation that each successive present could achieve a more comprehensive, better integrated selection. Becker indicated that historical facts are as much a product of the present as are historical interpretations or syntheses. His thoroughgoing subordination of past to present left no basis for the other side of the New History—its faith in becoming more and more of a social science. He even suggested, at the end of the 1910 essay, that the very ideal of objectivity, to which he was personally attached, was itself a part of a transitory present, unlikely to survive in the evolutionary process for very long.[9] While cherishing progress and reason, he lacked confidence in them, and so in historical knowledge as well.

Thus the intellectual origins of Becker's early skepticism about objective history are sufficiently clear. A combination of philosophy and temperament, his relativism resulted from the impact of a pragmatic conception of truth on a homeless spirit. He was also responding, evidently, to concrete circumstances. It is undoubtedly more than coincidence that his earliest disenchanted reflections on history appeared just at the time when the historical profession was losing momentum, when criticism of its labors was becoming widespread, and when the importance of history in American intellectual life was declining. George Burton Adams' outburst in 1908, the complaints of Jameson and Channing about the state of historiography two years later, Robinson's strident tone, and Becker's disturbing questions came out of a common milieu. Becker began that first speculative essay in 1910 by remarking on the disparaging attitude of contemporary scientists toward history, and his argument was on one level a diffident apologia for history's limitations, though on another it was a criticism of his fellow historians. In Becker the crisis in American historiography first reached full theoretical expression. Until much later, the discontent of the rest of the New Historians remained at a more superficial level. Doubly shielded from heresy—

[9] Phil L. Snyder, ed., *Detachment and the Writing of History: Essays and Letters of Carl L. Becker* (1958), pp. 3-28.

first by their profession's deafness to philosophical discussion, second by their own progressive faith—they too easily blamed history's difficulties on the pettifogging conservatives in their midst.

Becker sounded again in the 1920's essentially the same disenchanted, relativistic note he struck in 1910. It chimed now with the general, postwar disillusion so fashionable in many intellectual circles and with the pessimistic view of history so poignantly phrased in Henry Adams' posthumous autobiography. All of this awoke only an occasional echo among Becker's colleagues. One old scholar, Clarence W. Alvord, confessed that the science of history as he had practiced it now appeared "mere bunk," but for all his pessimism, he said, "I find it impossible to make myself over into a pragmatic historian." Another, convinced that the historian's purpose is to create credible myths and thus make a certain view of the world prevail, felt a sore need for a new philosophy of history. Finding none available, he concluded that historians could do no more than continue with business as usual.[10] Among the rank and file of the profession, the dogmas of scientific history, either in the orthodox or the reformed version, held fast.

Beneath the surface a subtle corrosion was occurring, and in the depths of the Great Depression it became visible at last. Becker's presidential address to the American Historical Association in 1931 received an ovation; now the profession was ready to listen. Now, restating his case, Becker put a recklessly unqualified emphasis on the necessity and value of conforming history to popular need, of satisfying Mr. Everyman, of keeping up to date his "useful myths." [11] A demand for participation, for shaping a disordered world in a more active and willful way than the pallid social-science movement promised, released a fullfledged relativist movement. The stage was set for Charles A. Beard.

[10] C. W. Alvord, "Musings of an Inebriated Historian" and "Changing Fashions in History," *American Mercury*, V (1925), 434-41, and IX (1926), 74; Joseph Ward Swain, "What is History?" *Journal of Philosophy*, XX (1923), 281-89, 312-27, 337-49, and "History and the Science of Society," in *Essays in Intellectual History Dedicated to James Harvey Robinson* (1929), pp. 324-25. Raymond J. Sontag remembers a long informal discussion of the causes of World War I at a meeting of the American Historical Association in the 1920's, when "the break between those whose minds were formed before 1914, and those, whatever their age, who began to think only in the years after 1918, became clear" (*AHR*, LXVII [1961], 91).
[11] *Everyman His Own Historian* (1935), pp. 233-55.

Whereas speculation about history was Becker's natural medium, Beard was driven to it by the course of history. Almost sixty years old in 1933 when he loosed the first of his relativist cannonades, Beard had taken a serious interest in historical theory only during the preceding two years. He turned to it not in a brooding mood of *Weltschmerz* but rather in a mighty effort to foresee and guide the future. Having grown up in a family of former Quakers, strongly tinged with eighteenth century rationalism, Beard had had no religious orthodoxy to lose; he had troubled himself little about the riddle of human existence. Instead, his warm, passionate nature had fulfilled itself in social issues and conflicts.

Always in the thick of things, as a college student he had visited the Chicago stockyards and had worked in Jane Addams' Hull House. While still a graduate student, he and another American had established a workingman's college at Oxford, England. During the years at Columbia (1902-1917), where Beard developed from a protégé to a partner of James Harvey Robinson, most of his teaching was on contemporary politics. He was active in the New York Bureau of Municipal Research and the National Municipal League, campaigned for a Socialist Congressman on the Lower East Side, and carried on an epic feud with the president of the university. In the 1920's he advised statesmen in the Balkans and in Japan. One of his favorite words was *dynamic,* and he once declared that the greatest passage in English literature was the conclusion to Shelley's *Prometheus Unbound.*[12]

While fighting the good fight, Beard nevertheless strained in his scholarly activity to maintain an unrelenting objectivity. Like Robinson, he associated progress with a steady extension of scientific control over human life and thought. Assuming that increasing knowledge furnishes an ever more adequate basis for political and economic policies, he rigidly excluded overt moral judgments from his own scholarly works. His early monographs were as austere as a surgical table.

In the 1920's, however, drawing on the hitherto buried resources of the English literary culture he had absorbed at Oxford, Beard's writ-

---

[12] Mary R. Beard, *The Making of Charles A. Beard: An Interpretation* (1955), pp. 12, 90-94; Harlan B. Phillips, "Charles Beard, Walter Vrooman, and the Founding of Ruskin Hall," *South Atlantic Quarterly,* L (1951), 186-91; Moses Rischin, *The Promised City: New York's Jews, 1870-1914* (1962), p. 233.

ing assumed a more humanistic cast. He began to defend, instead of merely putting to work, his basic values. He was worried by a widespread loss of nerve. Roused by pessimistic critics like Spengler, he turned to a defense of the cultural and moral underpinnings of modern and particularly American civilization. Beard became sharply aware that progress was not just evolutionary process but also a historical faith—"the guiding principle" of American civilization—and that belief in progress was essential to the kind of future he had before taken more easily for granted. Thus, when the Depression struck, Beard was already making articulate the philosophy of history that progressive historians had not quite known they had. The confusion and deterioration of the early Depression years thrust him deeper into a concern with values. Departing from his earlier hardboiled empiricism, he was calling by the beginning of 1932 for a scheme of ethics, "a recurrence to first principles, the hoisting of a moral standard to which all mankind may repair." [13]

Could science provide such a standard? Beard, along with Robinson and Dewey, had always thought so. Now he was not so sure. A "crisis in thought," he believed, had developed from "the discovery that science, facts, and the scientific method do not, and in the nature of things, cannot provide inescapable and irrefutable policies." [14] Like other historians who adopted a relativist position in the 1930's, he was learning that many scientists thought of themselves no longer as explaining an ultimate reality but rather as operating within sharp observational limits. [15] Perhaps more important for Beard was the criticism of natural science he encountered among European philosophers of history. Beard's plunge into philosophy apparently began with a reading of Benedetto Croce's *History: Its Theory and Practice* (trans. 1921), which taught him that the various

[13] Charles A. Beard, "A Search for the Centre," *Scribner's Magazine*, XCI (1932), 2. The best account of the gradual changes in Beard's outlook during the 1920's is in Bernard C. Borning's *The Political and Social Thought of Charles A. Beard* (1962), pp. 64-135.

[14] Quoted in Borning, *op. cit.*, p. 170.

[15] Charles A. Beard, *The Nature of the Social Sciences* (1934), p. 32, and *America in Midpassage* (1939), pp. 852-59; Carl Becker, *The Heavenly City of the Eighteenth-Century Philosophers* (1932), pp. 22-27; Charles W. Cole, "The Relativity of History," *Political Science Quarterly*, XLVIII (1933), 163, 167; Crane Brinton, "The 'New History' and 'Past Everything,'" *American Scholar*, VIII (1939), 154-55; Harry Elmer Barnes, *History of Historical Writing* (1937), pp. 266-68.

sciences are pragmatic abstractions from the more inclusive realm of history.[16]

Beard's son-in-law, Alfred Vagts, arrived on a visit from Germany in the summer of 1932 with a copy of a new book in the idealist tradition, Karl Heussi's *Die Krisis des Historismus*. Heussi described and analyzed the triumph of a subjective conception of historical knowledge in Germany in the early twentieth century. American historians were almost entirely ignorant of this development, having lost touch with German thought after the turn of the century; and Beard was amazed to learn of these "disclosures of contemporary thought." Now he saw Croce's ideas as part of a great movement. Under Vagts's tutelage, Beard went on to study other German historical theorists.[17]

As a consequence, Beard underwent a semiconversion that carried him beyond the point that Becker, in the native pragmatist tradition, had reached. Becker had humbled history, emphasizing its limitations as a science. Beard, following Croce, wanted to exalt history by restoring it to its rightful place as "the crown of philosophy." Becker argued history's inevitable bondage to the present. Beard turned the argument into a claim for freedom by announcing the emancipation of history from bondage to natural science. In contrast to Becker's somewhat fatalistic outlook, Beard centered his attack on determinism, which he associated with science and with the mechanistic causality of scientific history. He was rejecting, without openly saying so, the deterministic implications of his own earlier scholarship. He demanded that historians recognize the subjectivity of history in order to restore the primacy of values in the study of man, and thereby help to guide the history that was in the making.[18]

This first serious encounter between the American New History and German neo-idealism did considerable violence to both. It undermined, without really supplanting, the scientific theory; and left his-

16 Charles A. Beard, "A Historian's Quest for Light," *Proceedings of the Association of History Teachers of the Middle States and Maryland*, XXIX (1931), 12-21. Beard thought so highly of Croce that he tried as president of the AHA in 1933 to bring the Italian philosopher to its annual meeting. A letter from Croce on the current state of historiography was read to the meeting following Beard's presidential address (*AHR*, XXXIX [1934], 229-31).
17 Interview with Alfred Vagts, May 3, 1961.
18 Beard, *The Nature of Social Sciences*, pp. 61-62, 161-63, and "Written History as an Act of Faith," *AHR*, XXXIX (1934), 219-29. See also Minutes of the Program Committee, April 2, 1933, AHA Files 1933, Box 6.

torical thought in great confusion. While using German ideas to de-limit the claims of science, Beard clung to a positivistic conception of knowledge as a structure external to the observer. He continued to hanker for an objective grasp of the totality of things while denying the possibility of attaining it; he persisted in thinking of science as the only authoritative mode of inquiry while emphasizing the unscien-tific character of history. In spite of his desire to enhance history's status as an intellectual discipline, his argument had the effect, there-fore, of discrediting it.

Beard's pragmatism added to his difficulty in assimilating the ideas he borrowed from Europe. The subjectivity that Croce and Heussi upheld was a mode of understanding, an identification of the observer with the observed. It was not an obstacle to, but rather the essential condition of historical knowledge. For Beard, on the other hand, subjectivity referred more narrowly to the historian's social goals and values.[19] It had to do with molding the future rather than un-derstanding the past. As a pragmatist, he regarded the mind of the historian as an instrument that, in serving its owner's needs, re-shapes and necessarily violates the external reality of history. He could not conceive of the subjective action of the historian as much more than arbitrary and coercive: it related always to will or to faith in the kind of future that the historian desired.

By endorsing deliberate moral judgment in historical writing, Beard made a bold, refreshing departure from the colorless neutral-ity and impersonality that American scholarship had prized since the rise of realism. He upset the easy assumption of scientific history that values would take care of themselves if historians took care of the facts. But he was left in the end without much basis for taking care of either. He could only trust—pragmatically—that the future course of history would vindicate his present values, which in turn would justify his selection of past facts.

This insistence on writing history in accordance with a vision of the future should be understood against a background of hot and ur-gent activity. The Depression had roused Beard's Promethean spirit to unprecedented exertions, as if he would now grasp destiny by the

19 Lloyd R. Sorenson, "Charles A. Beard and German Historiographical Thought," *Mississippi Valley Historical Review,* XLII (1955), 274-87; Cushing Strout, *The Pragmatic Revolt in American History: Carl Becker and Charles Beard* (1958).

forelock and twist her once and for all in the right direction. While spelling out a philosophy of history in 1932-33, Beard was simultaneously engaged in sketching an ambitious blueprint for a planned economy to meet the domestic crisis. He was formulating a general conception of the national interest in foreign policy. He was goading an educational commission into an affirmation of collectivistic values as the foundation of all instruction in the social studies. He was even drafting a new state milk law for the angry Connecticut farmers who gathered for leadership on his lawn. In all of these respects Beard was engaged in a gigantic rescue operation, an attempt to reanimate by creative thought and purpose the progress that had lost its own momentum.

Beard's relativism, with its call to action and its renewed affirmation of progress, had a sledgehammer effect, far exceeding the impact of Becker's wistful disenchantment. Younger historians, by now thoroughly impatient with the stodginess of their profession, the stagnation of the American Historical Association, and the indifference of the public to professional history, responded eagerly to Beard's summons to controversy and interpretation. Unlike Becker, who seemed not to care much what other people did, Beard urged his colleagues to join him in reconsidering the nature of historiography; and the year after he delivered his thunderous address, "Written History as an Act of Faith" (1933), all three general sessions at the annual meeting of the American Historical Association dealt with philosophical issues.[20] Nothing like this had ever occurred before.

The indignation of conservative scholars added to the stir. In their eyes the ancient standard of objectivity was being trampled in the dust. The traditionalists guarded an essential truth, best expressed by Charles H. McIlwain, Arthur O. Lovejoy, and Robert L. Schuyler: that historical understanding requires us to transcend the biases of the present, and that history liberates us from parochialism to the extent that we succeed in doing so.[21] It was hard to listen to such voices in the midst of a world in tumult, particularly when the kind of scholarship they defended was so largely formalistic and old-fashioned. Deeply concerned about the state of their discipline but

[20] *AHR*, XL (1935), 425-28.
[21] C. H. McIlwain, "The Historian's Part in a Changing World," *AHR*, XLII (1937), 209-15; Arthur O. Lovejoy, "Present Standpoints and Past History, *Journal of Philosophy*, XXXVI (1939), 477-89; Robert L. Schuyler, "The Usefulness of Useless History," *Political Science Quarterly*, LVI (1941), 23-37.

unaccustomed to theoretical argument, historians quarreled in an atmosphere of growing confusion. Today we may look back ruefully at the partisanship that suffused this conflict between two versions of scientific history. Upholders of the orthodox version denounced the "relativists" as defeatists and sometimes associated their doctrine with fascism. They, in turn, implied that their opponents, puttering over harmless and distant facts, were practicing vicarious leisure and conspicuous waste.[22]

On the crucial matter of objectivity, the two arguments simply failed to meet. Orthodox scientific historians accused the relativists of abandoning the ideal of objectivity, when in fact they argued that the historian can become more objective by recognizing his limitations. The relativists, for their part, accused the orthodox of believing that bias can be eliminated from historical knowledge, when the latter insisted only that bias should be reduced to a minimum. One group, wishing to change the world, belabored the historian's shortcomings. The other, wishing to preserve the world, stressed his traditional ideal.

As an outgrowth of the New History, the relativist movement antagonized historians who were already hostile to a "social science approach" and appealed to historians who were sympathetic to the social sciences. Among these latter, a pragmatic desire to make history useful still united an emphasis on values with a search for scientific laws. Partly because of the ambiguities in Beard's own thinking, very few of the New Historians in the late 1930's and early 1940's realized how much the relativist argument jeopardized their own reformed version of scientific history as well as the conservative kind. The tangle did not unravel until after the New Historians made a final effort to present a coherent case.

This effort began in the interest, not of relativism, but of social science. The Social Science Research Council was looking for some concerted strategy to bring history into closer relation to the other social sciences. Roy F. Nichols in 1942 presented to the Council a report on the inadequacies of current historical research, together with suggestions for a large-scale program of fellowships that

[22] Cf. Allan Nevins's *The Gateway to History* (1938), pp. 43-44, and Eugene C. Barker's "The Changing View of the Function of History," *Social Studies*, XXIX (1938), 149-54, on one side, and on the other Walton E. Bean's "Revolt Among Historians: Interpretation in Historiography," *Sewanee Review*, XLVII (1939), 330-41.

would, he hoped, "encourage interpretive productions of value to other disciplines." At this point a major diversion occurred through the sudden entry of Beard into the deliberations. Nichols had sent a copy of his report to Beard. In reply the latter suggested that the SSRC might appoint a committee to consider not only the relation of history to the social sciences but also the basic characteristics of historical thought. The Council thereupon convened a conference of friendly historians to decide on a course of action and invited Beard to attend.[23]

Beard's recommendations, delivered in his usual grand manner, set the course that was followed. An SSRC committee chaired by Merle Curti prepared a handbook on historical methodology, which included—as Beard specified—a dictionary of terms, a treatise on historical theory, and a statement of fundamental propositions. Beard composed the propositions, wrote the introductory chapter, and exercised a predominant influence over the whole work.[24] Although the SSRC expected an analysis of the relations of history to the "other" social sciences, the book turned out instead to be a cautious, qualified elaboration of the relativist argument. Every written history, it was argued, is a product of a particular frame of reference; but we can and should become less biased by avoiding all absolutes and recognizing our preconceptions.

Theory and Practice in Historical Study, published in 1946 as Bulletin 54 of the Social Science Research Council, brought the controversy over relativism to a climax. For two or three years thereafter professional meetings resounded with discussions of the subject. But the debate was different now from what it had been in the Thirties. The profession was becoming more sophisticated, the concepts at issue were more familiar, and the whole atmosphere was less hectic and urgent. Historians of many persuasions now took a good part of the relativist argument for granted, and the division of opinion between progressive and conservative schools was no longer clear-cut. Perhaps the chief service of Bulletin 54 was an uninten-

[23] Minutes of the Committee on Problems and Policy, July 11, 1942, SSRC Files; Nichols to author, February 19, 1963.
[24] Beard's impact is clearly evident from a comparison of the final, published report with his recommendations as set forth in Beard to Nichols, July 15, 1942, and in transcript of conference on November 8, 1942, SSRC Files. The committee did balk at Beard's draft of Proposition X and accepted instead a version composed by Louis Gottschalk.

tional one. True to its divided origins, the SSRC committee had united a constant preoccupation with the relativistic limits of history and a basic allegiance to scientific objectivity. The most important chapter spoke obscurely of objective as opposed to subjective relativism. The attempt to codify the position made its internal inconsistency, and its failure to provide positive guidance in writing history, embarrassingly transparent. The pragmatic New History had reached a dead end.

~§ 4 §~

THE RENEWAL OF HISTORY

It was suggested in the first part of this book that changes in American society and culture since World War II have somewhat revived the prestige and influence of the humanistic scholar and diminished the alienation between the professional historian and the American public. A new basis has been forming for a richer historical culture. We are now in a position to observe a parallel development on the level of theory: a revival of confidence in historical knowledge. The restoration of intellectual self-respect that has taken place since 1945 has not in any simple way resulted from improvements in social status. The intellectual transformation began before a new social adjustment became apparent, and contributed to it. But emancipation from skeptical and derivative theories of history might not have gone very far if the historian's morale and his position in American culture had not hearteningly improved.

By the mid-1950's, it is worth recalling, McCarthyism was dead, and the big foundations were reacting nervously to outraged complaints that they had long neglected the humanities. A rising concern about the quality of American culture and its criteria of excellence was in the air. A reinvigorated American Historical Association was growing prodigiously in membership and activities. These and other signs of quickening vitality must be remembered as we follow the movement of historical theory.

The first indication of a new temper appeared during the late 1940's in the animated discussion of Bulletin 54.[1] Many who participated in the discussion were clearly floundering for solid ground, but the fixed point that everyone grasped was the simple axiom that history is basically an effort to tell the truth about the past. Unless the whole business is a bad joke, the historian must be able in some meaningful degree to understand the events of the past in their own terms. The label *present-minded* now loomed up as an epithet. Even

[1] Summarized in *The Social Sciences in Historical Study* (Bulletin 64, Social Science Research Council, 1954), pp. 4-16.

132

the relativists, who stressed the constructive role of present values in historical thought, recognized that the great problem was not to delimit but rather to realize more fully the possibilities of historical knowledge.

A clear indication of the change in atmosphere came from young scholars with obvious liberal, and even progressive, sympathies, who now drew back from the skepticism to which the relativist argument led. "I felt somewhat isolated," J. H. Hexter remembers, "from both the new-fangled and the old-fashioned historians of the thirties and early forties. . . . While wandering in the outer darkness, I felt that it might be useful—and would certainly be pleasant—to pelt the children of light, the historians à la mode, with whatever missiles came my way in the course of my groping about." Hexter and other disengaged spirits now argued that the relativists wrongly equated knowledge with certainty and truth with completeness: knowledge is always open to doubt, and all truths are partial. The historian's "frame of reference" includes present values, to be sure; but it also includes a large and growing mass of data about the past. The past is just as real, and just as capable of making itself felt in the formulation of historical generalizations, as is the present.[2]

At first critics hit Beard and Becker without repudiating the larger climate of opinion in which their ideas had formed. Morton White's influential book on the great liberal thinkers of the early twentieth century, *Social Thought in America* (1949), included a penultimate chapter sharply distinguishing "the later, non-synoptic gospel according to Beard" from the pragmatic and progressive ideas of the first three decades of the century. White rejected Beard's relativism as alien to the ideas of Dewey, Robinson, and Beard himself at an earlier date. Other postwar liberals, however, broke away from the whole pragmatic, evolutionist frame of mind. These historians observed that the weaknesses of historical relativism derived at least in part from its pragmatic origins. Chester M. Destler in 1950, and Burleigh T. Wilkins with more sophistication in 1959, pointed out that John Dewey stated a theory of history much like that of the rela-

---

[2] J. H. Hexter, *Reappraisals in History* (1961), pp. 1-13, 187-91. See also Harry J. Marks, "Ground Under Our Feet: Beard's Relativism," *Journal of the History of Ideas,* XIV (1953), 628-33; Perez Zagorin, "Professor Becker's Two Histories: A Skeptical Fallacy," *AHR,* LXII (1956), 1-11.

tivist historians; and that all of them slurred a necessary distinction between judgments of fact and judgments of value.[3]

A general reaction against pragmatic and progressive ways of thinking had much to do with the retreat of postwar historians from present-mindedness. Even philosophers like White, who felt a strong affinity with pragmatism, knew in the late 1940's that the movement had lost its momentum. It could not, in truth, survive the multiple catastrophes of the midcentury. It rested on a faith in progress; and the decline of the idea of progress left pragmatic philosophy and present-minded history invertebrate. Pragmatists had cheerfully trusted in the outcome of things to establish their truth or falsity. Similarly, the New Historians had subordinated past to present because they looked to the present and future direction of history for criteria of what is important and desirable. The relativism of Becker and Beard—precipitated as it was by a crisis in the progressive faith—arose from their unwillingness to surrender that faith. In disputing the historian's claim to objectivity, both of them were defending his participation in the forward thrust of life.

All of these tendencies received a decisive check when the course of history failed to vindicate progressive values. In some intellectual circles the dream of progress had faded after World War I. Among academic historians it persisted through the Twenties and into the Thirties, then dissolved during and after World War II. The breakdown of progressive assumptions freed historians, not from dependence on the present, but from an overdeveloped commitment to it. Past history escaped from deliberate subordination to future history; and a hardheaded unwillingness to rely upon the future restored a fuller integrity to the past.

An early sign of this change of heart appeared in an article entitled "Postwar Reorientation of Historical Thinking," which Roy Nichols published in the *American Historical Review* in 1948. Nichols had felt keenly the shortcomings of history vis-à-vis the social sciences; and as a great admirer of Beard, he was originally responsible for bringing the latter into the SSRC deliberations on historiography. Now, looking back over historical theory in the interwar period, Nichols concluded that historians had pushed a "doc-

[3] Chester M. Destler, "Some Observations on Contemporary Historical Theory," *AHR*, LV (1950), 517-20; Burleigh T. Wilkins, "Pragmatism as a Theory of Historical Knowledge," *AHR*, LXIV (1959), 878-90.

trine of uncertainty" too far. A "heedless optimism" about the future had entrapped them in the "slavery of present-mindedness." Now, he thought, less bemused by progress, historians could throw off the enslavement and become more positive and self-confident about their own intellectual functions.

In renouncing present-mindedness, Nichols also shifted ground on the question of history's relation to the social sciences. His call for a new self-confidence among historians was, in fact, a gentle "declaration of intellectual independence." In place of the widespread sense that New Historians had had of the backwardness of their discipline in comparison with supposedly more advanced social sciences, Nichols now affirmed that history will not bear such invidious comparison; for history is not science any more than it is art or literature. It is *sui generis*.[4]

This reaction against subordination of history to the social sciences was closely connected with the parallel reaction against subordinating the past to the present. Both strategies had arisen in the early twentieth century from an idolization of progress. Both reflected an urge to catch up with the exciting growth of the social sciences and to share in their influence. After World War II, the grim, intractable dilemmas of the contemporary scene, and the narrow range of alternatives it seemed to offer, sobered the claims of the social sciences. The progressive habit of grading intellectual activity according to its degree of contemporaneity diminished. In one sense the outlook of the professional historian had come full circle: the entrenchment of scientific history in the 1870's and 1880's had required a declaration of independence from literature and philosophy; the reform of scientific history in the early twentieth century brought it under the sway of the social sciences; and a declaration of partial independence from them after World War II reconstituted the historian's autonomous identity.

During the 1950's the attitudes vaguely prefigured in Nichols' essay of 1948 became the dominant outlook in the American historical profession. But the view—it can hardly be called a program, and it had no party label—spread undramatically, without the bitter de-

[4] Roy F. Nichols, "Postwar Reorientation of Historical Thinking," *AHR*, LIV (1948), 78-89. See also Max Savelle's autobiographical "Historian's Progress, or The Quest for Sancta Sophia," *Pacific Historical Review*, XXVII (1958), 1-26.

bate that raged in the Thirties and Forties. The absence of pyrotechnics suggests the constructive and temperate nature of the change. Neither the critique of relativism nor the affirmation of independence was dogmatic. Both trends made headway through an enlargement of intellectual sympathies and a reduction of the sharp ideological cleavage of the preceding decades.

On the score of relativism, historians did not swing back to the simple faith in a hard, external reality, and the accompanying distrust of their own shaping imagination, that characterized scientific history. The age of realism and naturalism in American culture had passed. Historians no longer considered their own subjectivity as exclusively a problem or a barrier to struggle against. It was that, of course. The task of historiography would always require the utmost divestment of bias and the penetration of a realm beyond the immediate self and its immediate society. But historians now knew that this achievement is not simply an act of self-effacement, not an effort to register passively the harmonies of an evolutionary pattern. It calls for a creative outreach of imagination and draws upon all the resources of the historian's human condition.

Accordingly, the historian can and should make use of his present in the very act of transcending it. Hexter wrote in 1954: "History thrives in measure as the experience of each historian differs from that of his fellows. It is indeed the wide and varied range of experience covered by all the days of all historians that makes the rewriting of history—not in each generation but for each historian—at once necessary and inevitable." [5] Thus the relativity of history can be accepted without apology as a challenge to intellectual adventure. Standing at the intersection between past and present, the historian can reject the pragmatic doctrine of his subservience to present purposes while welcoming the incentives and general awareness of the present in discovering new vistas of the past.

The relativity of history in this sense did not put it at a disadvantage in relation to science. The relativism of the Thirties, imprisoning the historian in his contemporary world, reflected a sense of the inferiority of history as a science. The relativity of the Fifties, emphasizing the positive opportunities of the historian's observational position, took the invidious sting out of the comparison. Physicists had learned to live as happily with their principles of relativity and un-

5 Hexter, op. cit., p. 13.

certainty as historians had learned to live with theirs. Both appreciated the importance of imaginative insight in the strategy of inquiry, and neither now drew extravagant conclusions from the downfall of the nineteenth century concept of science as a statement of absolute causal laws governing and explaining all things.

Similarly, the revival of the historians' self-respect relaxed the tensions between history and the social sciences. Less interested now in spurning others than in becoming themselves, historians seemed in some ways more receptive than they had been earlier to the teachings of their sister disciplines. Far from rejecting social science, Nichols coupled his call for independence with a continuing appeal for receptiveness to the methods of the social sciences. The principal statements of historical theory in the following years repeatedly attested the interest of leading historians in utilizing the thinking of their fellow workers in other fields. But many insisted now on utilizing such thinking in their own way and for their own distinctive ends. Instead of considering the social sciences as upstart rivals, in the manner of prewar conservative historians, or history as the handmaiden of the social sciences, after the usual fashion of the New Historians, postwar historians consider these disciplines as contributory to history. Once rid of the inferiority complex that provoked both antagonism and servility before World War II, historians look outward for intellectual stimulation and assistance without quarreling so much about the desirability of doing so. The new mood is enabling them to draw more fruitfully on the behavioral disciplines than they could under the influence of the indiscriminate enthusiasm and the reactive hostility of the 1930's.

Important differences of outlook in the profession certainly remain, and they still tend to be expressed in terms of relations with the social sciences. The debate is more temperate and constructive now. It usually presupposes a pluralistic appreciation of the many varieties of history and of social science; and hardly anyone denies that part of the contemporary culture with which historians interrogate the past resides in the social sciences. The issue goes rather to the nature of historical and scientific argument.

Some historians, in the positivist tradition, still regard scientific explanation—the testing of general laws by application to specific events—as the sole model of historical explanation. They expect by this means to achieve increasing agreement on problems of causation. They consider their colleagues regrettably vague, superficial, and short in analytical rigor. Against this view others contend that the historian is essentially a dramatist, whose narrative logic can never be simplified by any general theories and whose real task is to grasp the unanalyzable complexity of things.[6] Most historians occupy a position somewhere between these extremes: undaunted by the openness and imprecision of historical discourse, yet glad to have the help of any systematic concepts that can offer partial clarification of a particular historical problem. Most would probably agree with H. Stuart Hughes that "the historian's supreme technical virtuosity lies in fusing the new method of social and psychological analysis with his traditional storytelling function." [7]

The shift to an eclectic attitude on history's relations with its neighbors may even be followed in some of the postwar activities of the Social Science Research Council. At first the historians associated with the Council resumed their prewar campaign to teach their colleagues to be social scientists. Since Bulletin 54 had not done this, a new Committee on Historiography undertook to "sell" to the profession the "basic concepts" of the social sciences. All of the committee members earnestly espoused the "social-science approach" that had arisen in the 1930's. This they elaborated, though without the explicit present-mindedness evident before the war, in the Council's Bulletin 64, published in 1954 after many vicissitudes. Every page assumed that the social sciences provide history with its only reliable source of theory and techniques of proof; historians should therefore model themselves on their brethren.[8]

A different point of view emerged, however, from a separate conference of leading historians that the Council sponsored at Princeton in 1953. Whereas the SSRC committee concerned itself exclusively with what the historian should become, the conference discussed what he actually is. It concluded that the historian makes estimates of

[6] Lee Benson and Cushing Strout, "Causation and the American Civil War: Two Appraisals," *History and Theory*, I (1961), 163-85.
[7] H. Stuart Hughes, *History as Art and as Science* (1964), p. 77, and "The Historian and the Social Scientist," *AHR*, LXVI (1960), 35-38, 44-46. See also William B. Munro, "Clio and Her Cousins," *Pacific Historical Review*, X (1941), 403-10; René Albrecht-Carrié, "The Social Sciences and History," *Social Education*, XVI (1952), 315-18; W. Stull Holt, "History and the Social Sciences Reconsidered," *Kyklos*, IV (1955), 389-96; R. E. McGrew, "History and the Social Sciences," *Antioch Review*, XVIII (1958), 276-89.
[8] *The Social Sciences in Historical Study* (1954).

complex situations, judging which universals are present and to what extent; that he resembles in this respect an administrator rather than a scientist; and that he should not try to become a social scientist, though he should make use of abstractions drawn from social science or from any other reputable source. These sentiments did not come from old fogies, but rather from scholars like Robert R. Palmer and Oscar Handlin, whose intellectual antecedents went back to the New History and who had a healthy respect for the social sciences as well as an ability to employ their procedures.[9]

A third SSRC committee on historiography, appointed in 1956 to carry on the work of the first two, showed much less assurance about how to reform the historical profession. Composed largely of veterans of the earlier committees, the new one started with the same aim of promoting the explicit, systematic procedures associated with the social sciences. This committee was influenced, however, by the rising respect for the humanistic complexity of historical thought. It decided to find out what historians were doing for themselves in the way of arriving at sound generalizations, and accordingly solicited essays from specialists in several fields. The final report was an inconclusive confession of the difficulties of categorizing historical generalizations.[10]

Meanwhile among social scientists there were signs of a renewed appreciation for historical perspective. The predominant attitude in the decade after World War II remained—indeed became more —antihistorical under the influence of a "behavioral approach" pledged to precise quantification of the activities of the human machine. Nevertheless, in certain relatively backward fields, notably the new area studies, a genuine reciprocity between historical and systematic analysis developed. By the 1960's appreciation of the need for historical and speculative thought if the study of man was to escape triviality seemed on the rise.[11] If the vogue of behavioralism and

[9] R. D. Challener and M. Lee Jr., "History and the Social Sciences: The Problem of Communications," *AHR*, LX (1956), 331-38. See the wry comment on this and other conferences in C. Vann Woodward's "Report on Current Research: American History," *Saturday Review*, XXXVI (April 4, 1953), 16.

[10] Louis Gottschalk, ed., *Generalization in the Writing of History* (1963).

[11] It is significant that the new journal *Comparative Studies in Society and History* has attracted contributions most readily from students of non-Western areas. On the possibility of a larger historical dimension in the social sciences see Robert A. Dahl's "The Behavioral Approach in Political Science," *American Political Science Review*, LV (1961), 771.

the related vogue of cybernetics are indeed losing their sectarian exclusiveness, social scientists may be able to join historians in comparative historical studies with the mutual sympathy and advantage that have already developed in some of the area programs.

It should be evident from what has been said so far that historians, in acquiring a more confident and perhaps more sophisticated attitude toward the social sciences, have discovered more widely and deeply than ever before the humanistic implications of their own craft. As they ceased to feel inferior to, or resentful of, the social sciences, many came to regard as positive assets those human qualities of history that are neither reducible to formula nor susceptible of proof. This raised anew an old issue. Delivered from a parochial dispute over their standing as scientists, postwar historians faced the wider question of whether history is an art *or* a science. In view of the rough division of the American educational curriculum into "arts" and "sciences," it was perhaps inevitable that theoretical problems would again be posed in these classic terms. Yet the enhanced self-confidence and the eclectic outlook of most historians prohibit any simple choice. They assert the participation of history in art as well as science; they deny its possession by either.

One of the more obvious humanistic aspects of history that professional scholars have rated highly in recent years is its connection with literature and philosophy. The breach that the early scientific historians made, and most of the New Historians perpetuated, between history on the one hand and literature and philosophy on the other, began to close in the 1930's, chiefly through the influence of Becker and Beard and the search for values that they initiated. The concomitant awakening of a special interest in intellectual history among some professional scholars also pulled them toward the humanistic disciplines; and the penetration into professional circles of the popular interest in biography exerted another humanizing influence.[12] These forces were just beginning to impinge upon the still powerful currents of scientific history in the 1930's. Only since then has the academic schism between history and the humanities largely healed.

The engagement of postwar historians with literature goes beyond the question of "style" to reach the very form and texture of their

[12] J. R. Strayer, ed., *The Interpretation of History* (1943), pp. 121-48.

work. Many of them, to be sure, write better than all but a few of their predecessors, and some of them use literary sources with a sensitiveness never before attained by American professional historians. In addition, there is now a widespread awareness that reality does not present a natural, perceptible pattern for the organization of historical knowledge, nor can the historian rely on any extrinsic formula for arranging his facts. His knowledge becomes meaningful only as he shapes it into a symbolic design. "The unity of past action that is seen or sensed or understood by the historian is both the starting point and the goal of his art." [13] His task is therefore akin to that of a novelist or a playwright. Whereas academic historians traditionally considered "style" as an icing on the cake of scholarship, which some liked because it would improve the taste and others distrusted because it might spoil the appetite for solid nourishment, many now realize that style as an external application is inevitably artificial; for any authentic craft blends manner and matter, form and substance, in a single creative process.

A growing sensitiveness to philosophy has accompanied the new interest in aesthetic form, and both have sprung from the same root. Both reveal a new consciousness of the human and the problematical. Both have resulted from the breakdown of the old assumptions of scientific history, chief among which was an unexamined faith in evolutionary progress. Deprived of their erstwhile assurance that human affairs fall naturally into a sequence of adaptation and growth, historians have had to probe matters they once took for granted: the overarching patterns of history, the character of historical thought, and the form of historical work. The philosophic impulse, like the aesthetic, feeds upon the need for coherent design.

Although the ability of American historians to deal with theoretical and speculative issues has matured considerably since World War II, receptiveness to such issues really began with the relativist controversy of the Thirties. Perhaps the most lasting contribution that Beard and Becker made to the profession was in awakening a philosophical consciousness. If the relativists failed to reach their own immediate goals and even lost their way in confusion, they neverthe-

[13] Loren Baritz, "The Historian as Playwright," *Nation,* CXCV (1962), 341. See also C. Vann Woodward, *The Burden of Southern History* (1961), pp. 27-39.

less ended the age of innocence in American historiography. When the American Historical Association thirty years ago published a *Guide to Historical Literature* (1931), it listed just ten works on the philosophy of history, only one of which had appeared since 1875. Presumably nothing written in the late nineteenth or twentieth century, except Spengler's *Decline of the West,* merited the attention of a professional historian. A comparable section of the new *Guide to Historical Literature* that the AHA brought out in 1961 included 59 titles, almost all published in recent decades. The best work still came from Europeans. Although American scholarly journals now welcome theoretical and speculative essays, no American historian has yet produced a major book on the nature of history. It was, however, the relativist controversy, together with the concurrent influx of refugee scholars from Europe, that reopened American access to European historical theory.

In the thirty years since Beard came seriously to grips with Croce, Heussi, and others, that access has widened immensely. Uninterrupted intellectual communication across the Atlantic has, more than any other factor, raised the level of theoretical discourse in the American historical profession. Americans have learned in the last two decades from such notable refugees as Ernst Cassirer, Karl Löwith, Carl G. Hempel, and Hajo Holborn; from such Continental philosophers and historians as Friedrich Meinecke, Raymond Aron, Henri Marrou, Ortega y Gasset, Carlo Antoni, and Pieter Geyl; and from such various Englishmen as Herbert Butterfield, Isaiah Berlin, and E. H. Carr.[14] The single greatest influence has probably been that of a formerly neglected Oxford philosopher, R. G. Collingwood, whose posthumous work, *The Idea of History* (1946), quickly attracted an important following among American historians; its imprint was

[14] Ernst Cassirer, *An Essay on Man* (1944); Karl Löwith, *Meaning in History* (1949); Carl G. Hempel, "The Function of General Laws in History," in *Readings in Philosophical Analysis,* ed. Herbert Feigl and W. S. Sellars (1949), pp. 459-71; Friedrich Meinecke, "Values and Causalities in History," in *The Varieties of History,* ed. Fritz Stern (1956), pp. 268-88; Raymond Aron, *Introduction to the Philosophy of History* (1961); Henri Marrou, *De la connaissance historique* (Paris, 1955); Ortega y Gasset, *Toward a Philosophy of History* (1941); Carlo Antoni, *From History to Sociology* (1959); Pieter Geyl, *Debates with Historians* (1958); Herbert Butterfield, *History and Human Relations* (London, 1951); Isaiah Berlin, *Historical Inevitability* (London, 1954); Edward H. Carr, *What Is History?* (1962). See also Hans Meyerhoff's influential anthology *The Philosophy of History in Our Time* (1959), and W. H. Walsh's *An Introduction to Philosophy of History* (London, 1958).

already visible upon Nichols' essay of 1948.[15] On the whole, this in-pouring of speculative thought has confirmed and strengthened the association of history with the humanities; but it has done so in-directly, by clarifying the special character of historical knowledge.

Perhaps the most fundamental methodological proposition that has come out of this latest encounter with European thought is the necessity for historians to participate subjectively in whatever past they wish to understand. No amount of scientific analysis or synthesis can take the place of that crucial act of human empathy by which the historian identifies himself with another time and place, re-enacting the thoughts and reliving the experience of people remote from himself. Thus he tries to catch the distinctive resonance of a person, a situation, and an age, as it manifests itself amid the other phenomena among which it arises and into which it passes. Scien-tific historians, both of the orthodox and of the pragmatic school, neglected this empathic function. They located themselves outside of the people they studied. Today's historians feel much more need to get inside historical situations, for they depend less on an external scheme of meaning. Here too the contemporary historian departs from the evolutionist assumption that events can be adequately ex-plained as fixed links in a continuous chain of cause and effect. Un-willing to presuppose an all-embracing framework for history—rejecting both the old framework of evolutionary progress and the cyclical framework of the newer historical metaphysics—academic historians are finding meaning in history within the specific physi-ognomy of concrete human situations.

Few Americans, however, go all the way with Collingwood's ar-gument that history is "nothing but the re-enactment of past thought," a view that allows no scope for scientific thinking, for im-personal causes, or for general propositions in historical thought. No meaning is entirely intrinsic to a single situation. An adequate his-torical explanation should include a retrospective knowledge of con-sequences and conditions that the actual participants did not have. Most historians today seem to accept the responsibility of taking their stand at no one place, either inside or outside the scene of ac-tion. Instead, they move about, viewing a situation from within and from above, blending subjective identification with objective analy-sis, uniting art with science, recognizing the complementarity of per-

[15] Nichols, *op. cit.*, AHR, LIV (1948), 85.

spectives and the multiplicity of relationships by which the historian —and he alone—undertakes to grasp a transition in human affairs in its full contextual significance.[16]

It is unlikely that Americans will claim for historical knowledge the radical uniqueness and preeminence that European "historicists" like Collingwood insisted upon in their dispute with the natural sciences. For the typical American historian, if my story is correct, the special character of history inheres not in a definite and superior method of its own but rather in the convergence of all sorts of techniques and insights upon the explanation of human experience, in its full existential complexity, within the limits of a definite span of time. Having regained a strong position in American academic life by foreswearing isolation on the one hand and exclusive alliances on the other, historians are not likely to revert to either stance in the foreseeable future. Instead, they can rejoice in a mediating role. They can cheerfully concede the more systematic and intensive nature of other disciplines while maintaining their own unspecialized identity. Perhaps better than any other discipline in the American university, history can resist the partition of knowledge into two cultures.

[16] The following are in diverse ways illustrative: Leonard Krieger, "The Horizons of History," *AHR*, LXIII (1957), 62-74; Trygve Tholfsen, "What Is Living in Croce's Theory of History?" *The Historian*, XXIII (1961), 283-302; W. B. Willcox, "An Historian Looks at Social Change," *Journal of Social Issues*, XVII (1961), 50-65; John T. Marcus, "The Changing Consciousness of History," *South Atlantic Quarterly*, LX (1961), 217-25; "The Nature of History," AHA *Newsletter*, II (April 1964), 5-7.

∾ III ∾

AMERICAN HISTORY

ക§ചൈ

In turning from the theories that historians have professed to the actual history they have written, we should not expect to find a simple, one-to-one correlation. Connections between theory and practice in historical work are usually circuitous and indistinct. The fluid, unsystematic character of the historian's enterprise rarely permits him to go directly from a general theory to a particular proof. He is even likely to be a bit unclear about what his historiographical assumptions are. Trying to discern the shape and order of a concrete situation, he may feel his way into it quite successfully without clearly formulating the preferences that guide him.

In fact, a taste for theoretical niceties, a strong urge for clarity and precision in basic assumptions, can actually prove a handicap in dealing effectively with historical data. To move freely through the complex web of human experience, historians need to employ simultaneously a multitude of causal hypotheses. Accordingly, a good historian is not likely to operate consistently within a single theoretical framework: any one perspective restricts his range of vision. Like literature, history can gain richness from the interpenetration of conflicting ideas, from the tensions of a divided allegiance.

On the other hand, a scholar does not readily change his basic cast of mind. Although his theoretical premises may be various and ambiguous, they are relatively stable influences on the history he writes. The general view of history a man acquires at an early age may not be fully displayed for many years; for the patient, aggregative nature of historical research often postpones the publication of major books until relatively late in life. A recent analysis of the most highly regarded books on American history published between 1920 and 1950 shows that the median age of their authors at date of publication was forty-nine. Some of these books had been in preparation for only four or five years, others for twenty or thirty.[1]

During this slow gestation, the prevailing intellectual milieu is constantly changing. New theories of history gain currency. As a result, the most substantial studies may appear after the principal as-

[1] John W. Caughey, "Historians' Choice: Results of a Poll on Recently Published American History and Biography," *Mississippi Valley Historical Review*, XXXIX (1952), 295.

sumptions on which they rest have gone out of fashion. No strictly professional historian in America published a major book prior to the twentieth century. Thus the orthodox scientific historians—from whom we might offhand expect stately institutional histories in the Eighties and Nineties—produced their best work after a reaction against their philosophy had arisen in the historical profession and elsewhere. The New Historians published their master works between the two world wars, although Frederick Jackson Turner had sketched out much of their program of inquiry in the 1890's. The reaction against the New History that began twenty years ago has not yet come fully to fruition. A coherent story of historical practice must take account of this cultural lag.

It must also take account of the more specific intellectual influences that are always impinging upon and reshaping historical interests and interpretations. Even when our general conception of history remains relatively fixed, our grasp of a concrete past is continually in flux. Scholarship steadily heaps up new knowledge, testing and revising our understanding of events. Also, the unfolding of new history keeps altering the appearance of events further back. In many subtle ways the focus of attention shifts. These adjustments may go on for a long time before the theoretical framework itself gives way.

Thus the course of scholarship on American history is intricate indeed. Nevertheless, the general trends in historical theory do provide a rough guide to practice. Each of the major schools of professional historians has emphasized certain features of the American past at the expense of others. Each has also held a characteristic view of the meaning of America.

The orthodox scientific historians inherited an over-all view of American history from the leading amateurs who dominated writing in the late nineteenth century. Both the amateurs and the founders of the profession were chiefly concerned with the evolution of national unity. For them American history culminated in the achievement of a more perfect union. We may call these scholars conservative evolutionists. In contrast, it will be useful to call the New Historians progressives; for their notion of the American heritage stemmed from social protest. Rather than unity, they emphasized diversity. To the progressives the Civil War was not a culmination but an episode in a still unfinished conflict between sections and economic groups. Finally, the postprogressive historians who have emerged since World War II are taking neither unity nor diversity for granted. The old assumptions have dissolved and reformed. The central question has come to be the nature and extent of stability in American history.

1

THE CONSERVATIVE EVOLUTIONIST
AS AMATEUR

During the last quarter of the nineteenth century five American scholars published major works on American history. Moses Coit Tyler mapped out the history of American writing in the colonial period and later in the Revolutionary period. Theodore Roosevelt brought back to life the early American frontier. John Bach McMaster traversed the whole span of history between the revolution and the Civil War. Henry Adams concentrated on the years from 1800 to 1817. James Ford Rhodes, working on an equally large scale, studied the era of the Civil War.[1]

None of these men was basically a professional historian. None of them had any formal training beyond a regular college education. Roosevelt, Adams, and Rhodes did not need to engage in remunerative employment. They wrote history in the leisure afforded by their own ample financial resources. The other two, Tyler and McMaster, held academic posts during most of their adult life. Tyler, the product of a large family with modest means, and McMaster, who was left penniless as a young man by the collapse of his father's oil speculations, had to work for a living; but neither of them secured an appointment to teach history until after he had made a public reputation writing it. Tyler, escaping first from the pulpit and then from the press, launched his historical studies while teaching English literature at the University of Michigan. McMaster published his first volume while holding an instructorship in engineering at Princeton. A third member of the group, Henry Adams, taught history at Harvard during a seven-year interlude (1870-77) in his life as a literary gentleman; but his principal historical works were written later, and he left

[1] Tyler, *A History of American Literature, 1607-1765* (2 vols., 1878), and *The Literary History of the American Revolution, 1763-1783* (2 vols., 1897); Roosevelt, *The Winning of the West* (4 vols., 1889-96); McMaster, *A History of the People of the United States from the Revolution to the Civil War* (8 vols., 1883-1913); Adams, *The History of the United States during the Administrations of Jefferson and Madison* (9 vols., 1889-91); Rhodes, *History of the United States from the Compromise of 1850* (7 vols., 1893-1906).

more of an impression on Harvard than it left on him. In sum, the leading authorities on American history in the late nineteenth century were self-made scholars. They belonged, by background or by enlistment, to the patrician tradition of historical writing.

All five of these scholars derived from New England or New York, the areas with the oldest historical societies and the most vigorous historical culture. New England especially had dominated historical writing in America since the seventeenth century. This was largely due to the intellectual and moral earnestness of the Puritan heritage—a heritage that drove men to keep diaries, to remember the example of their ancestors and hold themselves accountable to posterity, to prefer fact over fiction, and to welcome solid instruction in the record of human responsibility. Of the five leading American historians in the late nineteenth century, only McMaster was neither by family nor by education a product of New England. The most accomplished historian of the lot, Henry Adams, had the strongest roots in that region, and the influence of New England also told on the others. Roosevelt began writing his first historical work while an undergraduate at Harvard; Rhodes yearned toward and eventually moved to Boston from the Western Reserve, in itself an extension of New England; and Tyler, who spent most of his adult life elsewhere, never mentioned the region without mentally genuflecting.

All five wrote, nonetheless, as national historians, making a conscious effort to overcome the limitations of sectional prejudice. During the late 1870's and 1880's, when they embarked upon the works that made them famous, a mood of sectional reconciliation was softening the acerbities of the mid-nineteenth century. In literature the nostalgic "local color school" transformed the vanishing peculiarities of individual regions into national possessions. In philosophy an Hegelian taste for reconciling antitheses prevailed: it expressed a similar impulse to unite conflicting values into a national synthesis.

Accordingly, the leading patrician historians in the late nineteenth century took as a dominant theme the forging of national unity and power in a crucible of sectional diversities. These historians remembered the Civil War as the great public experience of their early, formative years. Indeed, it contributed largely to their interest in history: it inspired Henry Adams' first excursion into historical scholarship, it turned McMaster's interests from science to American history, it helped to divert Tyler from the ministry to journalism and literature, and it furnished Rhodes with the subject of his master work.[2] Looking back in the aftermath of the war at earlier American history, these scholars read it throughout as a story of nationalizing principles overcoming the selfish, parochial interests of individual groups or areas.

Moses Coit Tyler explored the intellectual history of the colonial period in *A History of American Literature, 1607-1765* (1878), and in doing so he focused attention on the transition from isolated, disparate settlements to a growing "colonial fellowship." "Henceforward," he concluded, "American literature flows in one, great common stream, and not in petty rills of geographical discrimination. Our future studies will deal with the literature of one multitudinous people, variegated, indeed, in personal traits, but single in its commanding ideas and in its national destinies." Henry Adams also qualified a special fondness for New England with an embracing sense of national destiny. Like Tyler's account of colonial thought, Adams' *History of the United States during the Administrations of Jefferson and Madison* (1889-91) dwelled heavily on a contrast between the principles of New England and Virginia. Yet Adams, again like Tyler, rebuked the narrowness of both sections. He too closed his work with an apostrophe to a united people, advancing victoriously in spite of the mistakes of both the Virginia Republicans and the New England Federalists.[3]

John Bach McMaster, entirely a product of the Middle Atlantic states, carried the story of national progress forward to the eve of the Civil War. His *History of the People of the United States* (1883-1913) was distinctively the history of a whole people, observed not in prismatic patterns but in a single kaleidoscopic movement. McMaster disparaged the South for its backwardness, its sluggish response to the forces of improvement. In general, however, he sub-

[2] Adams' first historical essay, a deflation of the Pocahontas legend, was a covert attack on the southern aristocracy written in London in 1862 when his propagandist activities went awry. See Henry B. Rule, "Henry Adams' Attack on Two Heroes of the Old South," *American Quarterly*, XIV (1962), 174-84. Cf. Eric F. Goldman, *John Bach McMaster, American Historian* (1943), pp. 8-10; Howard Mumford Jones, *The Life of Moses Coit Tyler* (1933), pp. 110, 148; Robert Cruden, *James Ford Rhodes: The Man, the Historian, and His Work* (1961). Theodore Roosevelt, the youngest of the group, was less than seven when the war ended.
[3] See the fine analysis in William Jordy's *Henry Adams, Scientific Historian* (1952).

ordinated sectional differences to nationwide trends. In examining the Negro problem, the Industrial Revolution, political ideas, public schools, and a host of other topics, his eye ranged methodically from place to place across the length and breadth of the land, suggesting an infinitude of local variations upon a common theme. His work ended with Lincoln's invocation in March 1861 of "the chorus of the Union."

James Ford Rhodes plunged into the maelstrom of sectional conflict, writing like McMaster from a decidedly northern point of view. Yet his was a northernism lacking in sectional bitterness and capable of understanding the Civil War not only as grand but also as tragic. Rhodes's *History of the United States from the Compromise of 1850* (1893-1906) tempered the northern tradition with an inclusive nationalism, a widespread distribution of responsibility for slavery, and a relatively generous view of southern motives. His *History* sealed the late nineteenth century compromise between the sections; for it upheld the North on the wartime issues of disunion and slavery while upholding the South on the postwar issues of military rule and Negro suffrage.

Although a number of amateur scholars in the late nineteenth century—notably Charles Francis Adams Jr. and William B. Weeden—studied local and regional topics in a broad critical perspective,[4] only one of the most eminent patrician historians chose a sectional setting for his principal work. Theodore Roosevelt's *The Winning of the West* (1889-96) recounted the history of the trans-Appalachian frontier from 1760 to 1807. Significantly, he approached it as an arena of national adventure. His was not a story of conflicts between East and West, nor of differences between Northwest and Southwest. It was essentially a military history of how the advance agents of American destiny wrested the possession of a continent from Indians, from Englishmen, and from nature. For Roosevelt, as much as for his peers, national solidarity was the permanent result of a disappearing sectional past.

Woven through the theme of national unity was a second motif

---

[4] Charles Francis Adams Jr., *Three Episodes of Massachusetts History* (2 vols., 1892); William B. Weeden, *Economic and Social History of New England, 1620-1789* (2 vols., 1890). See also Robert L. Beisner, "Brooks and Charles Francis Adams Jr., Historians of Massachusetts," *New England Quarterly*, XXXV (1962), 48-70, and William S. Powell, "Philip Alexander Bruce: Historian," *Tyler's Quarterly Historical and Genealogical Magazine*, XXX (1949), 165-84.

that defined the nineteenth century historians' sense of America: its dedication to freedom. In the historical thought of the 1880's freedom and union did not stand opposed to one another; they formed a single national design. If America was the testing ground and the standard bearer of freedom, every step forward in its unification strengthened the fabric of freedom. Looking back from the 1880's, historians beheld the Revolution as the confluence of American history, the Civil War as its climax; and the war recapitulated the meaning of the Revolution. Both demonstrated that freedom and unity triumphed together in American experience.

From this point of view, freedom was not a particular strand of American history, distinct from and opposed to other dominant strands and therefore requiring its own particular explanation. It was a presiding genius, a pervasive energy that needed only to be exemplified. While respecting America's indebtedness and affiliation to Europe, the leading historians assumed that liberty was distinctively the essence of American nationality. Adams sketched the national character by contrasting America's open society with the "artificial," class-ridden societies of Europe.[5] Tyler interpreted the American Revolution as the outcome of principles so deeply held that the mere anticipation of possible tyranny could rouse rebellion. Roosevelt celebrated the restless initiative of western men as the essential American spirit. McMaster described the growth of national power and wealth and the widening of political and social opportunities as aspects of a single process. Rhodes felt no inconsistency in acclaiming the emancipation of the Negro from slavery and the emancipation of the postwar South from northern oppression, because both developments extended the sphere of freedom.

While the principal amateur historians shared a somewhat similar view of the meaning of American history, in choice of subject matter they displayed an impressive breadth and range of interest. Several of them, of course, concentrated on political and military events. As successors to Parkman and Prescott and Bancroft, they inherited the special interest of patrician scholarship in wars and in the actions of heroic leaders. Adams built his masterpiece upon a

[5] See especially Volume I, Chapter 6, and Adams' comment to a friend: "I have pretty much made up my mind not to attempt giving interest to the society of America in itself, but to try for it by way of contrast with the artificial society of Europe." Worthington C. Ford, ed., *Letters of Henry Adams* (1938), vol. I, p. 328.

groundwork of international relations, which he considered "the only sure base for a chart of history." Both he and Rhodes gave their best efforts to the appraisal of statesmanship. Both were also shrewd students of military affairs, as were Roosevelt and the great historian of seapower, Alfred T. Mahan. On the other hand, most of the leading amateur scholars took a wider view of the historical process than had their midcentury predecessors. Even Rhodes, who professed a sovereign disdain for "the routine of work and the round of pleasures of the majority—those blank pages of history which, if written over, could indeed be tiresome," wrote more than a few such pages.[6] Adams, a much greater historian, tried more seriously to extend the limits of political history. Troubled by "the want of some formula" to explain the social forces underlying governmental policies, he depicted individual leaders as manifestations of national traits; and he enclosed his political narrative within an elaborate cross-sectional analysis of American society at the beginning and at the end of the period he covered.

Although Adams and Rhodes never felt really at home at a distance from the centers of power, other amateur historians with a less toplofty outlook had a positive zest for exploring the common experience of the great mass of the American people. Roosevelt, while acknowledging Parkman as his master, gained from his own intimate frontier experience an unParkman-like familiarity with ordinary folk. Roosevelt's annals of border warfare embraced all the multifarious activities of the western settlements. He described vividly not only wilderness adventures but also the creation of a civilization. Tyler, in gathering up for the first time the intellectual history of early America, did not confine himself to great ideas but instead treated literature as an expression of the life and spirit of the people. McMaster made the life of the people his grand, distinctive theme, for he wrote in the conviction that no nation had ever before advanced so wonderfully in material prosperity and moral sensibility.[7]

[6] Harvey Wish, *The American Historian* (1960), p. 226.

[7] McMaster, *op. cit.,* vol. I, pp. 1-2. In this brief sketch I have perhaps unjustly passed over Edward Eggleston, whose one important scholarly book, *The Transit of Civilization from England to America in the Seventeenth Century* (1901), was in some ways unique. A free-lance writer without either personal means or institutional support, Eggleston had a more genuinely democratic outlook and a correspondingly broader sense of the historical process than either Tyler or McMaster.

Thus, two of the five foremost historians of the United States in the late nineteenth century, Tyler and McMaster, fixed upon previously neglected dimensions of history as their special concern, and the others widened the scope of political narrative.

In venturing out upon a broad terrain, these men were following the example of the most celebrated English historians of the third quarter of the century: the example, above all, of Lord Macaulay, who gave a model of how social history might be written; of Henry Buckle and his disciple W. E. H. Lecky, who created a kind of intellectual history that seemed to measure the progress of society; and finally of John R. Green, whose *Short History of the English People* (1874) outsold any other historical work in America during the latter decades of the century.[8] American historians were writing then in an atmosphere charged with increasing deference toward English society and thought. Such deference was virtually a hallmark of the American aristocracy of culture. Although American historians valued the distinctive vigor and freedom of American life, they relied on English models for improving its tone and expression.

Like their English mentors, most of the leading American historians in the late nineteenth century had not broken completely with the older romantic approach to the past. Their outlook, to be sure, was realistic and evolutionary. We may call them, on balance, scientific historians; for they wrote as modern men appraising the past from the outside, observing events and individuals as loosely connected fragments of on-going experience, more interested in the literal accuracy of photographic statement than in the intuitive grasp of a unified, symbolic design. Yet their style of thought was transitional and eclectic; their approach to history was in some ways traditional.

Most of them considered themselves engaged in a literary as well as scientific task. For Rhodes, Tyler, and Roosevelt especially, history remained a branch of literature. Objectivity must temper but should not supplant the claims of art. This, in effect, was Henry Adams' position too. Although he tried, more rigorously and strenuously than any of his contemporaries, to make history a genuine science, an unyielding dedication to aesthetic objectives irradiated his history. Adams' greatness as a historian is partly due to a sustained tension between these allegiances.

[8] Frank Luther Mott, *Golden Multitudes: The Story of Best Sellers in the United States* (1947), pp. 241-42, 310.

As inheritors of a literary tradition, the gentlemen-historians still had an interest in the role of individuals. Rhodes, for example, excelled in judicious estimates of political and military leaders. Tyler—following St. Beuve—cast his narrative in the form of a succession of biographies. McMaster, to be sure, moved steadily away from personalities, eliminating biographical vignettes in his later volumes; and some of the less prominent amateur historians in the late nineteenth century eschewed this sort of thing altogether. Nevertheless, even the pedestrian McMaster, who derived his conception of history from Macaulay, retained some sense of the scenic and pictorial.

Finally, historians who conceived of themselves as men of letters relished the making of moral judgments on men and events. The office of distributing praise and blame, and pronouncing the magisterial verdict of history, was always dear to patrician hearts. The gentlemen of the late nineteenth century, convinced of their independence from partisan bias and zealous to instruct their often misguided countrymen in the lessons of national experience, agreed with Tacitus's injunction "to let no worthy action be uncommemorated, and to hold out the reprobation of posterity as a terror to evil works and deeds." Adams did this indirectly, behind an arch and mannered pose of aloofness. Roosevelt, Tyler, McMaster, and Rhodes spoke out directly and loudly. A secure faith in evolutionary progress enabled them to suppose that they, standing at the summit of history, could truly judge the actions and standards of earlier times by their own without loss of scientific objectivity. Each of them aligned himself with the successful forces in American history, with the national unity and orderly freedom that now seemed well established.

2

THE CONSERVATIVE EVOLUTIONIST
AS PROFESSOR

Much the same can be said of the first professional historians. Drawn into graduate work in the 1870's and early 1880's, when egalitarian ideas were at a discount, they entered through the gates of the modern university into the earnest and confident world of the aristocracy of culture. They acquired, if indeed they did not already possess, the high-minded conservatism of the patrician historians. They embraced the same vision of American history as a story of freedom realized and stabilized through the achievement of national solidarity. In general, this first generation of professional historians received the work of Adams, Rhodes, McMaster, Tyler, and Roosevelt with great respect. For all their desire to set the record straight, the earliest professionals avoided challenging the interpretations of the most illustrious contemporary amateur writers. The difference between the two groups lay not in their respective social values but in the form of their historical work.

Most of the early professional scholars broke more sharply with the literary tradition. Carrying further the impersonality of scientific history, they paid little attention to the role and less to the character of individuals. They scorned scenic display and dramatic incident. They tried to withhold explicit moral judgments on people and circumstances, not because they questioned history's didactic usefulness but because they supposed that objective scholarship would reveal the evolution of morality in the march of events without intrusive comment by the writer. They assumed that the reader could make his own fair and independent judgment if given an unobstructed view of the past.[1]

Finally, the professional historians gave up the effort to encompass a wide range of social and intellectual life. Instead, they concen-

[1] The classic argument for scientific neutrality was made, however, by an amateur historian, Henry C. Lea. See his presidential address, "Ethical Values in History," AHA *Annual Report* (1903), vol. I, pp. 53-69, and Charles Homer Haskins' endorsement in "Henry Charles Lea," *Studies in Medieval Culture* (Oxford, 1929), p. 262.

trated on institutions. Whether it was the town meeting, the business corporation, Negro slavery, or something else, the institution was a form of organization, a gradually evolving structure. To study institutions was to study the morphology of history, to trace through time the skeleton of a society as biologists were tracing the underlying structure of other organisms. Not all institutional studies were specifically political by any means. At Johns Hopkins Herbert Baxter Adams encouraged the study of educational systems. G. E. Howard of the University of Chicago published a three-volume *History of Matrimonial Institutions, Chiefly in England and the United States* (1904). A vigorous interest in the history of economic institutions led Harvard in 1892 to call W. J. Ashley to the first chair of economic history and inspired the newly formed Carnegie Institution in 1904 to plan a multivolume economic history of the United States.[2] Regardless of subject, however, the approach of the institutional historians was essentially constitutional. On marriage and divorce, Howard confined himself to successive legal and ceremonial prescriptions. Herbert Baxter Adams and his students dealt chiefly with legislation, and the economic historians also focused attention on the operations of government.

Part of the appeal of institutional history derived from its impersonal, presumably objective character. To fix attention on the formal constitution of group activities was to simplify and clarify historical problems, to delimit the issue of motivation, and to bypass fortuitous, individual behavior. Institutional history lent itself to coordinated effort. A number of scholars could study the same institution—each in a different setting—in the hope of deriving by comparative analysis a larger grasp of historical development. One of the chief stimuli for institutional history came from the rise in the nineteenth century of historical jurisprudence, which in the hands of Sir Henry Maine and others revealed apparent continuities and connections between widely separated eras.

Another part of the attraction of institutional history sprang from the conservative, organic nationalism of the post-Civil War decades. Believing that the national state, now evolving toward empire, constituted the highest form of organization mankind had yet achieved, scholars studied its polity and its sanctions with profound respect. In-

[2] N.S.B. Gras, "The Rise and Development of Economic History," *Economic History Review*, I (1927), 12-34.

stitutional history taught a sober regard for constitutional processes, for "a government of laws rather than men," as the phrase went. It recorded the slow upbuilding of national organization, thereby demonstrating that neither abstract theories nor selfish interests counted for much in human affairs in contrast to the structural principles gradually unfolded over a long span of time. In sum, the institutionalists had two closely related biases: in favor of homogeneity in society, and in favor of continuity in history. At a time when leaders of opinion rejoiced in the attainment of national unity and feared the outbreak of new social cleavages, there was much satisfaction in studying the unifying ligaments within a sequence of historical development.

Before this conservative evolutionism affected American academic thought it permeated the German universities, where the study of institutional history centered. Thence institutional history spread to England, through John M. Kemble, the magisterial Bishop Stubbs, and Stubbs's successor at Oxford, Edward A. Freeman.[3] It reached America partly through the students who flocked to Germany after 1870 and partly through the influence of the English Teutonists.

One of the special fascinations of institutional history lay in a search for origins. Tracing continuities and unearthing antecedents, the institutionalists were drawn backward especially to the colonial period. There they left their strongest mark. Moreover, they characteristically sought the origins of colonial institutions in earlier European experience. The first professional historians were more consistent than some of their amateur associates in rejecting the popular patriotism that imputed a radical uniqueness to American history. In writing institutional history, conservative professors felt the solid ground of the European past beneath their feet.

At first, by an easy combination of Anglophile and Germanophile sentiment, the Americans simply followed the lead of the English Teutonists. Pursuing an hypothesis of Sir Henry Maine, the early professional historians at Harvard and Johns Hopkins tried to prove that American local institutions originated in the forests of Germany. Primitive Teutonic forms of local government—so the theory went —had been transplanted to England by the Anglo-Saxons and then carried by their descendants to New England, where they re-emerged

[3] G. P. Gooch, *History and Historians in the Nineteenth Century* (1959), pp. 271-72, 317-29.

in the shape of the town meeting. Herbert Baxter Adams made the study of Germanic origins the mainstay of his seminar in the 1880's.[4] Similarly, at Harvard in 1883 Albert Bushnell Hart included the Teutonic hypothesis in a set of "fundamental principles of American history" that defined the initial program of the conservative evolutionists:

    1. No nation has a history disconnected from that of the rest of the world. . . .

    2. Institutions are a growth, not a creation: the Constitution of the United States itself is constantly changing with the changes in public opinion.

    3. Our institutions are Teutonic in origin: they have come to us through English institutions.

    4. The growth of our institutions has been from local to central. . . .

    5. The principle of union is of slow growth in America: the Constitution was formed from necessity, and not from preference.[5]

The program soon had to be amended: the shallowness of the Teutonic thesis was already being demonstrated in England. In 1883 Frederic Seebohm's *The English Village Community* argued forcefully that this institution derived from the Roman villa rather than the German mark. Several years later a skeptical young student of Herbert Baxter Adams, Charles McLean Andrews, challenged the whole theory. Having made in his doctoral dissertation a careful study of the early settlements on the Connecticut River, Andrews read a paper before the American Historical Association in 1890 pointing out that the Teutonists relied at every point on superficial similarities rather than demonstrable genetic connections. The New England town differed significantly from its supposed ancestors. Moreover, the very existence of self-governing communities of free men in Anglo-Saxon times rested on no reliable evidence. Another young colonial historian, Edward Channing, supplemented Andrews'

[4] Herbert Baxter Adams, *The Study of History in American Colleges and Universities* (U.S. Bureau of Education Circular No. 2, 1887), p. 173; Edward N. Saveth, *American Historians and European Immigrants*, 1875-1925 (1948), pp. 16-26.
[5] G. Stanley Hall, ed., *Methods of Teaching and Studying History* (1886), p. 3.

argument two years later by explaining the genesis of Massachusetts towns in terms of immediate political experience.[6]

Thereafter the investigation of European origins turned from the remote to the immediate English background of American colonial history. Interest in local institutions correspondingly diminished. The Teutonists had postulated that the towns were the original units from which larger political organizations evolved. Andrews showed, on the contrary, that the general government created the towns. Central institutions came first. One must therefore look to the framework of British policy to understand the American colonies. From the ruins of the Teutonic school rose in the 1890's the much more impressive and lasting Imperial school. English historians had largely neglected the study of imperial organization: the Americans now told the Old World something new about itself.

The pioneer was another young man, a student of John Burgess at Columbia named Herbert Levi Osgood. In 1887 while supporting himself by teaching high school in Brooklyn, Osgood published an article identifying "the central thread" of American colonial history. It is, he said, the growth of a system of imperial administration and the problems that system engendered.[7] Osgood felt keenly the general desire of conservative intellectuals in the late nineteenth century to understand American history in a wider transatlantic context. He wished above all to show that early America had not made a sudden, radical break from the European past. The patriotic insularity of mid-nineteenth century historians like George Bancroft and Richard Hildreth had outlived its usefulness. By looking at the colonies from the vantage point of the central government in London, one could learn that all of the truth and justice did not lie on either side of the eventual quarrel. Such a point of view strengthened Anglo-American sympathies much more concretely and directly than any fanciful Teutonic thesis. Moreover, the imperial framework gave coherence to the data of early American history and permitted a realistic comparison of institutions.

On receiving his Ph.D. in 1889, Osgood quit his high school job and used his little savings to live in London. For fifteen months he

[6] A. S. Eisenstadt, *Charles McLean Andrews* (1956), pp. 14-20; Saveth, *op. cit.*, pp. 26-31.
[7] "England and the Colonies," *Political Science Quarterly*, II (1887), pp. 440-469. See also Dixon Ryan Fox, *Herbert Levi Osgood, An American Scholar* (1924).

burrowed into the vast stores of documents in the Public Record Office. It came as a great liberation to learn how the colonies looked from the unifying perspective of London. Colonial history ceased to be a mere prelude to later American history and acquired a new interest and amplitude of its own. Establishing himself at Columbia University on his return from London, Osgood embarked on a lifelong task from which he never swerved. He wrote the institutional history of the colonial period as a whole.

An address to the American Historical Association in 1898 announced his program. Here Osgood stated his most important single contribution. a classification of the colonies according to constitutional structure. Historians had conventionally grouped the colonies by region—New England, middle, and southern. Osgood divided them into chartered colonies (corporate and proprietary) and royal colonies. This grouping offered a sounder basis for comparative political analysis than either a loose geographical division or remote Teutonic analogies. A comparison of colonial constitutions revealed the gradual improvement in imperial organization that accompanied the emergence of the royal colony, which provided a better balance between local and central power than either the corporate or the proprietary form.[8] The early stages of this transition Osgood expounded in great detail in *The American Colonies in the Seventeenth Century* (3 vols., 1904-1907). Before his death in 1918, he had largely completed four volumes on the colonies in the eighteenth century, which analyzed the further development of the royal colonies and the growing opposition between British executives and colonial assemblies.

In his first years of teaching at Columbia, Osgood was fortunate to have an extremely talented student, George Louis Beer. Beer concentrated on the economic aspects of British imperial policy. Like the other conservative evolutionists who investigated economic history, he concerned himself not with economic motives but rather with the political organization of economic progress. His four volumes on British colonial policy from 1578 to 1765 treated mercantilism as an honest and progressive effort to balance and harmonize the interests of all parts of the empire.[9]

[8] "The Study of American Colonial History," AHA *Annual Report* (1898), pp. 63-73.
[9] *British Colonial Policy, 1754-1765* (1907), *The Origins of the British Colonial*

Meanwhile, Charles M. Andrews was working independently along lines very similar to those Osgood followed. A strong interest in European history delayed Andrews' full commitment to early American history until the turn of the century; but a trip to England in 1893 to explore medieval sources disclosed to Andrews the wealth of colonial records that Osgood had discovered four years earlier. In 1898, addressing the American Historical Association, Andrews expounded an approach to American colonial history that was largely identical with the one Osgood outlined at the same session.[10]

Andrews went a step beyond his confrere in taking the imperial point of view. A genuinely comprehensive and unprovincial history, he argued, can not confine itself to the thirteen colonies that later became the United States. It should embrace the whole Anglo-American Empire before 1776. Ultimately Andrews' far-flung research extended to the Canadian and West Indian as well as the mainland colonies. Significantly, his design did not call for similar attention to the non-English empires and peoples that contributed to the formation of the United States. After discarding explicit theories of racial continuity, the conservative evolutionists remained Anglophiles, and their American history was wholly a continuation of English history.

In the long run Andrews surpassed Osgood in mastery of British administrative history, in command of the English sources, and in finesse of craftsmanship. He advanced with careful, unhurried steps. Much of his time in the early twentieth century went into producing for the Carnegie Institution two superlative guides to unpublished English sources for early American history. He contributed a volume to the "American Nation Series," sketched out his view of the whole span of colonial history in a short book of 1912,[11] but withheld his major books until very late in life.

Although the Imperial historians disregarded both the remote

System, 1578-1660 (1908), *The Old Colonial System, 1660-1754* (2 vols., 1912).

[10] "American Colonial History, 1690-1750," AHA *Annual Report* (1898), pp. 49-60.

[11] *Guide to the Manuscript Materials for the History of the United States to 1783 in the British Museum* . . . (1908); *Guide to the Materials for American History to 1783 in the Public Record Office* (2 vols., 1912-14); *Colonial Self-Government, 1652-1689* (1904); *The Colonial Period* (1912).

Teutonic "germs" of colonial history and its connection with subsequent American national history, they never questioned the prevailing bias of amateur and Teutonist scholars in favor of political unity and historical continuity. In respect to unity, they found in the imperial framework an integrating principle similar to that which national organization supplied for later American history. In respect to continuity, the colonial period became in itself the matrix of a slow evolutionary process. In effect, the Imperial historians greatly lengthened American colonial history. Both Andrews and Osgood pointed out in 1898 that the middle decades between colonization and revolution, the years from 1690 to 1760, had never been studied carefully. Colonial history would lack continuity until this neglected period was brought to light. Moreover, the origins of the American Revolution should be sought in the gradual alteration of British and colonial institutions during that long span of time.

When Andrews at length published his interpretation of the causes of the American Revolution, he framed it in these terms, as did Claude H. Van Tyne and other conservative evolutionists. Imperceptibly, over many decades, said Andrews in *The Colonial Background of the American Revolution* (1924), the mother country and the colonies drifted apart. The development of new British policies of imperial control eventually precipitated a constitutional crisis, in which a rigid, aristocratic society confronted a growing individualistic one. Irresponsible agitators with an impractical philosophy of natural rights made matters worse, but no individual or group was crucially responsible. The Americans were "obeying a law of general evolution of human society toward higher and broader forms of government and social relations." [12]

Insofar as it was a genuinely revolutionary struggle, the American Revolution did not make a congenial subject for writers of the Imperial school, and most of their work lay further back in studies of the Board of Trade, British land policy, vice-admiralty courts, rights of Parliament, and the like. Meanwhile other conservative evolutionists looked past the Revolution to American national history with much the same tendency to play down dramatic ruptures in historical continuity. In studying American national history as well as

[12] P. 208. See also Claude H. Van Tyne, *Causes of the War of Independence* (1922); Charles H. McIlwain, *The American Revolution: A Constitutional Interpretation* (1923).

American colonial history, orthodox scientific historians interpreted change in terms of a unifying structure of institutions and principles.

Inevitably, for the period after 1776, the history of the federal constitution provided a focus comparable to that which imperial organization gave to colonial history. Andrew C. McLaughlin, one of the best of the constitutional historians, pointed out this continuity forcefully. He saw that the great problem of the early republic was the old colonial problem of reconciling liberty with central authority, and that the framers of the Constitution in 1787 in effect reestablished the old division of powers between local and central government. McLaughlin's contribution to the "American Nation Series," *The Confederation and the Constitution, 1783-1789* (1905), hailed the reorganization of these years as a conservative triumph of experience over impractical theories of pure democracy. Indeed, all of McLaughlin's writings breathed a deep respect for the continuity of the Anglo-American legal tradition.[13]

The same may be said of Edward S. Corwin, perhaps the finest of the historians of the American constitution. Corwin taught politics at Princeton from 1905 until his retirement more than forty years later. Many of his writings were historical commentaries on contemporary problems, and much of his best work appeared in the form of long articles in law reviews; so he did not leave an easily accessible corpus of historical scholarship. No one, however, matched the subtlety and precision with which he laid out the history of constitutional ideas. He looked upon constitutional law as designed primarily to set limits to legislative power. In tracing the evolution of such related concepts as judicial review, due process, and "vested right," Corwin emphasized the widespread desire of great American lawyers to give national protection to private rights threatened by legislative majorities. He depicted constitutional history as a stately interplay of doctrines that, at their best, vindicated not equality or state rights, but freedom and national power.[14]

---

[13] Pp. 35-42, 275; *The Foundations of American Constitutionalism* (1932).

[14] "The Doctrine of Due Process of Law Before the Civil War," *Harvard Law Review*, XXIV (1911), 366-85; "The Basic Doctrine of American Constitutional Law," *Michigan Law Review*, XII (1914), 247-76; *The Doctrine of Judicial Review* (1914); *John Marshall and the Constitution* (1919); "The 'Higher Law' Background of American Constitutional Law," *Harvard Law Review*, XLII (1928-29), 149-85, 365-409.

Constitutional issues also bulked large in the professional historians' treatment of the Civil War. Here was a time when unity and continuity had obviously and drastically broken down. Nevertheless, the main strategy of conservative evolutionists was to examine that fierce struggle as a stage in the consolidation of a united nation. In doing so, they strove to transcend sectional bias just as the Imperial school was striving to transcend a provincial bias. Most of the professional scholars went a step beyond James Ford Rhodes in withholding blame for the war and in taking a broadly national point of view. A constitutional approach was most useful in this regard; for one could argue that the South fought at least in part to defend an old-fashioned doctrine of state sovereignty that was being outmoded by the march of progress. By linking the slavery issue to a dispute over constitutional principles, historians dignified the position of both sections. The South clung to the original conception of the Union as a compact of states, whereas the North fought for the integral nation that the Union had become.[15]

On the subject of Reconstruction, the most recent period with which scholars dealt at all carefully, the acknowledged master was William A. Dunning. His doctoral dissertation, submitted at Columbia in 1885, concerned the history of the Constitution from 1860 to 1867. Although he taught a notable seminar in political philosophy and spent much of his scholarly energy on a history of European political theories, his influence on the study of the Reconstruction period proved much more enduring. Dunning published two outstanding books on that era, one a collection of essays on constitutional problems, the other a general volume in the "American Nation Series."[16] In these he maintained such Olympian aloofness from the northern bias of previous scholars that southerners flocked to Columbia to study under him. Their monographs on the reconstruction process in individual states gave substance to the "Dunning school."

---

[15] This was the view of Woodrow Wilson in *Division and Reunion, 1829-1889* (1893), p. 211. A residue of antisouthern feeling survives in John W. Burgess, *The Civil War and the Constitution* (2 vols., 1901). See Thomas J. Pressly, *Americans Interpret Their Civil War*, 2nd ed. (1962), pp. 162-63, 202-206.
[16] *Essays on the Civil War and Reconstruction* (1897); *Reconstruction, Political and Economic, 1865-1877* (1907). On the Dunning school see Wendell H. Stephenson's *The South Lives in History: Southern Historians and Their Legacy* (1955).

Essentially, Dunning agreed with the view that Rhodes was simultaneously expounding. Turbulent and unlovely as the post-Civil War years were, they could be shaped to the evolutionary pattern of national progress if one endorsed their final outcome: the reunion of North and South through the overthrow of military despotism and the restoration of white supremacy. Thus Dunning, like Rhodes and the vast majority of American historians, ratified the results both of the Civil War and of its aftermath. In the first, national unity triumphed over slavery in the South; in the second it triumphed over radical democracy in the North. This approach required, of course, a disapproval of the Radical policies of Congress in the late 1860's— a disapproval that paralleled Corwin's distrust of legislative majorities, Andrews' disdain for irresponsible agitators, and McLaughlin's criticism of the excessively democratic spirit unleashed by the Revolution.

In the case of Reconstruction, the conservative interpretation inevitably disparaged Negro claims to equality and Negro participation in government. Dunning shared the almost universal anti-Negro bias of white Americans of his day; and it is now common to assume that racial stereotypes determined his treatment of the period. Yet the distinctive feature of Dunning's book, *Reconstruction, Political and Economic, 1865-1877* (1907) was not his distaste for "barbarous freedmen" but rather the careful balance he held in discussing conditions in the South and in the North. His primary theme was the temporary breakdown and eventual recovery of probity and constitutional order in all parts of the country. Believing in reason as a restraint upon popular passions, in the educated man as a saving remnant, and above all in the majesty of the law, Dunning held no brief for the lawless tactics of the southern whites in regaining power. To him it was not only the rule of ignorance, force and fraud in the South that was deplorable but the misgovernment and commercial chicane of the whole period. The Negro was not simply an inferior race; he was a symbol of the political and economic corruption that pervaded the postwar era.

While these intensive studies of particular periods and topics were coming out, a crusty, determined little man at Harvard, Edward Channing, was methodically working his way through the whole sweep of American history on the basis of original sources. A proper

Bostonian descended from illustrious families, Channing was converted as an undergraduate from law to history by the teaching of Henry Adams. Only after establishing himself as a full professor, however, did Channing at the turn of the century take up the single task of the rest of his life. Thereafter he renounced church attendance, scholarly meetings, social engagements, and general faculty business in order to concentrate completely on *A History of the United States* (6 vols., 1905-25).

This was the most ambitious, and in some ways the crowning result of the conservative evolutionist approach to American history. The preface to the first volume declared Channing's grand theme: "the victory of the forces of union over those of particularism." "The guiding idea in the present work," he continued, "is to view the subject as the record of an evolution, and to trace . . . the story of living forces, always struggling onward and upward toward that which is better and higher in human conception." On the colonial period Channing adopted by and large the imperial point of view, arguing that the colonies and the mother country "drifted apart" in the century before 1760 through a gradual divergence of institutions. On the national period he applauded the growth of large-scale organization, praised Jefferson's loyalty to national interests, treated Jackson as a narrowly sectional man, and allowed the Old South a generous measure of sympathy.

Yet Channing's *History* does not fit neatly within a consistent style of historical thought. It was in one respect more old-fashioned than orthodox scientific history, and in another respect more modern. Educated entirely in Boston by men unblessed with German seminar training, Channing had about him something of the amateur litterateur. He gave much more attention to the role and traits of leading individuals than a true institutionalist would have done; his pages twinkled with personal comments on men and events. On the other hand, Channing also modified the conservative, institutional approach under the influence of new ideas being advanced by the reformers in the historical profession. By 1912, when Volume III dealing with the Revolution and the Constitution came out, the author was convinced that these had resulted chiefly from economic forces. "All historical development," he observed, "is founded upon industry, upon the necessity of supporting life, and the way in which it is done. . . . The historian owes a debt of deepest gratitude to the economist." [17] The last volumes of the *History* made much of the Industrial Revolution, underscored a conflict between agrarianism and capitalism, and depicted a great gulf between the divergent civilizations of North and South. Channing failed to relate effectively his social and economic data to his political narrative. He remained always in a special sense a conservative Boston Brahmin. Yet his work illustrates the fruitful interplay of competing ideas in a sensitive historical mind.

.

[17] J. F. Jameson and Edward Channing, *The Present State of Historical Writing in America* (1910), p. 25. In general see Samuel Eliot Morison, "Edward Channing: A Memoir," Massachusetts Historical Society *Proceedings*, LXIV (1931), 250-84.

❧ 3 ❧

THE RISE OF PROGRESSIVE HISTORY

In 1907 at a session of the American Historical Association devoted to American constitutional history, Professor William MacDonald read his colleagues a warning. Danger has arisen, he said, that an overemphasis on the economic and social aspects of American history will lead to neglect of the part that law has played in shaping our development.[1] At a time when legalism was so clearly dominant in historical scholarship the warning seems absurdly premature. The Imperial school and the Dunning school had only just emerged; the major works of Andrews, Corwin, McLaughlin, and others were far in the future. Yet MacDonald knew what he was talking about. A powerful undertow was at work, pulling younger men more sharply in the direction in which Channing was turning. It was the pull of the New History, already tugging strongly in those early years before James Harvey Robinson popularized its program.

To understand the history that the New Historians actually wrote we shall have to look behind Robinson's formal creed. The desire to widen the scope of history, to relate it to the present, and to link it with the social sciences were conscious objectives at a very early date; Frederick Jackson Turner espoused them in the 1890's. But these objectives do not in themselves explain what he and his successors did. The crucial fact underlying both their theory and their practice was a broad sympathy with the spirit of reform then developing in contemporary life. This sympathy induced an attitude toward change and continuity quite different from that of their conservative colleagues.

As progressives, the New Historians had a vivid sense that a great turning point had arrived in American experience. They wanted to participate in the transformation and to explain it. Accordingly, they studied history with more interest in interpreting change than articulating continuity. Carl Becker spoke for his own generation when he commented that the eighteenth century *philosophes* had little use for the conception of continuity in history, which nineteenth century historians established: "The reason is that the eighteenth-century

[1] AHA *Annual Report* (1907), vol. I, p. 79.

Philosophers were not primarily interested in stabilizing society, but in changing it." [2] Moreover, the kind of change that seemed important to the *philosophes* of the twentieth century was not the slow unfolding of institutions through an inner logic of their own, but rather the kind wrought out of conflicts of interest and clashes of purpose. To be progressive was to believe that the progress of society was neither automatic nor secure, but had to be won at every step, over entrenched opposition.

For progressive historians, then, the dynamics of change constituted the great issue of historical inquiry. Their rebellion against the dominant kind of institutional history did not arise from indifference to politics or constitutions; much of their research concerned political organizations, particularly political parties. But they wanted above all to know how and why these agencies responded to and effected transformations in a wider field of action. Whereas conservative evolutionists concentrated on the character of institutions, understood in terms of their origins, progressives focused on changes in institutions, explained in terms of a surrounding environment.[3] Their insistence on broadening the scope of history was, therefore, in large measure a search for the causes and conditions of change. Earlier explorations of social and economic history had proceeded from other motives, so it is little wonder that progressive historians paid only grudging compliments to such predecessors as McMaster and Macaulay. Their portrayal of historical environments seemed too static for progressive tastes, too little designed to explain the changes in human affairs.

In turning outward from institutional to environmental history, progressive scholars were in another respect turning inward. They were becoming in a certain sense more nationalistic than their conservative colleagues. The latter, seeking the European origins of our institutions, had inveighed against a provincial Americanism. The progressives, by diverting emphasis to environment and change, tended to lose sight of European origins and backgrounds. They took the Old World heritage for granted and asked how the American environment modified it; or they associated that heritage with reactionary elements resisting the life-giving forces of change. This, of

[2] *The Heavenly City of the Eighteenth-Century Philosophers* (1959), pp. 96-97.
[3] Oscar Handlin, "The Central Themes of American History," *Relazioni del X congresso internazionale di scienze storiche*, vol. I (1955), pp. 152-53.

course, was the emotional significance of Turner's celebration of the frontier as the crucible of a new nation and the matrix of a unique society. The nationalism of conservative scholars was, on the whole, not so positive and assertive. For them the growth of national unity provided a great theme because it was synonymous with stability, order, and the preservation of an ancient freedom. The progressives, on the other hand, cared less about the form of American unity and more about the content of American uniqueness.

Accordingly, quite a different vision of America shone through the pages of progressive historiography. For one thing, it was a livelier America, constantly in flux, full of real and vital conflicts between contending groups. It was less stable and more deeply divided than the America of the conservatives; it was less securely anchored in traditions reaching back across the centuries. It was a nation that had progressed, and achieved its own special identity, by breaking away from the bonds of a European past. For another thing, the essential meaning of America was differently construed. To progressive historians that meaning inhered not so much in the achievement of national unity as in a continuing struggle toward democracy. Significantly, the emergence of the progressive school coincided with an immense growth in popularity of the principal symbols of American democracy. Around the turn of the century Lincoln overtook and surpassed Washington as the most popular biographical subject. Simultaneously the reputation of Jefferson recovered from the long eclipse of the preceding forty years.[4]

The new historical attitudes that progressivism engendered spread quickly, widely, and selectively. To a remarkable extent the outstanding progressive historians sprang from two sections of the country: the Midwest and the South. Turner hailed from a Wisconsin town that still served in his youth as a trading post for nearby Indians. Robinson came from Bloomington, Illinois. Becker and Beard grew up on midwestern farms, one in Iowa, the other in Indiana. James T. Shotwell was a product of a country town in western Ontario. The list might be greatly extended. Most of the prominent conservative professors of history, on the other hand, were easterners: Herbert Baxter Adams, Andrews, Osgood, and Channing bore the

---

[4] Harry R. Stevens, "Contemporary American Biographical Writing: Trends and Problems," *South Atlantic Quarterly*, LV (1956), 362; Merrill Peterson, *The Jefferson Image in the American Mind* (1960), p. 229.

indelible stamp of New England; Beer and Dunning were affluent sons of New York and New Jersey respectively.

Many midwesterners and southerners felt that an eastern elite had too long monopolized the writing of American history. Resentfully, they complained that the typical eastern historian could scarcely see west of the Hudson River and that American history was being written mainly as an extension of New England.[5] Though not entirely untrue, the complaint was exaggerated. Its very extravagance proclaims the sense of cultural inferiority with which a new generation of home-trained scholars confronted the established citadels of academic authority. Their drive to democratize American history, to embrace its continental dimensions, and to read it as a struggle against privilege reflected the democratization of academic life itself.

The first and most influential of the new men was Frederick Jackson Turner. Never has an American historian had so much impact in so few pages; rarely has one acquired great influence at so young an age. Alert, strikingly handsome, enthusiastic, and quite without idiosyncrasies, Turner arrived at Johns Hopkins in 1888 to study for a Ph.D. under Herbert Baxter Adams. He brought with him the conviction that the present age surpassed all previous eras, that its glorious hallmarks were science and democracy, and that its heroes were Darwin, Spencer, and Lincoln. He had already learned at the University of Wisconsin to write institutional history. He had already discovered a special interest in the history of his Midwest. Having little to learn from Adams, Turner reacted against the latter's overemphasis on European origins. He was more impressed by the pioneer progressive economist, Richard T. Ely, who opened to him the exciting possibilities of an economic interpretation of political and social change.[6]

Nevertheless, until after his return to Wisconsin to teach, Turner

[5] C. W. Alvord to Carl Becker, April 23, 1917, Archives of Illinois Historical Survey (University of Illinois); Curtis Nettels, "Frederick Jackson Turner and the New Deal," *Wisconsin Magazine of History,* LVII (1934), 258.

[6] The best biographical account to date is Fulmer Mood's "The Development of Frederick Jackson Turner as a Historical Thinker," *Publications of the Colonial Society of Massachusetts,* XXXIV (1943), 283-352. I am also indebted to Lee Benson's *Turner and Beard* (1960), pp. 1-91; Henry Nash Smith's *Virgin Land: The American West as Symbol and Myth* (1957), pp. 291-305; "The Reminiscences of Guy Stanton Ford" (Oral History Research Office, Columbia University, 1956), pp. 77-92; and *The Early Writings of Frederick Jackson Turner,* ed. Fulmer Mood (1938).

was somewhat of a conservative evolutionist, seeing America primarily in terms of continuity and connections with Europe. Then he took his stand against the "wise men from the East," as he called his conservative, European-oriented colleagues; and in a relatively few years all of his major ideas flowered. Impressed by the deep agricultural unrest of the early 1890's and the apparent exhaustion of good cheap land, he concluded that America had reached a momentous turning point. He came upon the writings of an Italian economist, Achille Loria, who taught that access to land dominated the evolution of society. These ideas, converging perhaps with similar theories of Henry George and with a rich legacy of popular myths about the West, convinced Turner that natural conditions largely determined American history. In effect, he turned to nature for the key to history. His famous address of 1893, "The Significance of the Frontier in American History," argued with a poetic lilt that the encounter with the wilderness explained the distinctive features of America: above all, its democracy and its amalgamation of many peoples and sections into a united nation.

In 1893 Turner was still more interested in national unity than in conflict and diversity. He still thought of the frontier as if it were an institution, to be described as a single, organically unfolding process. Consequently, his frontier thesis was relatively easy to accept. It evoked an old grass-roots pride; it explained all of America—East as well as West—as a product of the same experience; it did not break with the conservative emphasis on homogeneity. Thus the frontier thesis mediated between old and newer styles of interpretation. It greatly eased the transition to more abrasive types of progressive historiography.

Turner never repudiated his frontier thesis; indeed, he invoked its imaginative appeal on many subsequent occasions. But his empirical research turned in another direction. Keenly aware of tensions between East and West as well as North and South, he put his seminar to work on a study of sections, which he defined as "natural economic groupings in American history." [7] From the mid-Nineties to the end of his life, the character and interplay of sections was his principal scholarly interest. He organized the whole program of teaching in American history at Wisconsin along sectional lines. His only com-

[7] Preface to Orin G. Libby, *The Geographical Distribution of the Vote of the Thirteen States on the Federal Constitution, 1787-8* (1894), p. vii.

pleted, integrated book, *Rise of the New West, 1819-1829* (1906), had as its main theme the transition from a predominantly nationalist to a predominantly sectionalist outlook in the United States during that decade; and Turner treated the politics of the period as expressions of unstable sectional alliances. Laboring prodigiously to define his sectional units, he made original use of maps and statistical data.

The sectional interpretation went much beyond the frontier thesis in revealing conflict and diversity while stopping short of the rigid categories of a class interpretation. Sections appealed to Turner as historical configurations partly because of their fluidity and complexity. They offset a deadening uniformity in national life without destroying its organic wholeness. Turner thought of his own beloved Old Northwest not only as a section but also a balance wheel between other sections; he thought of sectional politics as a politics of compromise. Like many early twentieth century progressives, Turner both discerned and deplored class conflict. To him the "common man" was an undifferentiated American: and the section, as a "natural economic grouping," seemed more American than "artificial" class alignments. Professor Charles G. Sellers Jr. has pointed out that "Turner and his followers muted the discordant note of class struggle by transposing it into conflict between distinct geographical sections."[8]

In fact the sectional approach was so fluid that it proved for Turner a will-o'-the-wisp. The sections refused to remain distinct. The more intensively he studied, the more they blurred, overlapped, and subdivided. For many years he struggled to write a sequel to *Rise of the New West,* a sectional interpretation of the period 1830-1850. When he died in 1932, the magnum opus was still unfinished.[9] Nevertheless, he had reached some striking insights and opened an immense domain to others. It is not too much to say that he supplied the first dynamic design for a history of American society.

Although applied to all parts of the country, Turner's method was especially influential in raising to professional importance the history of the West and the antebellum South. Around 1910 scholars working independently of one another discovered that various major

[8] Charles G. Sellers Jr., "Andrew Jackson versus the Historians," *Mississippi Valley Historical Review,* XLIV (1958), 626.
[9] *The United States, 1830-1850: The Nation and Its Sections* (1935).

issues, previously interpreted in other terms, arose from western expansion. One put forward the thesis that western land hunger produced the War of 1812, another that it brought on the Mexican War. A student of British policies toward the frontier thought he found there a new key to the American Revolution. Behind the notorious Kansas-Nebraska Act a Kansas professor detected legitimate western aspirations for a transcontinental railroad.[10]

This kind of economic "realism" tended to downgrade both the constitutional and the moral aspects of the slavery question and to encourage a new look at the Old South. Inspired by the Turnerian approach, southerners probed the "natural economic groupings" within southern history, distinguishing between the planters of the Black Belt and the farmers of the up-country, and between the Virginia of Jefferson and the South Carolina of Calhoun. Some—notably William E. Dodd and Thomas Jefferson Wertenbaker—analyzed conflict and change in southern history with a strong democratic animus against the planter aristocracy. On the other hand, Ulrich B. Phillips, who was no less indebted to Turner, dedicated one of his books "To the Dominant Class of the South," with whom he largely identified himself.[11] As a conservative Turnerian, Phillips gave his best efforts to studying slavery not as an abstract legal system but as a way of life revealed in the account books and other records of the great plantations. His genial, immensely learned *American Negro Slavery* (1918) argued that it had failed as an economic institution but succeeded as a form of social accommodation between a superior and an inferior race.

Actually, all of the important Turnerian studies bore upon na-

[10] Warren H. Goodman, "The Origins of the War of 1812: A Survey of Changing Interpretations," *Mississippi Valley Historical Review,* XXVIII (1941), 173-74; William E. Dodd, "The West and the War with Mexico," *Journal of the Illinois State Historical Society,* V (1912), 159-72; C. W. Alvord, *The Mississippi Valley in British Politics* (2 vols., 1917); Roy F. Nichols, "The Kansas-Nebraska Act: A Century of Historiography," *Mississippi Valley Historical Review,* XLIII (1956), 190-94. Alvord's book was actually a hybrid offspring of the Imperial school and the Turner school.

[11] Phillips, *A History of Transportation in the Eastern Cotton Belt to 1860* (1908); William E. Dodd, *Statesmen of the Old South* (1911), and "Profitable Fields of Investigation in American History, 1815-1860," *AHR,* XVIII (1913), 522-36; Thomas Jefferson Wertenbaker, *Patrician and Plebian in Virginia* (1910). Turner's influence on Dodd and Phillips is elucidated in Wendell H. Stephenson's *The South Lives in History: Southern Historians and Their Legacy* (1955), pp. 29-94.

tional issues, if only because Turner approached sections and frontiers as parts of a larger whole. His specific influence intermingled
readily with other strains of progressive thought. For example, John
R. Commons, another Hopkins-trained student of Richard T. Ely,
cast the history of organized labor in a form similar to that Turner
gave to the history of the West. Commons and Turner sat in the
same seminar at Johns Hopkins, came from similar midwestern
small-town backgrounds, and carried on their historical studies in the
same milieu. Commons joined the Economics Department at Wisconsin in 1904, and when Turner went to Harvard six years later he
tried to persuade the Wisconsin History Department to appoint
Commons as his successor.[12] Commons shared Turner's conception of
history as a conflict between competing interests. He shared equally
an enthusiasm for the stabilizing effects of balance and compromise.
In 1893, the very year of Turner's epochal address, Commons published a book on the distribution of wealth in America, which argued that a momentous turning point had arrived now that free access to land was disappearing. Later, in a four-volume *History of
Labor in the United States* (1918-35), largely written by his students, Commons explained the distinctive traits of the labor movement in much the way that Turner explained the distinctive traits
of America as a whole. For both men the key was opportunity in the
form of free land. Commons' best student, Selig Perlman, brilliantly
restated the point. The American environment produced a labor
movement that was characteristically job-conscious rather than
class-conscious.[13] For more than a generation most labor historians
remained true to the spirit of Frederick Jackson Turner.

Turnerians were too sensitive to economic conflicts, however, to
ignore class struggle; and sectionalism was simply not relevant
enough to contemporary interests to contain fully the progressives'
sense of social reality. Most political discussion in the early twentieth
century transcended sectional lines. In all parts of the country progressives rallied against a presumably monolithic opposition. They
commonly thought of America as fundamentally divided between

---

12 "George Clarke Sellery Room Dedication," *Wisconsin Magazine of History*,
XLI (Autumn 1957), 50; John R. Commons, *Myself* (1934), pp. 43, 128-37;
George D. Blackwood, "Frederick Jackson Turner and John Rogers Commons—
Complementary Thinkers," *Mississippi Valley Historical Review*, XLI (1954),
471-88.
13 Selig Perlman, *A Theory of the Labor Movement* (1928).

two socio-economic strata: the democratic many and the privileged few. This simple dualism had been part of the ideology of democratic protest movements in America throughout the nineteenth century. Even conservatives customarily regarded American political history as an enduring contest between Jeffersonian and Hamiltonian principles.[14] Progressives simply restored a rich social content to a dualism that conservatives figured in abstract constitutional terms. In their rising desire to curb big business, progressives interpreted the polarity of American politics as a persistent struggle between the great mass of the people and an overly powerful economic class. By 1910 Turner himself was writing with a new sense of the solidarity of a "monied aristocracy" in American history. "We may trace the contest between the capitalist and the democratic pioneer," he averred, "from the earliest colonial days."[15]

Although chiefly attributable to American reformist attitudes, this hardening of the progressive view of social conflict also owed something to Marxist influence, now seeping into American scholarship for the first time. In the process of convergence, Marxism softened at least as much as progressive history stiffened. Following E. R. A. Seligman, some of the more advanced progressive intellectuals found they could separate Marxism as an analytical tool from socialism as an ideological credo. Moreover, they vastly simplified the tool. They dispensed entirely with the dialectical pattern of true Marxist analysis, and they diluted its historical materialism into a simple emphasis on the political importance of property. In effect, Marxism helped to educate American scholars to the historical significance of other sorts of property relations in addition to the ownership of land.

The conception of American history as primarily a conflict between over- and underprivileged classes emerged most clearly at Columbia University. There Seligman's influence was strong. There James Harvey Robinson declared early in the twentieth century that a "sober and chastened form" of Marxism "serves to explain far more of the phenomena of the past than any other single explanation ever offered."[16] There too Carl Becker, already a student of Turner's,

---

[14] John Fiske, *Essays Historical and Literary* (1907), vol. I, pp. 169-70; William A. Dunning, *Truth in History and Other Essays* (1937), p. 45.
[15] *The Frontier in American History* (1920), pp. 110-11, 325.
[16] James Harvey Robinson, *The New History* (1912), p. 51. Seligman's influence on Beard stands out in the latter's review essay, "A Socialist History of France," *Political Science Quarterly*, XXI (1906), 120.

came under Robinson's instruction; and Becker's powerful dissertation, *The History of Political Parties in the Province of New York* (1909), related the rise of a revolutionary movement to lower-class aspirations for a larger share of the political and economic power held by the great provincial magnates. In contrast to Turner, Becker identified the urban workingmen as the quintessentially revolutionary group.

It was at Columbia also that Charles A. Beard pressed the knife of class conflict to the very heart of American political institutions. In two famous monographs published in 1913 and 1915, Beard offered belligerently revisionist accounts of the writing of the Constitution and the subsequent formation of American political parties. More than other progressive historians, Beard aimed deliberately to overthrow conservative institutional history, with its emphasis on the slow unfolding of abstract principles.[17] He interpreted both the Constitution and the rise of Jeffersonian democracy as convulsive shifts of power dictated by severely materialistic considerations.

Beard's tough-minded zeal to purge history of false idealism drove him to specify the property interests of both sides—the interests of opponents of the Constitution as well as those of its makers. He was thus more consistent than many progressives, and in a sense more impartial; but his typology suffered from excessive concreteness. Adhering to the usual dualism of progressive thought, he fixed upon the small debtor farmers and the large holders of public securities as the central antagonists. Out of a desire to shock and to prove the case in a very literal way, his *An Economic Interpretation of the Constitution* attributed the Founding Fathers' statecraft to the immediate, personal gain they could realize through appreciation of their own security holdings.

This narrow attention to personal motivation gave the book much notoriety and obscured Beard's larger concern with general class interests. Actually, his stress on security holdings was functional to a broad distinction he drew between two classes of property owners.

17 This is especially apparent in Beard's attack on McLaughlin for exaggerating the continuity of the Anglo-Saxon legal tradition and the role of ideas in history (*AHR*, XVIII [1913], 379). See also Beard's *An Economic Interpretation of the Constitution* (1913), pp. 8-13, and *Economic Origins of Jeffersonian Democracy* (1915). On Beard's relation to his intellectual milieu see the suggestive essays by Richard Hofstadter and others in *Charles A. Beard: An Appraisal*, ed. Howard K. Beale (1954).

Beard divided American political society into "personalty" interests on one hand and "realty" interests on the other. The Constitution and the Federalist party were the instruments of merchants, manufacturers, and associated speculators and creditors; Jeffersonian democracy rested on a broad farming basis. Essentially, Beard arrayed capitalists, whom he considered for the most part creditors, against resident landowners, whom he regarded chiefly as debtors.

Behind this somewhat unreal distinction it is not hard to discern a rural midwesterner's sensitiveness to the alien world of commercial chicanery and financial manipulation. Although Beard approved of the concentration of political power the capitalists brought about, he disliked their speculative motives. Until late in life he avoided stock investments because he regarded them as gambling.[18] One may also see in Beard's interpretation how the ideas of a fellow midwesterner, Frederick Jackson Turner, were being adapted to a sharper class analysis of American history. In effect, Beard was combining Turner's stress on property in the form of land with Marx's stress on property in the form of capital.

Having written nothing on American history prior to 1912, Beard arrived on the scene of United States historiography late in the progressive era. His impact was chiefly felt after World War I. Two imposing dissertations that Beard's students at Columbia wrote before the war testify, however, to the immediate possibilities of extending his ideas backward and forward through American history. Arthur M. Schlesinger's *The Colonial Merchants and the American Revolution* (1918) and Dixon Ryan Fox's *The Decline of Aristocracy in the Politics of New York* (1919) were written under the formal supervision of Osgood, but their inspiration came primarily from Beard.[19] Studying the politics of the American merchant class in the 1760's and 1770's, Schlesinger interpreted its opposition to British policies in a manner quite similar to Beard's explanation of the role of that class in creating a national government. Both saw the merchants as defending existing business interests against hostile legislation, by Parliament in one case, by state legislatures in the other; but in the revolutionary situation the merchants confronted a cruel dilemma when popular mobs outreached their own limited in-

[18] Interview with Miriam and Alfred Vagts, May 3, 1961.
[19] Arthur M. Schlesinger, *In Retrospect: The History of a Historian* (1963), pp. 43, 53.

◄§ 4 §►

THE ASCENDANCY OF PROGRESSIVE HISTORY

Prior to World War I conservative evolutionists and progressives shared in approximately equal measure the work of a young, eagerly developing profession. The progressive view dominated Columbia and Wisconsin; conservatism ruled Yale; Harvard, after the coming of Turner, had some of both; and so did Chicago, the home base of McLaughlin and Dodd. Although the balance was clearly tipping toward progressivism after 1910, controversy and rivalry between the two schools was minimal. There seemed room enough and problems aplenty for all professional historians while they were staking out their claims. The common cause of superseding amateur scholarship united their varied undertakings.

In the 1920's and 1930's the old conservative school, although strongly entrenched in many institutions, suffered a steady and ultimately disastrous loss of intellectual vitality. Its work was far from finished; great parts of our institutional and administrative history remained still unwritten. But that kind of history no longer seemed relevant to an age in which, as Walter Lippmann said, "Whirl is king." Of the livelier young men entering academic life, very few felt the sense of national unity and historical continuity that had inspired so many of the first generation of professional historians. Change and a passion for modernity were the order of the day. At a time when all values were in flux, and government seemed either irrelevant to life or an instrument for remaking it, who could find in the formal constitution of political authority an inspiring theme?

By the early Thirties, the eclipse of constitutional history was widely recognized. "Constitutional history, with its emphasis on the permanent rather than the transitory aspects of government and politics, has been falling into neglect," one elder statesman mourned in 1934.[1] He might have added that constitutional history itself was becoming less concerned with the permanent and more with the transitory. The best of the younger men who stayed in the field turned their attention from the framework of law to a realistic appraisal of

[1] *AHR,* XL (1934), 426.

individual judges. This was the strategy that Carl B. Swisher and Alpheus T. Mason followed, a strategy that attuned them to behavioral changes rather than institutional continuities. Other young historians deserted the field, as James G. Randall did after publishing *Constitutional Problems under Lincoln* (1926).[2] Some of the established authorities carried on, of course, in a traditional vein. A scholar settled in an area of research does not ordinarily switch to another in response to new intellectual fashions. McLaughlin, for example, published his weighty *Constitutional History of the United States* in 1935. Corwin, on the other hand, shifted increasingly from history to contemporary problems; and when he retired in 1946 he remarked that he had outlived his subject.[3]

In American colonial history the constitutional or institutional approach retained for some years an appearance of continuing vigor because of the prestige of the Imperial school. Its London-centered view of early American history seemed to some scholars more valuable than ever after World War I; for the popular mind seethed with isolationist, 100 per cent American sentiments, to which a transatlantic perspective offered a salutary corrective. The Imperial school was also sustained by the massive, undeviating strength of Charles M. Andrews. Andrews survived to a ripe old age, producing good students, extending his indefatigable researches, and finally in the evening of his life releasing his long awaited magnum opus. The four great volumes of *The Colonial Period of American History* (1934-38) dealt largely with the seventeenth century. Andrews did not live to treat the eighteenth century in the same way, but he had the last and most authoritative word on what he covered.

Moreover, Andrews had one remarkable student who carried forward his lifework with the same matchless fidelity to a youthful purpose. Lawrence H. Gipson, a one-time Rhodes scholar who received his Ph.D. under Andrews in 1918, settled in the 1920's into writing a "definitive" history of the last twenty-five years of the old British Empire prior to the American Revolution. Gipson proceeded with complete fidelity to the social values of conservative evolutionism.

[2] But Randall pointed out the direction of future scholarship in "The Interrelation of Social and Constitutional History," *AHR*, XXXV (1929), 1-13. A detailed account of research trends is in Paul L. Murphy's "Time to Reclaim: The Current Challenge of American Constitutional History," *AHR*, LXIX (1963), 64-79.
[3] Reported to me by Professor A. T. Mason, May 1961.

His sympathy for the harmonious strength of old English institutions, and his distaste for the radical spirit of '76, quite exceeded that of his austere master. He lingered through nine affectionate volumes upon a description of the Empire in its last moment of tranquility and equilibrium.[4] Few now wished to read so leisurely a work; but Gipson considerably modernized the imperial approach. He reached well beyond the institutional framework, taking much account of individual motives and geographical groups and analyzing social and economic conditions. By assimilating the methods of both amateur and progressive historians, Gipson carried the Imperial school as far as it could go.

He had, however, no students and—by the 1930's—hardly any fellow workers. By then the Imperial school was breaking up in all the leading universities; the progressive approach was ascendant. Old J. Franklin Jameson, who had seemed serenely independent of any school or theory, thrilled younger scholars in 1926 by publishing an almost radical economic and social interpretation of the American Revolution.[5] Students trained in institutional history in the Twenties changed the direction of their research in the following decade. Leonard Labaree and W. F. Craven undertook studies of colonial society, Richard B. Morris investigated the control of the colonial labor force, Stanley Pargellis and Charles Barker moved into intellectual history.[6]

---

[4] *The British Empire Before the American Revolution* (1936-56). In the tenth volume, published in 1961 thirty-seven years after he began the work, Gipson at last moved into the story of the coming of the Revolution. The relation of his efforts to those of his predecessors is summarized in Max Savelle's "The Imperial School of American Colonial Historians," *Indiana Magazine of History,* XLV (1949), 123-34.

[5] *The American Revolution Considered as a Social Movement* (1926). In response to an enthusiastic review by Charles A. Beard, Jameson said that "nearly everything that is a matter of doctrine" was in an earlier text he had read in 1895 to a small audience at Columbia University. Nevertheless, the imprint of subsequent scholarship and of World War I on Jameson's thinking are visible. Elizabeth Donnan and Leo F. Stock, eds., *An Historian's World: Selections from the Correspondence of John Franklin Jameson* (Memoirs of the American Philosophical Society, vol. 42, 1956), p. 319.

[6] Leonard W. Labaree, *Conservatism in Early American History* (1948); Wesley Frank Craven, *The Southern Colonies in the Seventeenth Century* (1949); Richard B. Morris, *Government and Labor in Early America* (1946); Stanley Pargellis, "The Theory of Balanced Government," *The Constitution Reconsidered,* ed. Conyers Read (1938), pp. 37-49; Charles A. Barker, *Henry George* (1955). An older institutionalist, Evarts B. Greene, also devoted himself in-

Reviewers of Andrews' volumes complained that he wrote in a "legalistic" spirit, touched only incidentally on economic developments in the colonies, ignored sectional conflicts, and paid little heed to the common man. Progressive historians were rectifying these deficiencies. In the spirit of Turner, Thomas Jefferson Wertenbaker produced a panoramic account of the Americanization of a transplanted European civilization. In the spirit of Beard, Curtis Nettels published a strongly class-angled synthesis of American colonial history.[7]

The title of Nettels' book, *The Roots of American Civilization* (1938), suggests the particular interest progressive historians had in the indigenous aspects of the colonial scene. While infusing a democratic bias into the writing of early American history, these scholars were also linking it with subsequent national history. Imperial historians had reached a dead end on coming to the American Revolution. Although they cherished the principle of continuity, their special insistence on treating the colonies as part of English history blocked them from looking forward to American national history. The Progressive school studied the colonial period in the light of the national period as so integrated the two. But the progressives' nationalistic concentration on the internal dynamics of American development reversed the fault of the Imperial school: in uniting colonial history with later national history, progressive scholars separated it too much from European history.

Still, the progressive approach offered a valuable counterbalance to the extrinsic and formal emphasis of the Imperial school. If research had flourished under these new auspices, the change might have been a substantial improvement. Unfortunately, however, colonial history declined between the wars almost as much as constitutional history. In textbooks the space devoted to the period before 1776 contracted drastically; the research talent it attracted decreased markedly in comparison with more recent fields. Undoubtedly, pro-

---

creasingly to social history; see *The Revolutionary Generation, 1763-1790* (1943).

[7] Wertenbaker, *The Founding of American Civilization* (3 vols., 1938-47); Nettels, *The Roots of American Civilization* (1938). See also Thomas P. Abernethy, *Western Lands and the American Revolution* (1937); Robert A. East, *Business Enterprise in the American Revolutionary Era* (1938); Carl Bridenbaugh, *Cities in the Wilderness* (1938) and *Cities in Revolt* (1955); Merrill Jensen, *The Articles of Confederation* (1940). The reception of Andrews' work is summarized in A. S. Eisenstadt's *Charles McLean Andrews* (1956).

gressive ideas contributed to the diversion of talent both from the colonial period and from constitutional themes. If one was too formalistic, the other was too remote to engage fully the progressive mind. The so-called present-mindedness of progressive history was in effect a predominant interest in the outcome rather than the origins of a situation or period in the past. Progressive historians saw the colonial period as a time of origins, and their attention tended to move from that starting toward what followed. Most of them neglected the origins of American history in favor of the changes it subsequently underwent. Thus, the best of Osgood's later students, Schlesinger and Fox, worked largely in the nineteenth century. When Andrews on one occasion twitted Schlesinger for deserting the colonial field, Schlesinger replied that he regarded the Revolution as the beginning of the national era rather than the closing stage of the period of dependence.[8]

The drift of historical interest from colonial to national history after World War I opened a field of research in which some of the functions of the old Imperial school found a new and relevant application. This was American diplomatic history, an area of study not completely ignored before 1914 but very nearly so. On the whole, professional historians before the war had trained their sights either on the domestic scene or on the European origins of American history. The continuing relations of the United States with Europe remained largely neglected except in the work of a few amateur scholars like Henry Adams and Alfred T. Mahan. The war fostered in professional circles a somewhat clearer awareness of American involvement in European politics. Accordingly, diplomatic history emerged as a recognized subdivision of American national history.

One could, of course, study diplomatic history in various ways. Followers of Turner, such as Julius Pratt, Arthur P. Whitaker, and Frank Owsley, came at the subject from an interest in the internal social and economic pressures affecting American policies.[9] On the

[8] "The Reminiscences of Arthur M. Schlesinger" (Oral History Research Office, Columbia University, 1959), p. 60.
[9] Julius Pratt, *Expansionists of 1812* (1925); Arthur P. Whitaker, *The Spanish-American Frontier, 1783-1795* (1927); Frank L. Owsley, *King Cotton Diplomacy: Foreign Relations of the Confederate States of America* (1931); Frederick Merk, "Oregon Pioneers and the Boundary Settlement," *AHR*, XXIX (1924), 681-99, and subsequent publications; Thomas A. Bailey, *Theodore Roosevelt and the Japanese American Crisis* (1934).

other hand, American diplomatic history in the 1920's strongly attracted scholars in the conservative evolutionist tradition. It offered them a congenial yet up-to-date substitute for the formal, institutional scholarship that was going out of fashion. Diplomatic history, like constitutional history, called for a mastery of public documents. It required a discriminating eye for official phraseology and for the architecture of official policies. It offered scope for tracing the continuities underlying such policies as the Monroe Doctrine and the Open Door.[10] Moreover, diplomatic history carried down into the national period the conservative evolutionists' appreciation of an international framework connecting American with European history.

So it is not surprising that a good part of the research on American diplomatic history in the 1920's dealt with Anglo-American relations, much of it written with the attention the Imperial school had given to British views and strategies. The most considerable specialist who emerged at this time was Samuel Flagg Bemis, a student of Channing with a fine passion for archival research. From the outset Bemis took his stand in Europe. Largely disregarding domestic conflicts, he examined the evolution of early American foreign policy against a background of international rivalries and intrigues. Unlike most of the Imperial historians, Bemis harbored a strong patriotic animus against the "corrupt" statecraft of the European powers. His account of how Americans shrewdly reaped advantage from Europe's distress smacked of postwar disillusion with the Old World; yet his insistence on a transatlantic perspective was clearly an inheritance from the Anglophile spirit of conservative scholarship.[11]

The flush of postwar interest in American diplomatic history did not last. The ranks of conservative evolutionists thinned; and progressive historians, who regarded foreign policy as subordinate to domestic concerns, became more wholly absorbed in the latter. Probably what most discouraged scholarly activity in the diplomatic field was the increasingly isolationist atmosphere in the United States. Iso-

[10] Dexter Perkins' three-volume history of the Monroe Doctrine (1927-37), summarized in *Hands Off: A History of the Monroe Doctrine* (1941), is one of the notable works of the period. See also Tyler Dennett, *Americans in Eastern Asia* (1922).

[11] Bemis, *Jay's Treaty* (1923) and *The Diplomacy of the American Revolution* (1935); Ephraim D. Adams, *Great Britain and the American Civil War* (2 vols., 1925); Donaldson Jordan and Edwin J. Pratt, *Europe and the American Civil War* (1931); Dora Mae Clark, *British Opinion and the American Revolution* (1930).

lationist sentiment reached an apogee in the Thirties. In 1941 one scholar thought it was "fortunate" in view of the widespread disinterest that as many as three major universities gave a position of importance to the study of American foreign policy.[12]

Since historians engaged in studying other countries were relatively immune to isolationist influence, they took over a good share of the work. A disproportionate amount of the best research on American diplomacy was done by scholars primarily interested in the history of Europe, Latin America, or the British Empire. Such was the case with major books published by Charles Seymour and Alfred L. P. Dennis on America's assumption of the responsibilities of world power, by William Spence Robertson and J. Fred Rippy on relations with Latin America, and by John Bartlet Brebner and A. L. Burt on the interwoven destinies of the United States, Canada, and Great Britain.[13] Specialists in American history, if they did not neglect foreign policy, viewed it in a more parochial and carping way. In an atmosphere heavy with distrust of "power politics" and "propaganda," isolationists and their opponents agreed at least on a profound dissatisfaction with the general record of modern foreign policy. Accordingly, in the 1930's a fixation on the mistakes and shortcomings of our diplomacy conditioned much of the writing that American specialists did in this field.[14]

One may conclude, then, that diplomatic history encountered in the intellectual climate of the late Twenties and Thirties essentially the same difficulties that impeded work in constitutional and colonial history. All three fields came under the influence of progressive thought, which was critical of tradition, insensitive to institutional continuities, and preoccupied with domestic conflict. Neither diplomatic nor constitutional nor colonial history provided an entirely attractive or suitable medium for major progressive scholarship. Their

---

[12] Statement of Carroll S. Alden in *AHR*, XLVII (1941), 167.

[13] Seymour, *American Diplomacy During the World War* (1934) and *American Neutrality, 1914-1917* (1935); Dennis, *Adventures in American Diplomacy, 1896-1906* (1928); Robertson, *Hispanic-American Relations with the United States* (1923); Rippy, *United States and Mexico* (1926); Alfred L. Burt, *The United States, Great Britain and British North America from the Revolution to the Establishment of Peace After the War of 1812* (1940); Brebner, *North Atlantic Triangle* (1945).

[14] This is emphasized in Ernest R. May's "Emergence to World Power," in *The Reconstruction of American History*, ed. John Higham (London, 1962), pp. 186-92.

vicissitudes are one index to the dominant position the progressive school won between the wars. The other index is what that school accomplished in the realm that concerned it most: the history of conflict and change within an indigenous environment.

Between the two world wars progressive influence became so great in American historiography that it seemed for a time virtually to overwhelm all other conceptual possibilities. World War I neither interrupted nor diverted this widening stream of historical thought. Instead, the ideas of Turner, Beard, and their younger associates spread through the historical profession in the 1920's without any really sustained opposition. Certain new currents fed into the stream; and ultimately it grew vexed and turbulent. But these complications arose, for the most part, within the progressive tradition.

The outstanding achievement of progressive scholarship between the wars was a broadening of the scope of historical narrative. The New History had from the outset pledged itself to a grasp of the past as inclusive as life itself, and American historians were now redeeming the pledge. Clearly delimited research on specific institutions languished; loosely defined studies of situations and relationships abounded. It was an age of social history. Surprisingly little first-rate political history was written. The few good political histories that did appear, like John D. Hicks's *The Populist Revolt* (1931) and Howard K. Beale's *The Critical Year* (1930), stressed the social and economic context of political action. Economic history as such fared no better than political history. Most of the work in this field had been done by economists, who by the time of World War I were lured away from history by new developments in theory.[15] Historians, while busily applying economic interpretations, took the underlying economic processes largely for granted. Impatient of studying any single department of life in its own terms, they neglected economic history in pursuing the undifferentiated flux of life.

The quest for breadth received considerable impetus from a series of conferences that the American Historical Association sponsored in 1931 for planning future research. Both of the conferences on American history, one meeting in the East, the other in the Midwest, bewailed the relative neglect of local history and of sociocultural matters like education, religious folkways, and the impact of

---

15 Of the forty leading colleges and universities that had offered courses on economic history in 1902, nine had dropped the course by 1920; AHA *Annual Report* (1920), pp. 153-62. See also Thomas C. Cochran, "Research in American Economic History: A Thirty Year View," *Mid-America*, XXIX (1947), 6.

technological change. Roy Nichols prepared for the eastern conference a long list of such topics. Both meetings assumed that the most urgent task of scholarship was to reach beyond political, military, and constitutional themes. Published in a little volume entitled *Historical Scholarship in America* (1932), these recommendations accelerated a movement already strongly under way.[16]

One important dimension of the movement was a steady expansion of the progressive historians' conception of "the people." Before World War I the common man was an abstract figure in American historiography, hardly visible except in the classic image of the pioneer. This image revealed little of the multitudinous variety that democrats had long considered one of the glories of the American people. In the 1920's and 1930's many of the younger scholars became fascinated with the concrete experience of particular groups in distinctive environments. They wrote, usually with a close feeling of identification, about such folk as dirt farmers, indentured servants, cowboys, missionaries, Indians, and immigrants. In so doing, progressive historians were specifying the rich diversity of the American people.

They were also reacting against the repressive, 100 per cent Americanism of the war years, which contributed especially to a new interest in the religious and ethnic divisions in American society. Academic scholars had hitherto left the story of such groups in the keeping of their own amateur chroniclers. Progressive historians still give little heed to the Negro as a fullfledged participant in American history. Within the white population, however, they recognized that the American people were in significant ways Methodists and Catholics and Germans and Norwegians as well as frontiersmen, workers, and planters.

The first notable efforts to integrate religious and ethnic groups into the mainstream of American history came from midwesterners heavily indebted to Frederick Jackson Turner. It was Turner who inspired the leading authority on the history of American Protestantism, William Warren Sweet. A professor at DePauw and later at the University of Chicago, Sweet revised the old denomination-centered

---

[16] Committee of the American Historical Association on the Planning of Research, *Historical Scholarship in America: Needs and Opportunities* (1932).

"church history" by relating the major Protestant groups to political and social forces. All of his books, including the widely read *Story of Religions in America* (1931), emphasized especially the democratizing effects of the frontier.[17]

A similar stress on the frontier in general and the rural Midwest in particular attended the treatment of the foreign-born. After World War I several second-generation midwestern historians realized that the interaction of European emigrants with the American environment was one of the great, neglected aspects of the making of America. Arthur M. Schlesinger, himself an Ohioan of German parentage, called attention to this theme in an essay published in 1921. Other young midwesterners had recently embarked on just such studies. George M. Stephenson and Theodore C. Blegen specialized respectively in the Swedes and the Norwegians. Marcus L. Hansen, a second-generation Dane, took the whole sweep of emigration from northern and western Europe for his field. He began work on the subject in 1917 as a student of Turner's at Harvard; and like Turner he explained migration primarily in economic terms. His fundamental contribution was to internationalize the Turner tradition. He viewed America as the frontier of an expanding Europe and took as much account of the changing European environment as he did of the American. Hansen's work, almost all of it unpublished and incomplete at his untimely death in 1938, went far beyond the usual limits of progressive history.[18]

While these researchers were expanding the base of American history, other scholars were constructing a new synthesis of the whole story. The empirical knowledge for a genuinely democratic history they had only begun to amass. But the outlines of an interpretive pattern lay ready at hand, and the leading progressive historians were eager to sum up. The task of synthesizing the full sweep of demo-

[17] Sidney E. Mead, "Prof. Sweet's Religion and Culture in America," *Church History*, XXII (1953), 33-47.

[18] Arthur M. Schlesinger, "The Significance of Immigration in American History," *American Journal of Sociology*, XXVII (1921), 71-85; G. M. Stephenson, *The Religious Aspects of Swedish Immigration* (1932); Theodore C. Blegen, *Norwegian Migration to America* (2 vols. 1931-40); Carl Wittke, *We Who Built America* (1939); Marcus L. Hansen, *The Immigrant in American History* (1940) and *The Atlantic Migration, 1607-1860* (1940). See also Allan H. Spear, "Marcus Lee Hansen and the Historiography of Immigration," *Wisconsin Magazine of History*, XLIV (1961), 258-68.

cratic experience appealed irresistibly to their comprehensive spirit. Accordingly, most of the major works published in the 1920's were not strikingly original essays on particular topics. They were massive codifications of the progressive version of American history.

The most influential book of this kind came from Charles A. Beard. *The Rise of American Civilization* (2 vols., 1927) was his first serious historical work in a long time. He resigned from Columbia University in 1917 and subsisted principally thereafter on textbooks for elementary and high school students, which he and his wife turned out rapidly and successfully. Beard had long wanted to produce a general survey of a different order, one that would do for the United States what John R. Green's *Short History of the English People* had done for England. The ferment among postwar intellectuals over the quality of the American heritage quickened his resolve, and an extended visit to the Orient in 1922-23 gave him a deep sense of the differences between civilizations. He returned home determined to write a history testifying to the restless, inextinguishable vitality of the American people.[19] Cutting loose from the restrictions of the textbook, as he had already broken away from academic fetters, Beard created with his wife's assistance a work of great power and eloquence.

In line with his earlier interpretation of the Federalist period, Beard portrayed an ever renewed struggle throughout American history between a dominant minority of businessmen and their various adversaries, notably British ruling classes, American farmers and workingmen, and southern planters. In this perspective Jacksonian democracy became an uprising of farmers and workers, and the Civil War a "Second American Revolution" in which northern businessmen drove the planter aristocracy from power. Beard told the story with few regrets for the vanquished. He admired the daring enterprise and the technological innovations engendered by the acquisitive spirit, and with each upheaval he associated—as cause or effect —a forward thrust of democracy. To these political and economic forces Beard related an impressive array of educational, cultural, and social activities, venturing brashly into fields (like music) that he knew little about, dwelling on the progress of scientific and secular values, and seeking wherever possible to interweave material and

19 Interview with Miriam Vagts, May 3, 1961.

ideal phenomena. He conveyed a strong sense of the importance of rational purpose in human affairs, but his rhetoric was profoundly naturalistic. The Civil War he described as an "Irrepressible Conflict." In other contexts he wrote of "an inexorable process beyond the will of any man or group," of the "forces of the age beating pitilessly . . . driving . . . men and women before the storm," of the "havoc [that] fate play[s] with the little schemes of men."[20]

While Beard was writing *The Rise of American Civilization,* some leading academic historians were collaborating on another synthesis, much less compelling but more scholarly and painstaking. In 1922 Arthur M. Schlesinger inaugurated at the State University of Iowa a course entitled "Social and Cultural History of the United States," the first of its kind in any college. At the same time he proposed to a publisher a scheme for a multivolume, cooperative history of "the formation and growth of civilization in the United States." The first four volumes appeared in 1927; nine more came out in succeeding years. The series, under the general editorship of Schlesinger and Dixon Ryan Fox, was called *A History of American Life.*

Whereas Beard never underrated the importance of political power, Schlesinger wanted to get away entirely from the predominantly political substance of general history. In this·he followed consciously the example of another of his Columbia teachers, James Harvey Robinson. Schlesinger's original conspectus for *A History of American Life* defined as its theme the events and influences that touch the everyday life of the people. He relegated politics and government to the background, convinced that they impinge only remotely on the sphere of the average citizen. The series had much to say about health, social welfare, prosperity, depression, poverty, recreation, and agitation for reforms, but very little about the actual exercise of power. This was, in Schlesinger's view, not only the democratic but also the truly American way to write history.[21]

Through the editors' scrupulous care, the series achieved a high degree of uniformity in style and content. It did not, on the other hand, have a unified conceptual scheme. Although the authors often

[20] *The Rise of American Civilization* (1927), vol. I, p. 635; vol. II, pp. 479, 544.
[21] Schlesinger, "What American Social History Is," *Harvard Educational Review,* VII (1937), 57-65. On the genesis and execution of this project Professor Schlesinger's "Reminiscences" are much fuller than his published autobiography.

made cautious, implicit use of economic interpretations in organizing their material, their attempt to be comprehensive and eclectic without specifying the locus of power gave their work a largely descriptive cast. The editors had divided American history into chronological segments according to the prominence at one time or another of some general process like the *The Rise of the Common Man, 1830-1850, The Emergence of Modern America, 1865-1878,* and *The Rise of the City, 1878-1898.* Periodization of this sort sharpened the usual progressive emphasis on rapid social change; for no contributor could take a long-range view of the process in question.

The third of the major syntheses published in 1927 dealt with the history of ideas. It came from the pen of a teacher of English at the University of Washington, Vernon L. Parrington. Professional historians were barely beginning to write intellectual history. Although Robinson and John Dewey had assigned it a prominent place on the agenda of the New History, and Carl Becker demonstrated in *The Declaration of Independence* (1922) how beautifully a professional historian could handle it, nearly all of his colleagues clung to the tangible stuff of social and political affairs. A severe conception of scientific objectivity inhibited professional historians from venturing into a realm where subjective values, speculation, and opinion composed the very substance for investigation. Parrington, having missed the rigors of graduate training, was not afraid of ideas. He was much closer than were the professionals to the nineteenth century humanistic tradition, in which men like W. E. H. Lecky, Leslie Stephen, and Moses Coit Tyler turned to intellectual history as a historical-evolutionary substitute for metaphysical systems. Parrington followed their example in producing *Main Currents in American Thought* (3 vols., 1927, 1930), the first grand formulation of its subject.

While his sense of the sweep and range of ideas derived from a literary background, Parrington belonged essentially among the progressive historians. He started work on *Main Currents* in 1913 captivated by the economic interpretation of history and "impatient with the smug Tory culture which we were fed on as [Harvard] undergraduates." He considered himself part of a generation that had "dedicated itself to history and sociology, accepting as its immediate and particular business a reexamination of the American past in order to forecast an ampler democratic future."[22] To organize his narrative Parrington relied on a Turnerian dialectic that arrayed East, West, and South against one another; and within each section he pitted the spirit of capitalistic exploitation against that of agrarian democracy. His book richly elaborated the old antithesis between Hamiltonian and Jeffersonian principles. It traced the evolution of the latter from the chrysalis of Puritan autocracy through infusions of enlightened and romantic idealisms to an eventual encounter with industrial consolidation and scientific pessimism. The architecture of the book, though much too ambitious to withstand close examination, was imaginative, intricate, and splendorous.

Amid the hosannas that greeted Parrington's epic, few progressive readers noticed how profoundly troubled his vision of American history was. Unlike Beard, Parrington did not celebrate an advancing partnership of science, democracy, and faith in progress. Unlike the authors of *The History of American Life,* he did not at every stage emphasize the *rising* forces and the indications of progress. Many progressive historians escaped—or in the case of Beard deliberately combatted—the disillusion that invaded American intellectual life after World War I. Parrington, who in this sense resembled Becker, felt the bite of postwar disillusion keenly. He was a hopeful man, eager "to forecast an ampler democratic future," quick to praise the children of light and to scold the children of darkness; but the general movement of history since the Civil War seemed inimical to the Jeffersonian ideals he cherished. His discouragement arose only partly from nostalgia for a decentralized society, from repugnance for the consolidated power and colorless standardization of the twentieth century. As an idealist, he was also disturbed by the deterministic implications of his own intellectual weapons. The economic interpretation of history taught the subordination of ideas to material realities. The whole scientific, naturalistic outlook of his generation endangered humanistic values. Consequently, Parrington could not cast American intellectual history in the pattern of continual progress. He saw it rather as cyclical. Starting from the wasteland of Calvinistic pessimism, he traced the rise of liberal democracy to an

---

[22] *Main Currents in American Thought,* vol. III (1930), p. 403. I am indebted to the careful analysis by Robert A. Skotheim and Kermit Vanderbilt, "Vernon Louis Parrington: The Mind and Art of a Historian of Ideas," *Pacific Northwest Quarterly,* LIII (1962), 100-13.

apogee before 1860 and its descent thereafter into the realistic but disillusioning jungle of scientific pessimism. At the end of the story the best he could see were "sunset skies that gave promise of other and greater dawns." Just as Carl Becker's writings in the 1920's signaled a crisis in historical theory, Parrington's marked the onset of crisis in the progressive interpretation of American history.

❧ 5 ❧

CRISIS IN PROGRESSIVE HISTORY

All of the leading historical journals ignored *Main Currents in American Thought,* presumably considering it outside their purview. The profession as a whole came to accept intellectual history only gradually in the 1930's and 1940's.[1] Nevertheless, during the inter-war years the concerns that weighed so heavily on Parrington's mind did infiltrate professional scholarship. They appeared first in the handling of certain concrete topics, then provoked wider controversies over interpretation, and led finally to new perspectives on American history.

It was becoming evident in the Twenties, and increasingly so in the Thirties, that history had somehow gone wrong. The course of America's progress was strewn with too many mistakes, failures, and illusions to have unfolded with the neat, intrinsic logic that Turner and Beard had sketched. A number of progressive-minded historians between the wars dedicated themselves to explaining the failures and puncturing the illusions. We have already observed this highly critical approach in the study of diplomatic history; it appeared just as strongly in a re-examination of America's domestic record. Tough-minded progressives, though still intent on vindicating democracy and saving a faith in progress, set out to expose the most unpleasant "realities." This naturally led to an intensified use of economic interpretations. Some historians, however, recoiled sharply from the fatalistic implications of so impersonal a view of history. By the late 1930's an emerging revolt against economic determinism was beginning to threaten the intellectual foundations of progressive historiography.

The roots of these developments, most of which became visible in the 1930's, go back to the disillusion that followed World War I. The general influence of the postwar disillusion was to call into question the status of ideals in American culture. Many Americans in the Twenties wanted to exorcise the crusading, self-righteous ideal-

[1] John Higham, "The Rise of American Intellectual History," *AHR,* LVI (1951), 462-67.

ism of the war years. They associated much of it with New England —a land of Puritans, abolitionists, and other moral fanatics. Accordingly, the principal literary and social critics mounted a withering attack on New England culture and on traditional moral authority in general. In this assault some progressive historians joined. They were already skeptical of abstractions and appearances; they had already spied the cloven hoof of self-interest beneath the seats of the mighty; and they were already in revolt against New England. As southerners and midwesterners, progressive historians had never had any sympathy for the moneyed and patrician groups of the Northeast. They equated democracy with the common man, especially the frontiersman, not with the New England tradition. After World War I their economic and sectional animus interlaced with the popular "debunking" mood.

The explosive effects of the combination may be observed in the work of two amateur historians who became widely respected and influential in professional circles. James Truslow Adams gave the sanction of scholarship to the repudiation of Puritanism, and Albert J. Beveridge did the same to abolitionism, though neither had set out with any such intention. Both launched their historical studies in a highly conventional vein. Adams, a New York gentleman brought up to regard that city as an outpost of English culture, started in 1919 upon a history of New England with the simple purpose of presenting it from the viewpoint of the Imperial school.[2] About the same time Beveridge, a midwestern progressive who had written an adulatory biography of John Marshall, embarked on a biography of Lincoln intending to eulogize his exalted moral leadership.

The postwar disillusion hit both of them hard. The revulsion against Puritanism provoked Adams to inquire iconoclastically into the economic motives of the early settlers. He decided that they had come more largely to fish than to pray. Adams soon dropped the Imperial approach and made his history of New England a study of conflict between Puritan "theocracy" and frontier democracy. Beveridge, also looking behind appearances to realities, was appalled to discover a shifty, partisan Lincoln, entangled in vested interests. The

[2] In a book review in the *New England Quarterly*, III (1930), 742, Adams explains the original intentions with which he began work on the three-volume series, *The Founding of New England* (1921), *Revolutionary New England, 1691-1776* (1923), and *New England in the Republic, 1776-1850* (1926). The James Truslow Adams Papers at Columbia University are also illuminating.

splenetic, trouble-making abolitionists shocked him still more.[3] Beveridge managed to redeem Lincoln somewhat by contrasting his down-to-earth politics with the abolitionists' destructive fanaticism. In place of a noble idealism, both historians found jobbery and hypocrisy.

Along similar lines, a highly critical view of the whole Civil War experience was shaping up. Disillusion with World War I called into question the moral grandeur of the earlier holocaust; and progressive emphasis on the common opposition of the South and West to New England focused attention on northern misdeeds. The Civil War seemed now, in its consequences at least, a betrayal of democracy. Fred Shannon won a Pulitzer Prize for a book describing the inefficiency, corruption, and profiteering in the Union armies. The already unflattering view of Radical Reconstruction that conservative scholars of the Dunning school had sketched became positively lurid in the hands of southern and western progressives who championed the white masses against the Republican "oligarchs." [4] Perhaps the war itself was an avoidable mistake. So Charles W. Ramsdell argued, with a Turnerian faith in the natural environment, which he thought would inevitably have prevented further expansion of slavery. Thus, by the end of the Twenties the idealism of the North in the Civil War era was heavily discounted. As early as 1928 Professor Dumas Malone assured his fellow southerners, "The more important positions were long ago surrendered into our hands, and the honors of war have been granted nearly all our heroes." [5]

In the 1930's revulsion against the supposedly false idealism of the

[3] *Abraham Lincoln, 1809-1858* (2 vols., 1928). The fascinating story of Beveridge's intellectual struggle may be followed in Claude G. Bowers' *Beveridge and the Progressive Era* (1932), pp. 569-77, and in Elizabeth Donnan and Leo F. Stock, eds., "Senator Beveridge, J. Franklin Jameson, and Abraham Lincoln," *Mississippi Valley Historical Review*, XXXV (1948), 639-73.

[4] Shannon, *Organization and Administration of the Union Army, 1861-1865* (2 vols., 1928); Claude G. Bowers, *The Tragic Era: The Revolution After Lincoln* (1929); George Fort Milton, *The Age of Hate: Andrew Johnson and the Radicals* (1930).

[5] Dumas Malone, "A Challenge to Patriots," *Virginia Quarterly Review*, IV (1928), 486; Charles W. Ramsdell, "The Natural Limits of Slavery Expansion," *Mississippi Valley Historical Review*, XVI (1929), 151-71. There are detailed accounts of the rise of "revisionism" in Thomas J. Pressly's *Americans Interpret Their Civil War* (1962), pp. 265-306, and T. H. Bonner's "Civil War Historians and the Needless War Doctrine," *Journal of the History of Ideas*, XVII (1956), 194-97.

North blossomed into a fullfledged reinterpretation of the causes of the Civil War. A group of southern and miswestern historians with southern connections undertook to refute Beard's interpretation of the Civil War as a necessary step in the progress of the nation. It was rather, these "revisionists" argued, a horrible, needless blunder. Who then was responsible? Surely not the common man—the revisionists were too faithful to progressive values to blame the demos. Impractical extremists must have misled an innocent people. Thus George Fort Milton tried to show in a biography of Stephen A. Douglas how fanatical minorities got control of the machinery of government, flouted Douglas's "economic common sense," and brought on a war that the masses had not wanted.[6] James G. Randall's important synthesis, *The Civil War and Reconstruction* (1937), took essentially the same approach. Avery Craven of the University of Chicago set forth in *The Coming of the Civil War* (1942) the most careful analysis of how genuine economic disturbances were magnified into factitious moral abstractions. With a curl of the lip he had announced in 1935 the basic thesis of the "revisionist" school: "Each side, in the end, fought the other for principles and the glory of God, for the preservation of civilizations, for the maintenance of honor. The conflict was the work of politicians and pious cranks."[7]

While Civil War historians assailed the moral idealism traditionally associated with New England, other progressive scholars were questioning the democratic idealism traditionally ascribed to the frontier. It was, of course, more difficult for progressives to see deformities in the western spirit than to notice blemishes on eastern ideals. No one seriously criticized Turner's attribution of American democracy to the free land of the West until after World War I; no considerable dissent was heard in the historical profession until the 1930's; and even then skepticism met devout resistance from Turner's disciples. Yet the sudden outbreak of controversy revealed how serious the strains within progressive historiography were becoming.

Beard had never given much credence to the Turner thesis. From Beard's point of view, Turner was not enough of an economic realist: although starting from a materialistic basis (land), Turner had erected on it a quasi-romantic theory of Western society as free, vir-

---

[6] *The Eve of Conflict: Stephen A. Douglas and the Needless War* (1934).
[7] "Coming of the War Between the States: An Interpretation," *Journal of Southern History*, II (1936), 305.

tuous, and supremely American. Beard's reservations about the uplifting influence of the frontier, initially suggested in a book review
in 1921, were much more strongly put by disillusioned cultural
critics for whom the idealism of the frontier seemed as fraudulent as
that of New England. In the 1930's scholars joined in the assault.
Thomas P. Abernethy, one of Turner's own students, published in
1932 a path-breaking book on Tennessee politics. He described that
frontier area as dominated by grasping, illiberal land speculators,
among them none other than Andrew Jackson. "The first offspring of
the West," Abernethy concluded, "was not democracy but arrant op-
portunism." Similar findings emerged from the careful studies that
Paul W. Gates and Fred A. Shannon made of land disposal in the
Midwest. Clearly the frontier had never offered as much egalitarian
opportunity as Turner had imagined. The old notion that the frontier
had provided a "safety-valve" for urban discontent and a release
from urban poverty seemed a pernicious illusion in the deep economic crisis of the Thirties. Was not the escapist mythology of a western paradise somewhat responsible for America's failure to face up
earlier to basic social problems? To purge our history of such beguil-
ing fantasies, several scholars took pains to demonstrate that industrial workers had never escaped to western farms in significant numbers.[8]

In effect, economic historians were revolting against Turner while
Civil War historians revolted against Beard. The coincidence of the
two movements suggests their common basis in the disillusion of the
interwar period. Behind the immediate target—Turner in one case,
Beard in the other—the rebels were attacking older shibboleths.
Each group was undermining an established piety of American culture that progressive historians had hitherto accepted: the grandeur
of the Civil War and the glory of the frontier. By discrediting these
cherished memories, progressive historians intended to make American history less pretty and more "realistic."

[8] Beard, "The Frontier in American History," *New Republic*, XXV (1921),
349-50; Abernethy, *From Frontier to Plantation in Tennessee: A Study in Frontier Democracy* (1932), p. 359; Shannon, "The Homestead Act and the Labor
Surplus," and Gates, "The Homestead Law in an Incongruous Land System,"
AHR, XLI (1936), 637-81; Ellen von Nardroff, "The American Frontier as a
Safety Valve—The Life, Death, Reincarnation, and Justification of a Theory,"
Agricultural History, XXXVI (1962), 127-34. On the background of cultural
criticism see Warren I. Susman's "The Useless Past: American Intellectuals and
the Frontier Thesis, 1910-1930," *Bucknell Review*, XI (1963), 1-20.

In other respects the two revolts differed. The Civil War "revisionists" honored Turner's memory. As southerners and midwesterners still teaching in America's heartland, they looked back affectionately, as Turner had, to the old rural America of farmers and planters. Craven, who was one of Turner's students and who had begun his career in agricultural history, regarded the ascendancy that the urban-industrial Northeast won during the Civil War as one of its most regrettable aspects.[9] The revolt against Turner, on the other hand, attracted many eastern historians along with a few disillusioned midwesterners like Shannon. In some measure it was a declaration of independence from midwestern domination of progressive historiography. Thus many of Turner's academic critics argued that his influence had too long delayed appreciation of the constructive importance of the city and the industrial revolution in American history. In this vein Arthur M. Schlesinger countered Turner's frontier thesis with an urban interpretation of American history, which inaugurated a sustained interest in the history of the city.[10] Another of Beard's students, Louis M. Hacker, reacted against Turner's sectionalism by insisting on the primacy of economic classes. Hacker's *The Triumph of American Capitalism* (1940) went as far in the direction of a Marxist interpretation of American history as any academic historian would ever go.

There was also another side to the anti-Turner movement, for it temporarily gave vent to very diverse discontents. While critics in the Beardian tradition assailed Turner for underrating urbanism or capitalism as against the equally impersonal processes of nature, others complained that all such approaches allowed too little autonomy or influence to ideas. Benjamin F. Wright and George W. Pierson, among others, traced American values to the cultural heritage Americans carried westward with them. From this perspective, Turner was too materialistic and even parochial in grounding ideas and behavior in the immediate physical environment. Turner, said

[9] Avery Craven, "The Turner Theories and the South," *Journal of Southern History*, V (1939), 314, and "Frederick Jackson Turner," *The Marcus W. Jernegan Essays in American Historiography*, ed. William T. Hutchinson (1937), p. 268. Craven spent his formative years in a small town in Iowa; Randall, who was a student of William E. Dodd, grew up in southern Indiana. Both married southern girls.

[10] *The Rise of the City, 1878-1898* (1933), and "The City in American History," *Mississippi Valley Historical Review*, XXVII (1940), 43-66. Cf. *The Historian and the City*, ed., Oscar Handlin and John Burchard (1963).

Pierson, derived America from real estate, not state of mind.[11] If some attacked Turner's western idealism, others criticized his economic determinism.

Actually, the latter group was striking out in the same direction in which Civil War historians were moving. Pierson's criticism of Turner chimed with the revisionists' criticism of Beard. In denying the inevitability of the Civil War they too rejected a deterministic explanation of events. Contending that agitators and propagandists precipitated a needless holocaust, these historians made much allowance for subjective and unpredictable elements in history—for passion, chance, and individual idiosyncrasies. Randall and Craven were, in fact, united with their chief northern adversary, Dwight Dumond, in believing that the Civil War resulted from folly rather than fate. Dumond, who resurrected the abolitionist indictment of slavery, was just as intent as any revisionist on discrediting economic causation.[12] It is indicative of the confused ferment of the 1930's that both the reinterpretation of the Civil War and the reconsideration of the frontier arose from a need to exorcise idealism—to be more "realistic"—yet both led in the end to a reaffirmation of ideas.

Thus, in concrete interpretive controversies, the problem of determinism, which had obsessed Parrington a decade earlier, came to a head. As a result a significant minority of progressive historians moved toward the forms of history in which Parrington had excelled: toward biography and intellectual history. There the problem of determinism was most acutely posed. Both branches of scholarship had, of course, other roots in American culture. Biography, cultivated by journalists, had already tapped a new reading public. The study of ideas was part of the unfinished business of the New History. It could be employed, as Robinson and Becker employed it, to deflate outmoded beliefs or to provide a general framework for the multifarious data history was now encompassing. But the fact that a really working interest in biography and in intellectual history emerged simul-

[11] *The Turner Thesis Concerning the Role of the Frontier in American History,* ed. George R. Taylor, "Problems in American Civilization" (1956) reprints some of the major papers. Two concrete reactions against the environmentalism of the frontier thesis are H. R. Shurtleff's *The Log Cabin Myth* (1939) and Richard H. Shryock's "British versus German Traditions in Colonial Agriculture," *Mississippi Valley Historical Review,* XXVI (1939), 39-54.
[12] Dumond, *Antislavery Origins of the Civil War in the United States* (1939) and *Antislavery: The Crusade for Freedom in America* (1961).

taneously in professional scholarship suggests that they also served a new and common need. Each seemed to delimit the sway of impersonal forces in history. Each opened a dimension for reasserting the capacity of men to choose their destiny.

Until the Thirties relatively few professional historians took biography seriously. Biographical dissertations were becoming popular among the increasing throngs of Ph.D. candidates for the bad reason that an individual life is relatively easy to lay out and the principal sources are often ready at hand. Mundane considerations do not account, however, for the initiative that produced the great collaborative project of the decade, *The Dictionary of American Biography* (22 vols., 1928-44). Moreover, such major scholars as Howard K. Beale, Henry Steele Commager, James G. Randall, and Allan Nevins now gave their best efforts to biography. In fact it became one of the most conspicuous and distinctive features of American humanistic studies. Through biography a remarkable number of scholars were trying to disengage themselves from the impersonal and external approach to the past that had always prevailed in American academic scholarship.

Nevins, the most indefatigible of biographers, published his first biography in 1928. He had already written three solid books of social history that reflected the strong influence of Turner and Beard. Then, partly in reaction, he became intensely interested in the role of the individual in history.[13] The long series of biographies he wrote during the next decade sought to humanize scholarly history. In each of them Nevins exhibited the character and moral force of his subject against a dense background of resistive circumstance. His career as a biographer epitomized the counterthrust of a chastened idealism arising out of the crisis in progressive historiography.

[13] Nevins to author, June 1, 1961. Among the outstanding biographies that were begun if not completed in the Thirties are Commager's *Theodore Parker* (1936), Randall's *Lincoln the President* (4 vols., 1945-55), Nevins' *Grover Cleveland, A Study in Courage* (1932) and *John D. Rockefeller: The Heroic Age of American Business* (2 vols., 1940), Charles M. Wiltse's *John C. Calhoun* (3 vols., 1944-51), Samuel Eliot Morison's *Admiral of the Ocean Sea* (2 vols., 1942), and Dumas Malone's *Jefferson and His Time* (3 vols. to date, 1948-62). Samuel F. Bemis turned to biography in the 1940's and published a notable two-volume life of John Quincy Adams (1949-55). The most imposing undertaking in this tradition today is Arthur S. Link's *Wilson* (3 vols. to date, 1947-1960). On the function and appeal of biography see Matthew Josephson's "Historians and Mythmakers," *Virginia Quarterly Review*, XVI (1940), 92-109, and John A. Garraty's *The Nature of Biography* (1957).

In considering the writings of Allan Nevins in the 1930's we leave entirely behind the pungent exhalation of postwar disillusion. Nevins evinced, along with zest for the rich human possibilities of biography, a delight in the inspirational function of history. In 1938 he wrote: "History is the sextant and compass of states which, tossed by wind and current, would be lost in confusion if they could not fix their position. . . . By giving peoples a sense of continuity in all their efforts, and by chronicling immortal worth, it confers upon them both a consciousness of their unity, and a feeling of the importance of human achievement." [14]

A sense of continuity, a consciousness of unity! These words, set down at a time when economic instability was ramifying into a fearful breakup of international stability, were more than a protest against determinism. They carried also a distinctly conservative feeling for tradition and solidarity, a feeling wholly alien to the basic progressive accent on conflict and change. They pointed to a new quest for stable values. Doubtless such a reaction against disillusion would have occurred if there had been no Depression and no threat of totalitarian power. But these disturbances raised basic questions about the general course of history and made some intellectuals more eager to find strength and sustenance in the past.

It is not commonly appreciated how far Beard himself moved in this direction. Beard's assault on scientific history during the 1930's stemmed from his desire for moral rearmament in the midst of a great crisis in human affairs. His relativism was explicitly an appeal for freedom from the coercions of fate. Consequently, his own historical writing shifted—sometimes awkwardly—toward greater stress on individuals and particularly on ideas in history. In 1939 he declared: "As in physical nature the flash of lightning always precedes the roll of thunder, so in human affairs the flame of thought has always gone before a transformation in the social arrangements of mankind." [15] The metaphor was still naturalistic, but the order of cause and effect seemed now reversed.

After giving the best years of his life to a realistic demolition of mental "fictions" and disembodied ideas, Beard was groping now for

[14] *The Gateway to History* (1938), p. 3.
[15] Charles A. and Mary R. Beard, *America in Midpassage,* vol. II (1939), p. 860; Bernard C. Borning, *The Political and Social Thought of Charles A. Beard* (1962), pp. 165-81.

the inner spirit, the unique and enduring essence, of American civilization. He never quite put his finger on it. A first attempt to identify an integral "national interest" shattered on the rock of his stubborn economic realism. Beard's *The Idea of National Interest* (1934) showed only a clash of diverse material interests, for he deliberately excluded from consideration all nonmaterial elements. A few years later, just as deliberately, Beard cut loose from materialism. He added a supplementary volume to the *Rise of American Civilization*, calling it *The American Spirit* (1942). This he considered an essential complement to the earlier volumes. It would present the "interior" rather than the "outward" aspect of civilization, describing the "intellectual and moral motivation" of Americans. Unfortunately, Beard had no method for analyzing ideas apart from material interests, so the book was a disappointingly literal summary of the documents he had read.

Beard's last historical work, written at the end of World War II, was a scathing analysis of Franklin D. Roosevelt's foreign policy. This too reflected Beard's revolt against determinism.[16] Convinced in the mid-Thirties that another war would destroy democracy in America, Beard could not regard our involvement as inevitable. He could not think that economic forces would run so contrary to the true "national interest." Nor could he, as a good progressive, hold "the people" responsible, any more than the revisionists held them responsible for the Civil War. When intervention occurred, it had to be the work of malign individuals. In a sense, Beard joined Allan Nevins in putting a new emphasis on personal responsibility in history and on the preservation of traditional values. Though Beard and Nevins disagreed completely on foreign policy, and Beard remained a critic while Nevins became a laureate of heroes, both of them reveal the approaching disruption of the progressive school.

One major historian at the height of his powers in the 1930's had never in any real sense been part of that school. This was Harvard's Samuel Eliot Morison. As Channing's student and successor, Morison inherited eclectic sympathies together with a basically conservative allegiance to the continuities in history. As a proper Bostonian living still in the house of his ancestors, he knew that those continuities be-

---

[16] *President Roosevelt and the Coming of the War, 1941* (1948). Beard's change of outlook is also shown in *A Basic History of the United States* (1944) and *The Republic* (1943).

tween the present and the remote past were still unbroken.[17] He did not find them where the older conservative evolutionists had, in the formal structure of institutions. He was enough of a twentieth century man to know that institutions are not so self-sustaining as late nineteenth century professors had believed. For Morison continuity inhered in the very stuff that progressive scholars brought to the fore, the very stuff that postwar critics held up to scorn and derision. It inhered in social relationships, in ways of life, in accustomed values, in the web of culture. Although Morison was a gifted narrative historian rather than an architect of broad interpretations, the books he wrote in the Thirties adumbrated an essentially new view of American history. Against the progressive accent on change and against the postwar revulsion from ideals, Morison wrote of the tough, enduring qualities in his cultural heritage.

Being a vigorous, explicit opponent of determinism, Morison chose biography and intellectual history as his vehicles is the 1930's. These he employed in a spirited and sustained defense of New England Puritanism. The widespread debunking of the Puritan as a gloomy moral hypocrite, especially by James Truslow Adams and Parrington, aroused Morison's regional pride. His counterattack opened with an array of biographical portraits, *Builders of the Bay Colony* (1930); it widened through an influential series of lectures, *The Puritan Pronaos* (1936); and culminated in three solid volumes on Harvard College in the seventeenth century. These books launched a revival of respect for the early religious underpinnings of American thought and society.

Morison made the Puritans relevant in several ways to the broad defense of American culture that was appearing in the Thirties. First, he humanized and somewhat modernized the Puritan image. By depicting an intellectually vigorous, broad-minded folk, comprehensible to the modern mind, he pointed up the continuity between the first Americans and their latter-day descendants. "Primitive New England is the porch to the temple," Morison concluded, "a puritan *pronaos* as it were to the American mind of the nineteenth century, and of today." Second, he repelled the economic interpretation of the Puritan emigration; they came for idealistic reasons, to preserve a

[17] See W. H. Hale's "Historian of the Ocean Sea," *Reporter*, XVII (July 11, 1957), 44-47, and Morison's own memoir of his childhood, *One Boy's Boston, 1887-1901* (1962).

"rugged faith." Third, Morison denied that the Puritans were Calvinistic determinists, thereby associating them with his own assault on modern determinism.[18]

In much of this program Morison had the support of a brilliant young colleague in the English Department, Perry Miller. With extraordinary subtlety, gusto, and industry, Miller elaborated the meaning of Puritan ideas on a grand scale. A Chicagoan and an atheist, he did not have Morison's conservative zeal to re-establish continuity with the fathers of New England. Miller wanted to cut through all the myths, traditional and modern alike, to decipher the authentic, unsuspected otherness of the past. Certainly the Puritans attracted him partly because of the sheer difficulty of reaching them. Yet the main point to be made here is the repugnance he shared with Morison for all social and economic determinisms. By showing that the Puritans brought with them from Europe a fully developed system of beliefs, Miller's prewar books swelled the rising assault on the Turnerian school.[19]

Miller was little read by professional historians until after the war, and it would be wrong to suppose that Morison's restoration of cultural continuity, Nevins' hero worship, or Beard's search for the American Spirit made much impression on them either. Undoubtedly most historians, in spite of multiplying schisms, remained broadly loyal to the progressive outlook. Most of them apparently held to the basic faith in progress that Parrington had come to doubt; most of them looked for "realistic" explanations of human behavior; many still viewed society as a tumultuous extension of the flux of nature. Yet the old progressive consensus was clearly under increasing strain. The notion that material forces govern history was losing ground. All of the major authorities on the Civil War, and most of those who wrote on other wars as well, had rejected the thesis of inevitability. Interest in the decision making of powerful individuals and in the impact of powerful ideas was spreading. A disillusion that had sharpened economic realism had also revealed follies and failures

[18] *The Intellectual Life of Colonial New England,* 2nd ed. (1956), pp. 11, 274; *The Founding of Harvard College* (1935) and *Harvard College in the Seventeenth Century* (2 vols., 1936).
[19] In addition to *Orthodoxy in Massachusetts: A Genetic Study* (1933) and *The New England Mind: The Seventeenth Century* (1939), see the appraisals collected in "Perry Miller and the American Mind," *Harvard Review,* II (Winter-Spring, 1964).

that realism could not explain. Current events portended a grim future for democracy. The human prospect in the future and in the past seemed less predictable than progressive historians had hitherto supposed. In compensation, some now looked for the relatively permanent features of their culture.

Two books published on essentially the same subject in the early 1940's threw these divergent views of American history into dramatic contrast. Ralph Gabriel's *The Course of American Democratic Thought* (1940) and Merle Curti's *The Growth of American Thought* (1943) were broad surveys, which brought to maturity the study of American intellectual history by professional historians. Curti's book testified to the persistent vigor of progressive scholarship. Gabriel's sketched out a new pattern that was emerging from the crisis in progressive thought.

The two men had begun their studies from similar starting points. Although Gabriel was an easterner and Curti was a midwesterner, they started from a common background of Parrington, Turner, social history, and social science. Curti was a student of Turner, and Gabriel's first book, *The Evolution of Long Island* (1921), was strongly Turnerian. Both men were primarily occupied in the 1920's with what we would today call social history. Both were drawn to intellectual history partly by an idealistic concern over the impact of war, industrialization, and modern science on American values; both wished to resist the pessimism and disillusion of the time. Curti did so in the manner of John Dewey, combining an instrumental view of ideas with an unshaken faith in science. But Gabriel, influenced by an underlying religious commitment, joined in the outcry against scientific determinism.[20] His *Course of American Democratic Thought* consisted largely of biographical portraits; Curti's *Growth* completely subordinated individuals to general social and economic patterns.

Fearful also of the danger of totalitarianism in an unstable world,

[20] On the affinity between Gabriel and Morison and the linkage between Curti and earlier New Historians see Robert A. Skotheim's "The Writing of American Histories of Ideas: Two Traditions in the XXth Century," *Journal of the History of Ideas,* XXV (1964), 269-77. The attitudes that attracted the two men to the study of intellectual history are evident in Curti's "Literature in the Synthetic Study of History," *Historical Outlook,* XIII (1922), 129, and Gabriel's reviews of the *Encyclopaedia of the Social Sciences* in *AHR,* XL (1935), 305-07, and XLI (1935), 113-16.

Gabriel adopted a conservative view of the American past. His theme was the continuity of an essentially unchanged body of ideas through the vicissitudes of the last century. He argued that the American people were basically united, even in 1861, by a faith that had survived every adversity. Curti, on the other hand, celebrated conflict, diversity, and change. His book treated democracy not as a stable faith in man but as an expanding struggle waged by and for common men with the aid of scientific knowledge. Eager to make intellectual history genuinely democratic, Curti gave special attention to popular ideas and their dissemination. He widened to the utmost the scope of the progressive synthesis, and so in a sense completed the task to which the dominant school of historians gave their best energies during the interwar years.[21] Gabriel laid the foundations of another synthesis grounded in the persistence rather than the progress of American democracy.

[21] Curti's impressive range—his capacity to bring into history the data of all of the social sciences—is also displayed in his collected essays, *Probing Our Past* (1954) and his pioneering quantitative study, *The Making of an American Community* (1959).

⊷ 6 ⊶

A SEARCH FOR STABILITY

Although World War II caused a widespread lapse of scholarly activity, it did not seem for a time to change the interpretation of American history very much. In fact, as young historians came back to the universities from wartime assignments, progressive historiography entered a kind of Indian summer. Through the late 1940's and into the early 1950's most of the exciting books were written by scholars who had been trained during the Great Depression and who had responded ardently to the influence of Charles A. Beard. Their books in large measure were hearty evaluations of the tradition of democratic reform and protest. Merrill Jensen's *The New Nation* (1950) recorded the advancing struggle of democracy in the 1780's. Arthur M. Schlesinger Jr.'s *The Age of Jackson* (1945) told a similar story about the 1830's. Eric F. Goldman's *Rendezvous with Destiny* (1952) swept bravely forward from 1870 in tracing "the reform movements that culminated in the New Deal and the Fair Deal." C. Vann Woodward's *Origins of the New South, 1877-1913* (1951) focused on the upthrust of democracy under the impact of industrialism. Among somewhat older scholars, Alice Felt Tyler wrote about religious and humanitarian reform in a Turnerian vein; and Henry Steele Commager carried forward Parrington's unfinished story of modern American thought with an optimistic pragmatism the old master had lacked.[1]

A disquieting note sounded in one of the most brilliant of the postwar books. Richard Hofstadter's *The American Political Tradition and the Men Who Made it* (1948) commented mordantly on a cur-

[1] Tyler, *Freedom's Ferment: Phases of American Social History from the Colonial Period to the Outbreak of the Civil War* (1944); Commager, *The American Mind: An Interpretation of American Thought and Character Since the 1880's* (1950); Max Savelle, *Seeds of Liberty: The Genesis of the American Mind* (1948); Thomas C. Cochran and William Miller, *The Age of Enterprise* (1942); John C. Miller, *Triumph of Freedom, 1775-1783* (1948); John Hope Franklin, *From Slavery to Freedom* (1947); Daniel Aaron, *Men of Good Hope: A Story of American Progressives* (1951).

rent "lack of confidence in the American future" and on "the rudderless and demoralized state of American liberalism." This he attributed partly to the absence of really basic differences between liberal and conservative impulses throughout the national experience. The customary emphasis of American historians on conflict, Hofstadter said, has obscured the underlying agreement that major parties and movements have always shared. Ours has been "a democracy in cupidity," which offers no coherent guidance in a new, more dangerous era.[2] Hofstadter did not press this fateful challenge to progressive historiography. He delivered it as a casual afterthought to a narrative revealing a fascinating variety of political types. He wrote from a position otherwise so sympathetic to Beard and so critical of American business mores that his heresy seemed only a step to the left.

All of these books displayed a keen interest in the role of ideas, particularly as they bore on political action. Many of the authors still held to a primarily economic interpretation of history; but close attention to the impact of ideas on politics inevitably pushed economic causation into the background. From an original concentration on external, material reality, the progressive scholar was turning more and more to a preoccupation with values. And since the values that many of the best books examined were those of the progressive tradition itself, historians were obviously taking stock of their own ideological heritage. While some were assuring themselves of its strength, others probed soft spots. Hofstadter was not alone in showing a new awareness of failures and dilemmas in the liberal record. Goldman worried about the growing relativism it displayed. Other left-of-center historians, newly sensitive to the magnitude of American racial problems, discovered a vein of prejudice in liberal thought; they set about rectifying the insensitivity and disinterest older progressive historians had usually shown on the subject of race.[3]

A more central and thoroughgoing reappraisal of progressive history began in monographs challenging the significance of economic conflicts. No single monograph could make extensive claims or es-

[2] Pp. vii-x. This introduction was written, Professor Hofstadter recalls, at the behest of the publisher; he had not written the book with any such clear design.
[3] John Higham, "Anti-Semitism in the Gilded Age," *Mississippi Valley Historical Review*, XLIII (1957), 559-78; Kenneth M. Stampp, *The Peculiar Institution* (1956); C. Vann Woodward, *The Strange Career of Jim Crow* (1955).

cape the suspicion that its findings were exceptional. By the mid-Fifties, however, the new research was having a cumulative impact on the whole shape of American history. One after another, the great crises, which progressive historians had depicted as turning points in the battle between democracy and privilege, came under fresh examination. In each case the scale of conflict seemed to shrink. Sharp divisions between periods, sections, groups, and ideologies disappeared. Over all, the new digging amounted to a massive grading operation that smoothed and flattened the convulsive dialectic of progressive history. An unsuspected degree of uniformity and agreement appeared in the welter of America's historical experience. Instead of a polarized culture—a culture eternally divided betwen over- and underprivileged groups, between a party of the past and a party of the future, between noble ideals and ignoble interests—young scholars glimpsed an essentially homogeneous culture full of small, impermanent variations. The continuity that Gabriel had observed in the American "democratic faith" and that Hofstadter criticized in the American political tradition emerged as substantial social reality.

Among the various types of cleavage that progressives dwelled upon, the sectional principle gave way most easily. An attack on sectional differences as fundamental to American history had already developed in the 1930's. It stemmed partly from the revolt against Turner: all anti-Turnerians saw the West as an extension of the East, not its antithesis. The revisionist approach to the Civil War also ran counter to an emphatic sectionalism; for revisionists assumed that North and South were not incompatible civilizations, but basically one. These views simply gained further momentum in the 1940's and 1950's. Now the defensive and aggressive sectional feelings that motivated so much scholarship in the early twentieth century were rapidly dissolving. The standardized urban milieu in which younger historians grew up deprived them of strong regional identities.

Consequently, in postwar scholarship, much that had been described as southern or western either lost significance or merged into national configurations. Following a line of research that Frank Owsley opened in the late 1930's, many southern historians called attention to the democratic features of the Old South. It was, they maintained, primarily a land of middle-class farmers, not of plantation aristocrats.[4] The notion of the antebellum South as a distinctively aristocratic society was a myth; and a northern scholar wrote a book to prove that even the myth had rested on nationwide rather than purely sectional yearnings. *The Southerner as American* (1960) was the title of a collection of essays by a group of young southern historians, and it summed up the general trend of scholarship.[5]

One might equally say of western history that it now dealt with the westerner as American. Attention shifted increasingly to the post-frontier West, to cities, economic development, and the impingement of national politics and institutions on western areas.[6] For many readers Henry Nash Smith made America's mythology about the West more interesting than the reality. Smith's powerful book, *Virgin Land* (1950), capped the assault on Turner by relegating the frontier thesis—prematurely, it should be said—to the ash heap of dead myths. Simultaneously Walter P. Webb took that thesis out of a sectional context and put it in an international context. Before World War II Webb had dwelled on the distinctive features of his own West, the Great Plains. In 1952 he published *The Great Frontier,* in which America's frontier experience is linked to European history in a general interpretation of Western civilization.

In view of the reaction against sectionalism, it is little wonder that academic interest in political conflicts between East, West, and South fell off markedly. No one could deny, of course, that the Civil War was a tremendous rupture of whatever unity and continuity America had exhibited. But few of the younger professional historians coming along in the wake of Craven and Randall found the causes of the war an attractive subject for research. While journalists served up great gobs of Civil War drama to an avid public, the number of significant contributions from professionals declined. A notable exception was

[4] Frank L. Owsley, "The Economic Basis of Society in the Late Ante-Bellum South," *Journal of Southern History,* VII (1940), 24-45, and *Plain Folk of the Old South* (1949); Charles S. Sydnor, *The Development of Southern Sectionalism, 1819-1848* (1948).

[5] Edited by Charles G. Sellers Jr.; William R. Taylor, *Cavalier and Yankee: The Old South and American National Character* (1961).

[6] Earl Pomeroy, "The Changing West," in *The Reconstruction of American History,* ed. John Higham (London, 1962), pp. 77-80; Louis B. Wright, *Culture on the Moving Frontier* (1955); Douglas F. Dowd, "A Comparative Analysis of Economic Development in the American West and South," *Journal of Economic History,* XVI (1956), 558-74.

the monumental history of the Civil War era on which Allan Nevins embarked about 1940; but Nevins, writing in the spirit of James Ford Rhodes, had an old-fashioned appreciation of the triumph of union in the midst of strife.[7]

If antagonisms between North and South failed to stimulate younger historians, conflicts between East and West proved still less inspiring. Events that had been attributed to aggressive western initiative, such as the War of 1812 and the progressive movement, were reinterpreted in national terms.[8] Most remarkably, the Turnerian doctrine that the political democracy of the early nineteenth century came out of the West received hardly any effective support in postwar research.[9] A major controversy erupted over the nature of Jacksonian democracy without any of the leading participants taking seriously the specifically western elements for which it had been famous.

Not a sectional but a class thesis was at issue in the controversy over Jacksonian democracy. Not Turner but Beard was the main target of the newer historians. Turner, having died in 1932, bore the brunt of the historiographical discontents of the Thirties; Beard's death in 1948 released a similar but fiercer onslaught. While Turner's sectionalism faded gracefully into the background, Beard's vision of an America divided between the democratic many and a privileged economic class underwent searching criticism. Throughout the late 1940's and 1950's a host of scholars mined and sapped the old economic dualism over most of the span of American history. The first sustained attack developed on Jacksonian terrain simply because a new, highly vulnerable statement of the Beardian approach materialized there.

Arthur M. Schlesinger Jr.'s *The Age of Jackson* was the work of a

[7] *Ordeal of the Union* (2 vols., 1947); *The Emergence of Lincoln* (2 vols., 1950); *The War for the Union* (2 vols., 1959).

[8] Bradford Perkins, *Prologue to War: England and the United States, 1805-1812* (1961); George E. Mowry, *The Era of Theodore Roosevelt, 1900-1912* (1958).

[9] A partial exception was the ingenious reformulation of the Turner thesis in urban terms by two easterners, Stanley Elkins and Eric McKitrick, "A Meaning for Turner's Frontier," *Political Science Quarterly*, LXIX (1954), 321-53, 565-602. Turner's stoutest postwar champion, Ray Allen Billington, gradually modified the claims of the master, muting especially the theme of sectional conflict. See "The Frontier in American Thought and Character," *The New World Looks at Its History*, ed. Archibald R. Lewis and Thomas F. McGann (1963), pp. 77-94.

brilliant, ardent, and very young man charged with the antibusiness spirit of the 1930's. Building on postulates advanced earlier by his father and by Beard, Schlesinger depicted the urban working class as the cutting edge of the Jacksonian movement. That movement involved intellectuals and other "noncapitalist groups, farmers and laboring men." It was a phase of the pragmatic, realistic, "enduring struggle between the business community and the rest of society which is the guarantee of freedom." [10] The line ran straight and true from Jackson to Franklin D. Roosevelt.

Launched in 1945 on a great wave of praise, *The Age of Jackson* soon collided with a backlash of criticism. Many historians, it will be remembered, were turning away from the urgent present-mindedness of the 1930's. They distrusted Schlesinger's heavy emphasis on the features of Jacksonian politics that resembled the New Deal. Further probing into the impressive new evidence he had assembled dissolved the polarity between "the business community and the rest of society." Jacksonian "laboring men" were often merchants and professional people; the "working class" displayed no consistent political allegiance. In fact, acquisitive, business motives entered very largely into the Jacksonian program. Evidently the common man *was* a businessman.[11]

It also began to appear that the ideological cleavage between Jeffersonianism and Hamiltonianism, which progressive historians linked with the distinction between common men and capitalists, was equally misleading. Schlesinger endorsed the usual view that the Jeffersonian spirit triumphed in the 1830's over the monopolistic schemes of the Hamiltonians. But postwar scholarship undercut this dualism too. A modest revival in the study of economic history, beginning in the 1940's, brought out startlingly close relations between government and business in the Jacksonian era.

The revival of economic history owed something to the initiative of Edwin F. Gay, Arthur H. Cole, and the Rockefeller Foundation, and something also to a new climate of opinion. The waning of eco-

[10] *The Age of Jackson* (1945), p. 307.
[11] The most effective critics were Joseph Dorfman and Bray Hammond, whose own books, *The Economic Mind in American Civilization* (5 vols., 1946-59) and *Banks and Politics in America from the Revolution to the Civil War* (1957), were among the major works of the postwar era. For a summary of the controversy see Charles G. Sellers Jr.'s "Andrew Jackson versus the Historians," *Mississippi Valley Historical Review*, XLIV (1958), 615-34.

nomic interpretations of history enabled historians to reverse their chain of cause and effect. Attention shifted from economic motives to economic processes, from the economic causes of historical development to the historical causes of economic development. Doubtless the dramatic impact that governmental policies were having on national income and wealth created a special interest in the political sources of economic growth. A Committee on Research in Economic History, appointed by the SSRC in 1941, chose as its first area for investigation the role of government in economic development. The studies it sponsored over the next decade, notably those of Carter Goodrich and his students, revealed a thoroughly mixed economy in antebellum America. An intimate, pragmatic association of state and local governments with "private enterprise" overrode all ideological scruples. One economic historian actually concluded that "it is only meretricious to contrast Hamiltonian with Jeffersonian policy." [12] Others, notably Lee Benson in *The Concept of Jacksonian Democracy* (1961), are redefining party differences with a new grasp of what was constructively liberal in Whig and Federalist programs.

Inevitably, the reaction against an ideologically divided, class-structured history reached back to the Revolutionary era. The basic dialectic of progressive historiography had been established by contrasting the Revolution and the Constitution, the one a democratic social upheaval, the other a capitalistic counterrevolution. Here was the critical test of the progressive approach; and here the sharpest clash of interpretations occurred. In 1943 a modest monograph by Philip Crowl, demonstrating an absence of class conflict in Maryland politics during and after the Revolution, went largely unnoticed.[13] In the 1950's the tide turned. It drastically reduced, though it did not wholly eliminate, the antithesis between a Jeffersonian Revolution and a Hamiltonian Constitution.

Two slashing critics went straight for Beard's *Economic Interpretation of the Constitution.* Forrest McDonald closely re-examined

[12] E. A. J. Johnson, "Federalism, Pluralism, and Public Policy," *Journal of Economic History,* XXII (1962), 442. On the origins of this research program see Herbert Heaton's *A Scholar in Action: Edwin F. Gay* (1952), pp. 237-48; on its impressive results, Robert A. Lively's "The American System," *Business History Review,* XXIX (1955), 81-96. Another, more recent approach to economic growth, paying less attention to government and more to markets, is in C. Douglass North's *The Economic Growth of the United States, 1790-1860* (1961).
[13] *Maryland During and After the Revolution* (1943).

the sources of income of constitutional convention delegates in order to demolish Beard's distinction between personalty and realty interests. Robert E. Brown raked Beard's logic in one book and in another assailed Becker's thesis of an internal social revolution. The widespread participation in government in colonial Massachusetts, Brown claimed, shows that Americans did not gain democracy in 1776 but rather preserved it. Instead of creating a new social order, they defended an old one.[14]

Thus a minimization of class conflict deprived early American history both of a revolutionary and of a counterrevolutionary thrust. Scholars investigating the causes of the Revolution, notably Oliver M. Dickerson, Edmund S. Morgan, and Bernard Knollenberg, discounted the impersonal economic forces and the irrepressible conflicts of Beardian history. Instead, they put forward the old patriotic view that the revolutionists were defending traditional liberties against bungling innovations of British officials. Just as historians in the 1930's rejected Beard's explanation of the Civil War for a theory of inept American leadership, so historians in the 1950's replaced Beard's explanation of the Revolution with an emphasis on inept British leadership.[15] Although the new interpretation of the Revolution was sympathetic whereas the revisionist account of the Civil War was not, the similarity of the two cases suggests again how much a repudiation of determinism contributed to the breakdown of progressive history.

As controversial breezes eddied through the staid ranks of early American historians, a new vigor seemed to enter that field. Never before had professional scholars debated so seriously the issues of the seventeenth and eighteenth centuries. The imperial and progressive schools had worked different sides of the street and had only oc-

[14] McDonald, *We the People: The Economic Origins of the Constitution* (1958); Brown, *Charles Beard and the Constitution* (1956) and *Middle-Class Democracy and the Revolution in Massachusetts, 1691-1780* (1955). The Beardian approach, modernized and improved, persists in Jackson T. Main, *The Antifederalists: Critics of the Constitution* (1961).

[15] Dickerson, *The Navigation Acts and the American Revolution* (1951); Edmund S. and Helen M. Morgan, *The Stamp Act Crisis: Prologue to Revolution* (1953); Knollenberg, *Origin of the American Revolution: 1759-1766* (1960); Esmond Wright, *Fabric of Freedom, 1763-1800* (1961). Other studies are summarized in Jack P. Greene's "The Flight from Determinism: A Review of Recent Literature on the Coming of the American Revolution," *South Atlantic Quarterly,* LXI (1962), 235-59.

casionally encountered one another directly. Now a frontal challenge to the progressive school made early American history, for a time at least, the liveliest area of intellectual ferment. It began to recover from the relative neglect into which it had fallen because of the progressive bias in favor of more recent history. More scholars were willing to focus on the colonial origins of American experience and to understand remote situations in their own terms. Then too, the revulsion against determinism helped to quicken colonial history. A good many postwar historians followed Morison's example of humanizing the colonial scene. Much of the best research appeared in vivid biographies of such people as Jefferson, Ezra Stiles, and Edward Livingston.[16] Fortunately, all these impulses received the timely support of a new research organization, the Institute of Early American History and Culture, which Carl Bridenbaugh started upon a productive career in 1945.

Recent American history may not be faring as well. The study of the twentieth century has shared, of course, in the general reevaluation of the American past. There too the antibusiness spirit of progressive scholarship, with its emphasis on economic conflict, has diminished. There too a revolt against determinism and a more sensitive grasp of the role of political and economic leadership characterize the latest books.[17] But major interpretive revisions, such as we have had for the history of the eighteenth and nineteenth centuries, have been less in evidence, at least for the period since 1917. No established professional historian except Eric Goldman has written seriously about the period since World War II, and some are moving their research back from the twentieth century altogether. There may be some question whether or not the vitality recent historiography had in the 1940's will persist without the explicit present-mindedness of the progressive school.

Enough has been said, perhaps, about particular periods to enable us to ask what over-all meaning the new American past is assuming.

[16] Dumas Malone, *Jefferson and His Time* (3 vols. to date, 1948-62); Edmund S. Morgan, *The Gentle Puritan: A Life of Ezra Stiles* (1962); George Dangerfield, *Chancellor Robert R. Livingston of New York* (1961).

[17] In addition to books by Link and Hofstadter cited elsewhere, see the numerous studies of diplomatic history by Herbert Feis; Arthur M. Schlesinger Jr., *The Age of Roosevelt* (3 vols. to date, 1957-60); William E. Leuchtenburg, *Franklin D. Roosevelt and the New Deal* (1963); Ernest R. May, *The World War and American Isolation 1914-1917* (1959); Alfred D. Chandler Jr., *Strategy and Structure: Chapters in the History of the Industrial Enterprise* (1962).

The present generation has not produced a decisive leadership such as Turner and Beard supplied in their day. No one has written a major work shaping our history into a grand design as persuasive as theirs once were. Nevertheless, alternatives to the progressive scheme have been sketched in a number of recent books, all of which depict a relatively homogeneous society with a relatively conservative history.

Historians in an age of unceasing international peril, when national security and the capacity for survival are fundamental concerns, can hardly avoid a somewhat conservative view of their country's history. They can hardly avoid an appreciation of its more cohesive and deeply rooted qualities. Nevertheless, they may trace those qualities to quite diverse sources, and they may disagree widely on the worth and durability of such homogeneity as they perceive. In rejecting a simple cleavage between two Americas, some historians may be most impressed by the wholeness of the national fabric, others by the looseness and multitude of its many strands. Their common concern is with the nature and degree of stability in American experience. Yet their answers are various and often ambivalent.

A key to the present temper of historical opinion lies in the pages of Alexis de Tocqueville's *Democracy in America* (1840), today the most respected of all interpretations of the United States. Tocqueville treated American culture as an organic whole; and his work rested heavily on the concept of national character. During the heyday of progressive scholarship this approach was somewhat suspect, and Tocqueville's influence was at a low ebb. Although progressive intellectuals sometimes indulged in generalizations about national character, they distrusted its heuristic value. Referring as it does to the pervasive, persistent features of a whole culture, "national character" neglects the environmental determination of social conflict. No edition of *Democracy in America* was published in the United States between 1904 and 1945; during most of that time it was out of print. Since World War II, however, at least six hardcover editions have appeared. With them has come a torrent of scholarship and speculation on *the* American experience, character, traits, etc.[18]

---

[18] The revival of serious discussion of national character by scholars seems to date from Margaret Mead's *And Keep Your Powder Dry* (1942) and Arthur M. Schlesinger's "What Then Is the American, This New Man?" *AHR*, XLVIII (1943), 225-44.

In addition to its integral approach, Tocqueville's classic has the special appeal today of rendering a mixed verdict on American democracy. The genial French aristocrat observed a nation at once stable and full of flux. He noticed little class cleavage. But he described a democracy that produced oppressive conformity on the one hand and kaleidoscopic variety on the other. He rejoiced in America's stability while deploring its social fragmentation. These antinomies, which Tocqueville's genius held together, jostle and contend in contemporary historical writing. Today's historians affirm on one side a need for and partial attainment of community in America. They cling on the other to values of dissent and diversity inherited from the progressive tradition. The opposing schools of interpretation that clashed so sharply in the 1930's and 1940's have partially blended, just as general historical theories have done. But the tensions that formerly divided those schools have survived their mingling.

Some of the efforts to sum up American history in recent years primarily emphasize the stability—and therefore the continuity—of American experience over the centuries. Other historians have given more attention to the reverse side of Tocqueville's model, stressing instabilities and thus allowing for a greater degree of change. To the first group belong the Harvard political theorist Louis Hartz and the University of Chicago historian Daniel Boorstin. Both of them have dwelled on the remarkable persistence of basic characteristics throughout American history. Hartz, like Gabriel before him, locates continuity in certain unifying principles or beliefs. Boorstin finds it in the pragmatic, down-to-earth way of life progressive historians often admired. Yet it is Hartz who stands closer to the progressive sympathy for friction and dissent, regretting that America has not had more.

Hartz wrote *The Liberal Tradition in America* (1955) to substitute new categories for the overworked schema of Beard and Parrington. He argued that the absence of a feudal heritage had left America with just one rather than two traditions of thought. A liberal consensus has had so unchallenged a sway, Hartz said, that most American political debate has been shadowboxing. "America must look to its contact with other nations to provide that spark of philosophy, that grain of relative insight that its own history has denied." [19]

Boorstin was equally impressed by the massive stability and un-

[19] P. 287.

philosophic harmony of America. He too explained the mediocrity of American political thought as a consequence of the absence of the deep social antagonisms that have existed in Europe. Boorstin, however, had no regrets about this. In *The Genius of American Politics* (1953) and in *The Americans: The Colonial Experience* (1958), he contended that America from the outset flourished by scrapping European blueprints, dissolving European distinctions, and moving toward a homogeneous society of undifferentiated men. A naïve practicality enabled Americans to unite in a stable way of life, undisturbed by divisive principles.

Significantly, both Hartz and Boorstin got their accent on a stable, continuous national character by looking at the United States as Tocqueville had: from the outside. They too—Hartz especially— adopted an explicitly comparative approach to American history. Hartz came to a comparative approach partly by the accident of having to teach European political theory at Harvard instead of the American theory for which he had been trained. Boorstin came to it through a European education as a Rhodes Scholar (as Lawrence Gipson had many years before) and later as a visiting professor abroad. Certainly both men were responding in a large sense to the heightened awareness of the outside world that the history of the mid-twentieth century thrust upon American historians. The domestic conflicts so apparent in an age of reform had diverted progressive scholars from the international context of American history. The neo-Tocquevilleans of the 1950's partially restored that context and so widened the horizons of scholarship. Unfortunately, their comparative interests were largely confined to contrasts between America and Europe. The insecurities of the postwar era engendered such an urge to define America—to establish its distinctive character—that the parallels and reciprocal involvements of a truly international history remained little attended.

The search for the essential and the permanent in American experience led perhaps more readily in an interdisciplinary direction, for the pursuit of national identity animated literary critics and social scientists as well as historians. One of the most persuasive general historians of the 1950's, David M. Potter, developed an integral and comparative view of American history primarily through contact with anthropology rather than contact with Europe. Like an increasing number of his colleagues, Potter found the theories of contemporary social scientists indispensable to a grasp of American society now that the progressive pattern was dissolving. He stopped writing a conventional sort of political history and made an intensive study of recent findings on culture and personality. More than most postwar historians, Potter wrote in a deterministic vein. His *People of Plenty: Economic Abundance and the American Character* (1954) is an economic interpretation, which transmuted Turner's frontier thesis into the more inclusive and systematic formulas of behavioral theory. For the transitory, sectional abundance of the frontier, Potter substituted a broadly based aptitude for productivity. Whereas the generation of Parrington and Beard had explained basic cleavages on economic grounds, Potter showed our wealth shaping a common, distinctive, and successful way of life.

On a more concrete level of scholarship one of the finest historians who has illuminated persistent features of American history is Edmund S. Morgan of Yale. Hartz, Boorstin, and Potter have explained continuity and stability largely in terms of environment and institutions. Morgan, on the other hand, has looked for and discovered a dogged adherence to fundamental principles. In writing about the Puritan founders of New England, he has emphasized the maintenance of their religious and social standards in the face of many divisive pressures. In writing about the Revolutionary generation, he has shown its undeviating pursuit of consistent principles throughout the tortuous controversy with Britain.[20]

All these historians have been aware of the other side of Tocqueville's America. All of them have noticed the diffuse instability associated in America with rapid mobility; and Boorstin's latest book, *The Image* (1962), reveals a distinct uneasiness over the formless flux he had earlier celebrated. Still, it has remained for another group of scholars, less preoccupied with contrasts between America and Europe, to deal seriously with the dimension of change. It has remained for them to formulate into new patterns the frictions within American life. Although most of the latter historians work on a relatively small scale, close to the stream of events, some of them too have tried to sketch the general course of American history. As a

[20] Morgan, *The Stamp Act Crisis* (1953); *The Birth of the Republic, 1763-1789* (1956); *The Puritan Dilemma: The Story of John Winthrop* (1958); *Visible Saints: The History of a Puritan Idea* (1963).

group, they share a common fascination with the tendency of stable structures to break down in a free and fluid culture.

Movement through space and through the ranks of society forms the central theme of our latest students of conflict. Like Potter, they have taken Turner's emphasis on migration out of a sectional context. In effect, they have used the theme of mobility to explode the rigid categories of progressive scholarship while maintaining a sharp interest in conflict and change. In place of classes and sections, they have conceived of a politics of coalition between diverse interests and of a society of shifting status groups. The concept of status has seemed especially relevant because of the very fragility of the honorific and prestigeful considerations that define it. Status is something that is continually pursued and ever on the verge of being lost in a nation of mobile men. As they break free from traditional security in search of better locations, a vast process of disintegration and partial reintegration goes on.

Considering the crucial importance assigned to mobility in this version of American history, it is hardly surprising that one of the influential exponents is also the leading authority on immigration. Oscar Handlin has shaped each of his major books as a story of disintegration and mobility. Handlin's history begins, characteristically, with a stable, orderly community—a *Gemeinschaft* in the language of German sociology—which makes life meaningful and whole. Then the shock of migration disrupts the community, breeding strife and freedom; and uprooted men pursue their separate, clashing purposes. This is the story of *Boston's Immigrants* (1941), the story of antebellum Massachusetts in *Commonwealth* (1947), the story of nineteenth century immigration in *The Uprooted* (1951), and the story of us all in *The Americans* (1963). It is often an anguished story, heavy with a sense of loss and alienation. It is also highly ambivalent, for the author admires the growth of freedom while lamenting the decline of order.

A rather similar picture of American development lies behind the superficially quite different interpretations recently offered by William A. Williams and Rowland Berthoff, one of them a neo-Marxist, the other a self-proclaimed conservative. Both Williams and Berthoff look back to a time of stability and order at the beginning of American history. Both of them observe a breakdown of community in the laissez-faire world of the nineteenth century as a consequence of excessive mobility (Berthoff) or expansion (Williams).[21] The three accounts differ most sharply in their evaluation of the twentieth century. Handlin leaves the outcome confused and uncertain; Berthoff finds America gradually recovering a healthy balance; Williams sees a capitalist oligarchy restoring but perverting the ideal of community.

Through all these interpretations, through those that stress stability and those that stress change, runs a question previous generations of historians in America had never so insistently asked. Most of the major postwar scholars seem to be asking in one way or another, "What (if anything) is so deeply rooted in our past that we can rely on its survival?" This has become, perhaps, the great historical question in a time of considerable moral confusion, when the future looks both precarious and severely limited in its possibilities. The question is genuinely open-ended, because neither the partisans of stability nor the connoisseurs of change assume that history is on their side. Progressive historians, like the conservative evolutionists who preceded them, relied implicitly on a faith in progress in charting the relations between past and future. Assuming an upward gradient, they asked what each period or movement "contributed" or "added" to the march of progress. This faith, which was shaken in Parrington's day, has since 1940 been so shattered that historians must soberly ask what is permanent and what is transient in American history. Accordingly, the shedding of a progressive outlook has not left historians accoutered in the conservative evolutionism of the late nineteenth century. Conservative evolutionists were confident that unity would continue to overcome internal strife. They expected that the partnership between union and freedom, which defined their America, would continue to develop and to triumph over obstacles. Today's historians want to know how durable and meaningful are the unities and diversities that already exist. In our postprogressive culture, the relation between freedom and union seems no longer natural but tense and problematical.

Once released from the dream of progress, historians who were alert to conflict and change could face unflinchingly the tragic and

---

[21] Rowland Berthoff, "The American Social Order: A Conservative Hypothesis," *AHR*, LXV (1960), 495-514; William A. Williams, *The Contours of American History* (1961).

ironic elements in the past. In fact, many of our best historians acquired a positive relish for the burdens, the losses, and the intractable dilemmas of history. An early indication of how profoundly this
shift in sensibility could affect historical interpretation appeared in
the Civil War field. The revisionist school of the Thirties had viewed
the "needless" war and the "vindictive" Reconstruction as exceptional interludes in the normal progress of civilization. Like the philosophers of the Enlightenment, the revisionists believed such crimes
and follies avoidable if only reason were allowed to work matters
out. All of this began to look naïvely optimistic in the 1940's. Rely-
ing heavily on Reinhold Niebuhr's powerful critique of the idea of
progress, Arthur M. Schlesinger Jr. in 1949 assailed the revisionists
for simplifying great moral issues: "Man generally is entangled in in-
soluble problems; history is consequently a tragedy in which we are
all involved, whose keynote is anxiety and frustration, not progress
and fulfillment." Before these words were written, the leading revisionist, Avery Craven, was already modifying his position. His writings in the 1950's took more seriously the emotional realities and the
moral dilemmas that led to war.[22]

Indeed, much of the best scholarship of the 1950's struck the tragic
note. Instead of looking backward from the crest of a historical
movement to observe its rise, as progressives usually did, the newer
historians often looked forward from the crest to watch its decline.
Thus Perry Miller, in resuming the Puritan studies he had com-
menced in the Thirties, wrote one of the finest books in our historical
literature, the second great volume of *The New England Mind*
(1953), as an epic of unrelieved defeat. Remorselessly, even glee-
fully, Miller followed the agonizing, century-long breakup of the
intellectual system he had presented in Volume I in its original
wholeness. In later work that reflected a growing obsession with the
"meaning" of America, Miller shifted to more nationalistic themes.
Meanwhile, the stable features of Puritan experience came into view
again in Edmund Morgan's writings. But others carried on the analysis of dispersion and loss. Bernard Bailyn, a young historian with a
keen understanding of instability in early America, traced through

[22] Schlesinger, "The Causes of the Civil War: A Note on Historical Sentimen-
talism," *Partisan Review*, XVI (1949), 891; Craven, *The Growth of Southern
Nationalism, 1848-1861* (1953) and *Civil War in the Making, 1815-1860*
(1959).

the seventeenth century the fragmentation of social and educational patterns as Miller had traced the fragmentation of beliefs.[23] In writing about the first half of the nineteenth century Stanley Elkins and David Donald discovered similar trends. Where earlier historians had seen a rise of democracy they found a disastrous erosion of all institutional authority.[24]

Into recent history also passed an unprecedented fascination with decline and defeat. Richard Hofstadter's very influential *Age of Reform* (1955) dwelt on the failings of the populists and the progressives. Instead of one evolutionary sequence culminating in the New Deal, he observed the degeneration of each movement into a perverse illiberalism. Henry May's *The End of American Innocence* (1959) examined the cultural ferment on the eve of World War I not as the beginning of a new era but rather as the destruction of a pre-existing scheme of things. C. Vann Woodward, who was perhaps as deeply attached to progressive values as any of our leading historians, nevertheless discovered that experiences of guilt, alienation, and defeat defined the distinctive value and pertinence of southern history.[25]

A crucial book in this mode was Henry Nash Smith's *Virgin Land* (1950), which we have already noticed for its attack on Turner's kind of western history. Although written with deceptive detachment, *Virgin Land* was essentially a study of the death of ideas. It traced three major images of the American West from the late eighteenth century to the end of the nineteenth. In each case Smith's attention fixed on a loss of imaginative richness and social relevance as the image became increasingly debased, exploited, and false to fact. An adequate account of the rise of western myths and symbols remains to be written. *Virgin Land* was the valedictory of a man alienated from the Texas in which he grew up in the 1920's.

---

[23] Miller's *The New England Mind from Colony to Province* (1953) is complemented in social and political history by Bailyn's *The New England Merchants in the Seventeenth Century* (1955), *Education in the Forming of American Society* (1960), and "Politics and Social Structure in Virginia," in *Seventeenth-Century America*, ed. James Morton Smith (1959), pp. 90-115.
[24] Donald, *Lincoln Reconsidered: Essays on the Civil War Era*, 2nd ed. (1961), pp. 209-235, and the critique by A. E. Campbell, "An Excess of Isolation: Isolation and the American Civil War," *Journal of Southern History*, XXIX (1963), 161-74; Elkins, *Slavery: A Problem in American Institutional and Intellectual Life* (1959).
[25] Woodward, *The Burden of Southern History* (1960).

Smith's book also announced another theme of great significance in recent historical writing, particularly in the kind that emphasizes instability and change. He handled ideas with a psychoanalytical awareness of their emotional import. *Virgin Land* shares with Hofstadter's *American Political Tradition* (1948) the credit for introducing into professional historical scholarship a large, effective grasp of the nonrational elements in human conduct. Both authors had nourished themselves on modern literary criticism, which became penetrated by psychological interpretations in the late Thirties and Forties. Hofstadter called upon psychology primarily to explain aggression and frustration. Smith, as a professor of English, was less interested in motives than in meanings. A product of the new American Studies movement that was linking literature with history in an integrated study of art and society, he studied the dramatic symbols and pictorial images in which Americans had expressed their deeply rooted hopes and fears. He wrote the history of myths.[26]

Professional historians had been quite slow to make any real use of depth psychology. The first major study of myths in American history, *The Mind of the South* (1941), was written in the 1930's by a tormented literary and social critic, W. J. Cash; but professional historians did not follow up his brilliant insights until the 1950's.[27] Perhaps this was partly because they got little encouragement from the behaviorism that ruled academic psychology. More importantly, a reluctance to accept the nonrational as a legitimate and pervasive dimension of reality was integral to the progressive heritage of American historians. The progressive expectation of steady improvement in human affairs rested on the assumption that men are rational: they ordinarily pursue their individual or collective self-interest, and such interest is either rationally perceived or—at worst —coherently rationalized. Progressive historians treated ideas not as myths, full of extravagant fantasy, but as ideologies that interpret

[26] Smith took the first Ph.D. in American Civilization at Harvard (1940), an experience that made him a historian; but his essential intellectual experience came earlier as an editor and literary critic in the late 1920's in the Southwest, where his interest in myth was shaped by contact with the New Critics and through the influence of Hans Vaihinger and Henri Bergson. Hofstadter owed more to sociologists like Karl Mannheim and to Sigmund Freud, though his style of historical analysis was also much influenced by the approach of literary critics.

[27] E.g., Charles G. Sellers Jr., "The Travail of Slavery," *op. cit.,* pp. 40-71, and Taylor, *op. cit.*

life in terms functional to some interested group. Such, for example, was the method of Charles A. Beard. In the last weeks of his life in 1948 the old man still insisted, "Economics explains the mostest!" Then, after a pause, he added, "But I may have neglected the irrational." [28] The comment was an epitaph to more than one man's career.

In recent years scholarly journals have teemed with articles and university presses with books on historical myths, symbols, images, and the like. A psychological approach may, if it continues to gain momentum, reopen every question in American history. It is seductively congenial to the present climate of opinion; for it enables restless historians who are impressed by the over-all stability of their country to subjectivize the stresses within it. Psychological history turns conflict and change into an interior drama. Divisions, which the previous generation understood as basic opposition between distinct groups, become generalized tensions running through the whole culture. Acts of protest and defiance often acquire defensive, compensatory implications, so that reformers for example are seen acting out their personal and social maladjustments.[29]

Also, the study of myths and images has a special attraction in the postwar period because it focuses on kinds of thinking that unite a people rather than those that divide them. The concept of ideology refers to exclusive and rival creeds. It relates directly to social conflict. The concept of myth, on the other hand, refers to the integrating values that bind men together.[30] All in all, the psychological vogue has given an implicit sanction to harmony or adaptability. It has sustained our sense of the dynamic while expressing our need for social solidarity. It has also raised our appreciation of tragedy in history and depressed our appreciation of rational purpose.

Fortunately, American historians have not yielded wholly to the psychologizing trend. Among those who still respect the force of overt principles, a strain of rationalism persists. It is also reappearing

[28] Diary of Alfred Vagts. Evidently World War II set Beard—as it set many others—thinking more seriously about irrational motivations.
[29] See, for example, Emery Battis, *Saints and Sectaries: Anne Hutchinson and the Antinomian Controversy* (1962), David Donald, *Charles Sumner and the Coming of the Civil War* (1960), Marvin Meyers, *The Jacksonian Persuasion: Politics and Belief* (1957), and Samuel P. Hays, *The Response to Industrialism: 1885-1914* (1957).
[30] Ben Halpern, " 'Myth' and 'Ideology' in Modern Usage," *History and Theory,* I (1961), 136-37.

among a small but rising number of historians who are taking a fresh look at organizational patterns. The latter wish to know how groups and agencies—such as political parties, corporations, and communities—have molded behavior and regulated the distribution of power. Deriving partly from studies in entrepreneurial and business history and partly from contemporary American sociology, this kind of history is less concerned with motives than with structure and process. It shows men managing and being managed through rational systems of control and communication. Perhaps we may call this the new institutionalism; for it is bringing back to life a morphological study of organizations, now freed from the formalistic, evolutionary emphasis of nineteenth century scholarship.[31]

Although institutionalists thus far have not gone much beyond the monographic level, the breadth and importance of their contribution seem sure to grow. Yet it is not easy to anticipate that institutional history will in itself alter the main thrust of current scholarship. Institutions are, by their very nature, means of stabilizing the flux of society. If psychological history uncovers in the past the insecurities and pervasive anxieties that trouble many scholars and intellectuals today, institutional history projects the other side of the contemporary spirit: its rage for order. Both the psychological and the institutional approach reflect our fixation on the nature and extent of stability in our past and present. To move beyond that preoccupation historians will need more than a panoply of analytical techniques. They will need a larger and braver vision of the future than most of them now possess.

Meanwhile the profound changes in historical interpretation in the last twenty-five years have left today's scholars with plenty to do. Simply to master the new conceptual resources they have acquired is a herculean task. And the task must be well in hand before one can feel confident that the postwar generation is writing history that will live as a monument of its era, as the history of Henry Adams, of Turner, of Beard, and of Parrington lives as monuments of theirs.

31 William Miller, ed., *Men in Business: Essays on the Historical Role of the Entrepreneur* (1952); Lee Benson, *The Concept of Jacksonian Democracy: New York as a Test Case* (1961); Morton Keller, *The Life Insurance Enterprise, 1885-1910: A Study in the Limits of Corporate Power* (1963); Chandler, *op. cit.* Far from being mutually exclusive, the institutional and psychological approaches are joined in the impressive works, already cited, by Elkins and McKitrick, and in McKitrick's *Andrew Johnson and Reconstruction* (1960).

On the concrete, empirical level, many of the newer research objectives remain substantially unfulfilled. The intricate study of social organization demanded by the collapse of the simple categories of progressive scholarship has just begun. The long stultified outward reach of American history into international and comparative dimensions, which suffered first from the environmentalism of progressive scholarship and later perhaps from the inwardness of the American Studies movement, is only now going beyond a few simplified contrasts. The sophisticated moral criticism of the past implicit in our growing psychological awareness has barely revealed its potentialities.

There is work to do also in cultivating a point of view wide enough to integrate these new interests with the unexhausted heritage from which they sprang. Much was sacrificed when the progressive historians largely ignored the constructive insights of the institutionalists. The diverse tendencies in contemporary scholarship suggest that the fault may not be so glaringly repeated. After the stirring historiographical revisions of the Thirties, Forties, and Fifties, it is a good sign that some historians are pondering "the delicate problem of developing an attitude appropriate to the process of absorbing the contributions of predecessors while trying to advance beyond them." [32] Management of this problem would seem to require all the sensitivity historians can muster—sensitivity to progress as well as decline, to the smiling as well as the tragic aspects of life, to the international background as well as the internal narrative, to social patterns as well as psychic tensions, to rational controls as well as irrational impulses, and to the great river of change as well as the bed of continuity.

[32] Lee Benson, *Turner and Beard: American Historical Writing Reconsidered* (1960), p. 96.

LEGACY

❧ 1 ❧

A TIME OF TROUBLES

The concluding sentence of the first edition of this book seemed, at the time I set it down, to be little more than an appeal for cultivating inclusive sympathies. Now, looking back, I can see that my image of a "great river" flowing within a "bed of continuity" betrayed the central location of this book within the main body of historical studies in the postwar era. My summing up was an endorsement. History had renewed itself, finding directions that altered without abrogating earlier forms and achievements. Affluent, respected, and absorbed in studies of unchallenged worth, American historians could contemplate an enticing future continuous with their effective past.

Continuity has proved in hindsight to be the last thing one should have expected from the 1960's. Before the words I wrote early in 1964 were in print, the first of the ghetto riots of the decade had erupted in Harlem, and the Free Speech Movement at Berkeley had opened the floodgates of student protest. Thereafter, year by year, dissent and alienation cut more and more deeply into the promises of the past.

Two consequences ensued. First, the significance of history as a dimension of experience and understanding diminished. Many educated people, especially the young, were overcome by an apocalyptic sense of a rupture in time, separating the present from everything hitherto known or experienced. Some coined a label, "the now generation," describing the children of the Sixties who felt little relation either to the past or to the future. Yesterday's solutions seemed irrelevant to today's problems; yesterday's burdens seemed just as inessential, just as easily cast off. Somewhat in this spirit, a radicalized American historian advised his readers that they could best formulate and pursue present goals if they avoided intense involvement with the past. Professor J. H. Plumb thought that no emotional involvement at all might be better yet. Reviving the message of the New History of the early twentieth century, Plumb argued that industrial society "does not need the past. Its intellectual

235

and emotional orientation is towards change rather than conserva-
tion. . . . The new methods, new processes, new forms of living of
scientific and industrial society have no sanction in the past and no
roots in it."[1]

Second, those who still looked for meaning and guidance from
history now found the principal interpretations of American history
that had emerged in the 1950's insupportable, and impatiently
brushed them aside. In the midst of an earthquake, what use could
one make of histories that described a persistent national ethos or
treated change as erosion rather than explosion? America might
well be a conservative society, as the postwar historians had indicated, but it was also a volatile one; and suddenly everyone wanted
to hear from historians who savored that volatility and who might
be able to explain the repressive forces that usually held it within
narrow bounds. What this new line of thought produced will occupy
us in due course. Here it is enough to notice the speed with which
a sweeping repudiation of so-called consensus history spread from
small radical coteries to the main body of American historians. In
July 1967, the staid *American Historical Review* published a long
appraisal, at once judicious and responsive, of the impact of the
"New Left" on United States historiography.[2] That impact had
seemed so inconsequential three years earlier that I had not mentioned it at all.

As the political turbulence of the late 1960's mounted, an economic crisis engulfed the learned professions, adding immeasurably
to the depth and scale of discontent. The study and teaching of
history in American colleges and universities had flourished in the
Fifties and early Sixties as never before. Enrollments in history
courses had benefited in those years not only from a huge expansion of higher education but also from a near doubling of the
proportion of students majoring in history. Then, suddenly, the
tide turned. The first substantial losses of undergraduate enrollment

[1] J. H. Plumb, *The Death of the Past* (1969), p. 14; Martin Duberman, *The
Uncompleted Past* (1969), p. 206. See also Kenneth Keniston, *The Uncom-
mitted: Alienated Youth in American Society* (1965), pp. 224-27; Edward B.
Fiske, "History Means Little to 'Now' Generation," *New York Times*, May 9,
1976, sec. E, p. 16; Margaret Mead, "The Future as the Basis for Establishing
a Shared Culture," *Daedalus* (Winter, 1965), 135-55.
[2] Irwin Unger, "The 'New Left' and American History: Some Recent Trends
in United States Historiography," *AHR*, LXXII (1967), 1237-63.

in history courses occurred at the leading schools in 1967–68, apparently as a result of student restlessness. A year later the headlong expansion of facilities for higher education came to a halt: the Ph.D.'s pouring in ever-larger numbers out of the graduate schools encountered a sudden shortage of jobs.[3]

At the end of the decade, in December 1969, C. Vann Woodward's presidential address to the American Historical Association articulated a disturbing consciousness that historians could be entering a new era of shrinking opportunities and narrowing horizons. Woodward spoke in a somber interlude between tumultuous sessions, some of them wildly applauding philippics against "mainstream historians," others wrangling far into the night over the withdrawal of American troops from Vietnam. It was the right moment to suggest, as Woodward did, that a long, twenty-year boom in the study of history might be coming to an end.[4]

The job crisis worsened in the early 1970's. A thousand petty ambitions fed the pell-mell growth of every academic discipline, and there was no way suddenly to change direction. Forty-three percent of all the Ph.D.'s in history ever produced in the United States had been awarded in the 1960's; yet the flood did not crest until 1973, when 1,213 doctorates were granted.[5] Meanwhile, the number of sessions at the annual convention of the American Historical Association escalated to 120, compared to fewer than 50 in 1962. Total paid membership peaked at 18,403 in 1971, up 100 percent in a single decade. The Organization of American Historians continued to add members until 1974, when the number of manuscripts submitted to the *Journal of American History* also climbed to an all-time high.[6] Thus, it was not until the mid-1970's that the growth of the historical profession really stopped. Only then, as the

---

[3] C. Vann Woodward, "The Future of the Past," *AHR*, LXXV (1970), 715-18; AHA *Annual Report* (1970), p. 3.

[4] Woodward, *AHR*, LXXV (1970), 711-26; AHA *Annual Report* (1969), pp. 42-50. For a vivid description of a similar convention two years later, see J. Anthony Lukas, "Historians' Conference: The Radical Need for Jobs," *New York Times Magazine*, March 12, 1972, pp. 38ff.

[5] Oscar Handlin, *Truth in History* (1979), p. 24; AHA *Annual Meeting* (1980), p. 85.

[6] AHA *Annual Report* (1972), p. 54; (1971), p. 21; OAH *Newsletter*, IX (July, 1981), 10; "News and Comments," *Journal of American History*, LXVIII (1981-82), 462.

total output of books on history reached a plateau, did the proliferation of scholarly journals begin to slacken.[7]

Painfully, in the late 1970's, a better adjustment between supply and demand came about. The number of undergraduate history majors in American colleges and universities dropped year by year, registering a total decline of 57 percent between 1971 and 1980, but the number of Ph.D.'s in history also fell sharply, from 1,213 in 1973 to 744 in 1980. The most vulnerable young Ph.D.'s quit the profession. Academic publishers, hard hit in 1972 and 1973, learned to cope with declining sales per title by adopting new technologies and other economies.[8] Perhaps partly in response to these adjustments, the radical impulse flagged. Altogether, the sense of crisis eased. It was now apparent that the historical profession was going to survive, certainly on a scale somewhat reduced from that of the early 1970's, but in a form not greatly altered by the upheaval.

All in all, through these troubled decades, a surprising continuity had been maintained in the general character of the profession. Perhaps the most striking continuity was the remorseless advance of specialization. In hard times every specialty offered an unforeseen attraction to those who could define themselves as within its bounds. It was a kind of bomb shelter—a little stronghold to defend against budget-cutting attacks, the safest and most familiar place in a time of troubles. In the absence of any authoritative standard or any generally accepted scheme of priorities, nobody could claim that one discipline, field, or subfield was more promising or intrinsically worthier than any other. Small was beautiful, and every manifestation of diversity deserved to survive. Thus, in a pluralistic climate of opinion adversity intensified the specializing energies that prosperity had earlier fostered.

What suffered in the late Sixties and Seventies was not specialized research but rather the larger aspirations of postwar historiography. At the same time that the general interpretations advanced by the postwar historians were losing credibility, the general audience that

---

[7] *Scholarly Communication: The Report of the National Enquiry* (1979), pp. 41, 85-87.

[8] Curtis O. Baker, *Earned Degrees Conferred: An Examination of Recent Trends* (National Center for Education Statistics, U.S. Department of Education, 1981), p. 28; AHA *Annual Report* (1981), p. 76; *Scholarly Communication*, p. 128.

the most successful of them had sought to reach was receding from the consciousness of the historical profession. A vision of the historian as an intellectual, nourished by and serving an increasingly responsive national culture, had inspired some of the best historians throughout the twentieth century. This dream had been in every generation a counterpoise to excessive specialization, and during the great history boom of the postwar era it had seemed closer to realization than ever before. History shared then in what was called "the cultural explosion."[9] Though academic historians rarely produced the popular histories that were prominent on the best-seller lists,[10] they could feel a vital connection with an expanding body of contemporary opinion that drew its historical consciousness from such leading intellectuals as Reinhold Niebuhr, William Faulkner, Eric Erickson, Lionel Trilling, and David Riesman. In the late Sixties that body of opinion dissolved. The unspecialized public that many of the best postwar historians had courted was now preoccupied with the present. Yet it is difficut to say whether the public abandoned history or historians abandoned the public. In the late Sixties and after, the most literate historians who had gained prominence in the postwar decades fell largely silent.

Three of the most imaginative of them died prematurely: Perry Miller in 1963 at the age of fifty-eight, Richard Hofstadter in 1970 at fifty-four, and David Potter a few weeks later at sixty. To some of their stricken colleagues the passing of the latter two seemed a dark portent, which the following decade woefully confirmed. The best and the brightest of that extraordinary generation of American historians who had come to the fore in the 1940's and 1950's— C. Vann Woodward, Oscar Handlin, Louis Hartz, Arthur M. Schlesinger Jr., David Donald, Frank Freidel, Eric Goldman, and others a few years younger—published little of consequence after

---

[9] Stanley Kauffmann, "Can Culture Explode?" *Commentary*, XL (August, 1965), 19-28.

[10] During the early 1960's popular historical works appeared regularly on the best-seller lists. Sometimes as many as half the top ten nonfiction best sellers were histories. As late as April 3, 1966, the *New York Times Book Review* listed the following (p. 8): Barbara Tuchman, *The Proud Tower* (no. 2); John Toland, *The Last Hundred Days* (no. 3); Arthur M. Schlesinger, Jr., *A Thousand Days* (no. 5); Cornelius Ryan, *The Last Battle* (no. 6); Larry Collins and Dominique Lapierre, *Is Paris Burning?* (no. 10). Nothing like that is even conceivable any more.

the mid-Sixties and less after 1970. There were, to be sure, distinguished exceptions. Daniel Boorstin, for example, produced in 1973 the third and final volume of his extraordinary trilogy, *The Americans*; Henry May brought out *The Enlightenment in America* in 1976; and Alfred D. Chandler Jr. pursued undeviatingly his remarkable studies in business history.[11] Nevertheless, one senses the spread of a deadly blight among the senior historians who might have been expected to do their culminating work in the 1960's and 1970's. All sorts of personal reasons obviously contributed to the dryness of those years. Behind the personal distractions, however, it is possible to glimpse the loss of a fructifying rapport between the historians and the audience they had addressed.

It would be heartening to be able to say that younger scholars created in the 1960's a fresh conceptualization of American history to replace the postprogressive themes of continuity, homogeneity, and national character. There was indeed a widespread (though far from unanimous) conviction that "conflict" rather than "consensus" should be the keynote of a new American history. But how to formulate that conflict and how to stipulate the terms of its enactment were far from clear. In truth, the historians of the United States during the 1960's and 1970's very largely lost interest in comprehensive themes and overarching generalizations.

Many of the rising scholars of the Sixties believed that the pursuit of big ideas and general audiences was just what had led their predecessors astray. Particularly in intellectual history, the study of which had generated the principal interpretive schemes of the postwar era, the reaction against grand theory was sharp. At the Wingspread Conference, which met in 1977 to reconsider the status and tasks of American intellectual history, the note that sounded again and again was the need for rigor, precision, and specificity rather than sweeping statements about a national character or the "mean-

---

11 *The Visible Hand: The Managerial Revolution in American Business* (1977). For two further exceptions, both in early American history, see discussion below. Here and elsewhere in this chapter I have been guided by a list of the books in American history, published since 1960, that were judged most significant by two panels of professional historians; this list is in Michael Kammen's "Clio and the Changing Fashions: Some Patterns in Current American Historiography," *American Scholar*, XLIV (1975), 486. I have also used the lists of annual Bancroft Prizes in American History and the comparable prizes awarded by the American Historical Association.

ing" of America. Looking back at what he described as the "pre-tentiously grandiose" scholarship of the 1950's, Laurence Veysey spoke for the younger historians at the conference in arguing that the most important and constructive shift in recent historical writing had been a methodological recognition that generalizations "to be credible must be extremely hard earned. They require far more arduous preparation, far more careful spadework, far closer atten-tion to logic than many of our predecessors a generation ago were aware." Veysey permitted a wan hope that intellectual historians might some day be able "to return to a grander level of synthesis" but quickly warned that such endeavors would always be extremely difficult.[12]

It was not a warning that intellectual historians needed during the 1970's; the main tendencies in the field were already deeply defensive. Intellectual history no longer seemed to many historians, as it had in the postwar era, to offer the master key to the inner secrets of the American past. No longer did a fascination with the ideologies of liberalism, reform, and democracy give a spacious sweep to the writing of American political history. No longer did the evocative methods of literary criticism empower historians of myth and symbol to claim special insight into American culture as a whole.[13] In the bitterness of the late 1960's, when holistic views of America suddenly appeared transparently false and claims for the causal significance of ideals rang hollow, intellectual historians re-treated to safer ground. Instead of refining and improving the study of myth and ideology, American historians (with some important exceptions, which will be noted in due course) simply gave them up. On one side of intellectual history, political historians restricted their attention more and more to the concrete behavior of voting blocs. On the other side, literary criticism moved away from the historian's concern with time and place. Intellectual historians were left to cultivate more intensively than ever a delimited and partic-

[12] "Intellectual History and the New Social History," in *New Directions in American Intellectual History*, ed. John Higham and Paul K. Conkin (1979), pp. 22-23.
[13] On the decline of the myth-and-symbol school see Gene Wise's " 'Paradigm Dramas' in American Studies: A Cultural and Institutional History of the Movement," *American Quarterly*, XXXI (1979), 318-25, and Bruce Kuklick's influential critique, "Myth and Symbol in American Studies," *American Quarterly*, XXIV (1972), 435-50.

ularized terrain: the ideas of and about specific social groups, such as abolitionists, artists, soldiers, judges and jurists, philosophers, Indians.[14]

It would be wrong, however, to see the narrowing of the focus of research altogether—or even primarily—in negative terms. What may, from the vantage point of the 1980's, strike one as a retreat was felt by most scholars at the time as liberation: the liberation of social history from its postwar subordination to intellectual history; the liberation of a new, multitudinous generation from the familiar questions posed by a national synthesis; the liberation, finally, of every special field from any agenda other than its own. In this broad sense the triumphant advance of specialization in historical research has been part of a wider movement in the United States and in other complex, postmodern societies. Every social interest that could define itself as distinctive because of the possession of special skills, knowledge, life-style, or heritage has striven with some success during the last two decades to enhance its autonomy and influence. In this challenge to centralizing institutions and hierarchical values people of all kinds found in the 1960's and 1970's an available means for seeking more control over their own lives. Here was the underlying meaning and appeal of "pluralism," a protean word that acquired an almost incontestable authority outside of the technical discourse of political scientists.[15] A pluralistic ethos—a celebration of group autonomy and social diversity— supplied an ideological sanction for the disaggregation of American history.

Pluralism necessarily discouraged any encompassing interpretation or full-scale historical synthesis, but it was too engaging a credo

14 Ronald G. Walters, *The Antislavery Appeal: American Abolitionism after 1830* (1976); Neil Harris, *The Artist in American Society: The Formative Years, 1790-1860* (1966); Marcus Cunliffe, *Soldiers and Civilians: The Martial Spirit in America, 1775-1865* (1968); Morton J. Horwitz, *The Transformation of American Law, 1780-1860* (1977); Bruce Kuklick, *The Rise of American Philosophy: Cambridge, Massachusetts, 1860-1930* (1977); Robert F. Berkhofer, Jr., *The White Man's Indian: Images of the American Indian from Columbus to the Present* (1978). There were of course other tendencies. Here and elsewhere I confine myself to a few illustrations of what seems to me a predominant concern.
15 Compare Philip Gleason's "American Identity and Americanization" on pluralism with the treatments of the same subject by Michael Novak and Michael Walzer in *Harvard Encyclopedia of American Ethnic Groups*, ed. Stephan Thernstrom (1980), pp. 50-58, 772-87.

to be contained entirely within specialized monographs. Of the few general books about the American past published by academics during the time of troubles, three in particular tried to create a pluralistic framework for American history.

Michael Kammen's *People of Paradox: An Inquiry Concerning the Origins of American Civilization* (1972) was the first considerable attempt to replace the "consensus" interpretations of Hartz, Boorstin, Handlin, and others. Undaunted by the deflation of the idea of national character, Kammen described Americans as a people peculiarly at home in the midst of contradictions, ambiguities, and intersecting cross-purposes. Institutionally, he argued, America is a country of "unstable pluralism," in which diversities proliferate because they do not fully congeal. Kammen was answered by Robert Wiebe's more severe interpretation of American pluralism. In *The Segmented Society: An Introduction to the Meaning of America* (1975), Wiebe replaced Kammen's lively kaleidoscope with a set of tight little boxes. Throughout their history, Wiebe averred, Americans have insisted on living within small, internally homogeneous compartments (churches, neighborhoods, occupations), which have minimized both conflict and human sympathy by the simple device of keeping other people out. Pluralism, in short, is a structure of exclusivity and repression. Finally, Robert Kelley put American pluralism again in an affirmative light, making it the central theme in the history of American politics. From the eighteenth century to the twentieth, according to the first volume of Kelley's *Cultural Pattern in American Politics* (1979), the crux of political conflict has been a struggle between a Yankee host culture, pressing for a homogeneous society, and a shifting coalition of outgroups fighting persistently and effectively for the right to be different.

The three books had scarcely anything in common except their view of America as everlastingly heterogeneous. Each was a formulation of the prevailing diversity, but none (at this writing) has become a focus of it. None aroused anything like the interest and controversy their predecessors had inspired in the 1950's. To locate the most vigorous scholarly undertakings of the last twenty years we shall have to look beyond these disparate attempts to give some shape to pluralism. We shall have to identify the particular initiatives it helped to release.

Some roots of the new scholarship of the 1960's went back to the early twentieth century. Progressivism, tinged with a simplified Marxism, laid down part of the historiographical program many young scholars embraced in the Sixties, specifically the part that championed the underprivileged sectors of society and examined divisions between the few who wield power and the many who do not. But the more immediate sources of upheaval and innovation are to be found in the historiographical world of the late 1950's and early 1960's. Imbedded in the dominant paradigm were tensions and dissatisfactions that needed only the events of the mid-Sixties to erupt with explosive force.

As indicated in the preceding chapter, the postprogressive out-look of leading historians in the postwar era was not all of a piece. It was loose, pliant, and shot through with cross-purposes. On one side the most influential books projected a vision of America as essentially stable and homogeneous. On the other side they stressed psychological conflicts and a pervasive, destabilizing social mobility. An especially rich vein of scholarship dealt with the breakdown of stable structures, the loss of unities, the failure of ideals, and the turning of affirmations into ironies. By the end of the 1950's the genuineness, strength, and durability of the unifying forces in American history were more and more in question.

Thus consensus historiography lacked the strong conceptual underpinnings that had sustained the earlier progressive and conservative-evolutionist schools; it was vulnerable to internal frac-tures. It was also exposed—more than I realized at the time—to unexpected intrusions from other academic disciplines. These ex-ternal stimuli were not frontal challenges to the dominant para-digm; at first they seemed to reinforce it. At a deeper level, however, they were diversions. Social scientists, newly interested in the sys-tematic, quantitative study of historical problems, invited historians to join in agendas of research that led in many different directions. It will be useful to consider this diversionary influence first, since it was already at work before the paradigmatic revolution of the mid-Sixties and would certainly have continued to flourish had nothing else changed.

In the first edition of this book (pp. 139–40) I noted that some American social scientists in the late 1950's and early 1960's were showing a fresh interest in historical data. This was a surprising development in view of the distinctive, longstanding preoccupation of American political scientists, sociologists, and economists with the construction of abstract, ahistorical theories on the one hand and the facts of contemporary life on the other. At the time the only explanation I had to offer for the obvious intellectual congeniality arising between a number of historians and sympathetic co-workers in the social sciences was the interdisciplinary spirit that the area programs, created since World War II, had fostered. It is now apparent that a wider purpose was also at work outside the area programs.

Certain hard-headed empiricists in the social sciences had become dissatisfied with the temporal shallowness of the statistics and the generalizations on which prevailing theories of human behavior rested. Analyses of why Americans voted as they did were confined to recent elections; the survey data that political scientists studied could very well obscure longstanding attachments in the electorate. Economists and sociologists attempting to understand the sources of modern economic growth found themselves increasingly perplexed by differential growth rates between countries and by the inability of existing historical knowledge to yield reliable explanations of such differences. They pressed for statistical series that would permit comparisons between countries and regions, between periods, and between various factors in an ongoing process.[16] In putting theories to the test of specific historical sequences, social scientists had something to give to, and something to receive from, historians. For some of the latter the interchange promised not only immediate benefits but also a new opportunity to realize the old dream of making history a social science.

The partnership was facilitated by lavish funding and implemented by powerful new means of computation. The federal government, to say nothing of the great private foundations, handsomely supported these massive, collaborative projects of data collection and analysis. Promising much, offending no one, and certain to produce a concrete product, the data projects took a good share of

[16] Douglass C. North, "Economic History," in *International Encyclopedia of the Social Sciences* (1968), VI, pp. 468-73; Seymour M. Lipset, "Introduction," and Richard Jensen, "History and the Political Scientist" and "American Election Analysis," in *Politics and the Social Sciences*, ed. Seymour M. Lipset (1969), xii-xiii, xix, 13-25, 239-40.

the tenfold increase, between 1956 and 1965, in federal grants for "basic research" in the social sciences, including history.[17] Yet this was just the beginning. The pioneers in quantitative history used nothing more than adding machines and punched cards, which were threaded with a needle or fed into the hopper of a machine that would sort the cards into various bins and count them as they fell. Historians began to learn to use electronic computers in the mid-Sixties. Immediately, vast possibilities for linking records and testing new variables opened up. Interinstitutional training programs in quantitative methods appeared at the University of Michigan, the Newberry Library, and elsewhere.[18] The first textbooks on quantification for historians followed about 1970.[19]

The earliest significant achievements in the new quantitative mode came from economic historians who had the advantage of working within departments of economics and thus being in daily touch with theoreticians and with statistical analysis. The first monographs and articles tackled traditional problems in American economic history, such as the profitability of slavery and the role of government in financing the building of railroads. The novelty of these studies lay in the employment of formal economic theory to make traditional hypotheses testable by identifying the numerical evidence that could decisively confirm or disprove them. Soon larger questions, such as the exact contribution of technology to advances in productivity and the relative performance of the American economy over time, came to the fore.[20]

17 *Federal Funds for Research, Development, and Other Scientific Activities* (Surveys of Science Resources Series, XIV, National Science Foundation, 1965), p. 150.

18 Robert P. Swieringa, "Computers and American History: The Impact of the 'New' Generation," *Journal of American History*, LX (1974), 1045-70.

19 Don Karl Rowney and James Q. Graham, Jr., eds., *Quantitative History: Selected Readings in the Quantitative Analysis of Historical Data* (1969); Edward Shorter, *The Historian and the Computer: A Practical Guide* (1971). Far more influential than textbooks, however, was Robert Berkhofer's theoretical synthesis, *A Behavioral Approach to Historical Analysis* (1969).

20 Robert W. Fogel, *The Union Pacific Railroad: A Case in Premature Enterprise* (1960), pp. 9-10; Douglass C. North, *The Economic Growth of the United States, 1790-1860* (1961). See also Robert William Fogel, "The New Economic History: Its Findings and Methods," in *The Reinterpretation of American Economic History*, ed. Robert William Fogel and Stanley L. Engerman (1971), pp. 1-12. This volume also contains the pioneering work on slavery by Alfred H. Conrad and John R. Meyer and other important essays.

The econometric historians were a tight-knit intellectual community, proud of their scientific standing and largely cut off from the rank-and-file of American historians. With remarkable consistency their findings fit within an economist's version of the idea of a national consensus. The "new" economic history described a system in which competition functioned as "a socially meliorative process"[21] while a dynamic economy produced a wide distribution of material rewards. This conservative, consensual point of view persisted without effective challenge until 1974. Then Robert W. Fogel and Stanley L. Engerman in a daring and celebrated study of slavery, *Time on the Cross* (2 vols.), went too far. Arguing that rational, economic calculations motivated both slaves and masters, Fogel and Engerman made the case that American slaves benefited substantially from American capitalism. This brought from social historians and some econometric historians as well a roar of criticism and rejection.[22]

The same methodological program that inspired the new economic history captured the imagination of several young political historians about the same time. Here, too, as in economic history, a framework of consensus and continuity shaped the initial efforts. The early quantitative reassessments in American political history by Richard McCormick and Lee Benson were designed to test the Beardian idea that class conflict explains the composition of political parties. Both men concluded that Beard was wrong. American voters in the nineteenth century shared (in Benson's words) "broad and deep agreement . . . upon the very issues which elsewhere have provided the fundamental bases of political conflict."[23]

However, the new political history speedily became a paradise for pluralists. Unlike the new economic historians, the political

---

[21] Robert Higgs, *Competition and Coercion: Blacks in the American Economy, 1865-1914* (1980), "Preface to the Phoenix Edition."

[22] "Symposium on *Time on the Cross*", *Explorations in Economic History*, XII (October 1975); Paul A. David et al., *Reckoning with Slavery: Critical Study in the Quantitative History of American Negro Slavery* (1976); Herbert G. Gutman, *Slavery and the Numbers Game: A Critique of* Time on the Cross (1975).

[23] Richard P. McCormick, "Suffrage Classes and Party Alignments: A Study in Voter Behavior," *Mississippi Valley Historical Review*, XLVI (1959), 397-410; Lee Benson, *The Concept of Jacksonian Democracy: New York as a Test Case* (1961), p. 275.

historians broke away from any single, integrative model. What fascinated Benson's readers and gave *The Concept of Jacksonian Democracy* (1961) an extraordinary influence in the 1960's and 1970's was not his interest in ideology and comprehensive theory but rather his identification of ethnic and religious groups as the most important components of the electorate. This aspect of Benson's work was elaborated by Samuel P. Hays, Hays's students, and many others. The ethnic and religious allegiances of voters proved readily quantifiable by microscopic analysis of local electoral units. Attention shifted from national policies to local issues, from a center of power to a myraid of constituencies. Following different insights and examining different variables, researchers brought out more and more complex alignments and realignments of groups. Far from establishing any consensus among present scholars or past voters, the new political history revealed an extremely heterogeneous polity.[24]

A quantitatively oriented social history lagged somewhat behind the parallel developments in economic and political history. Consequently, Stephan Thernstrom's stunning doctoral dissertation on Newburyport, Massachusetts, published in 1964, was immediately recognized as an overdue breakthrough. Thernstrom focused on the widely held belief that class lines had hardened in the course of industrialization, and he demonstrated that a team of social scientists who had drawn that conclusion in a classic study of Newburyport (the famous "Yankee City" series) had been completely misled by their static categories and ahistorical cast of mind.[25] The striking feature of Thernstrom's research was the tracing of hundreds of ordinary manual laborers and their families across three

---

[24] There has been substantial agreement on the importance of a distinction between "pietists" and "ritualists," to use Hays's terminology, but also increasing skepticism about the primacy of these categories. See Paul Kleppner, *The Third Electoral System, 1853-1892: Parties, Voters, and Political Cultures* (1979), pp. 358-71; Melvyn Hammarberg, *The Indiana Voter: The Historical Dynamics of Party Allegiance during the 1870's* (1977). See also Allan G. Bogue, "The New Political History in the 1970's," in *The Past Before Us: Contemporary Historical Writing in the United States*, ed. Michael Kammen (1980), pp. 231-51; and Richard B. Latner and Peter Levine, "Perspectives on Antebellum Pietistic Politics," *Reviews in American History*, IV (1976), 15-24.
[25] *Poverty and Progress: Social Mobility in a Nineteenth-Century City* (1964). Thernstrom wrote about his objectives in "Reflections on the New Urban History," *Daedalus* (Spring, 1971), 359-75.

decades to observe their changing social position. No one before had so effectively addressed a prevailing sociological construct with systematic historical research.

For about a decade the study of social mobility was one of the hottest projects in American history. It became a comparative study of different ethnic groups, different localities, and different kinds of mobility. The entire enterprise came under attack as a legacy of consensus thinking, since its conclusions seemed to back up the old American dream of success, and its relentless focus on achievement imposed middle-class criteria on people who may not have wanted to judge themselves in that way.[26] The criticism had some merit. The main attraction of research on mobility was not, however, an ideological commitment to the process or to the society that fostered it. Most social historians were ambivalent about both. Their ambivalence about success undoubtedly contributed to their fascination with the subject, but what drew them most strongly to mobility studies was rather the same human appeal that invested the new political history: the opportunity to probe beneath the formal structures of history, to touch the daily lives of ordinary people, to infer their otherwise inaccessible states of minds from their behavior, to write history "from the bottom up."[27] Nearly all of the new tendencies of the 1960's were anti-elitist, and the study of mobility was paradoxically one of the avenues by which historians moved downward into the experience of anonymous individuals within particular local settings.

This was obviously the case also with a second strand in the new social history that appeared in the mid-1960's, the history of the family. Almost simultaneously with Thernstrom's monograph, three young colonial historians brought out the first close-up, quantitative studies of the population of early New England towns.[28] They were responding to encouragement from a group of English scholars at Cambridge University, who were in turn following the lead of a

26 James Henretta, "The Study of Social Mobility: Ideological Assumptions and Conceptual Bias," *Labor History*, XVIII (1977), 168-78.
27 Charles Tilly, *As Sociology Meets History* (1981), pp. 23, 32.
28 Philip Greven, "Family Structure in Seventeenth-Century Andover, Massachusetts," *William and Mary Quarterly*, XXIII (1966), 234-56; Kenneth Lockridge, "The Population of Dedham, Massachusetts, 1636-1736," *Economic History Review*, XIX (1966), 318-44; John Demos, "Notes on Life in Plymouth Colony," *William and Mary Quarterly*, XXII (1965), 264-86.

French demographer, Louis Henry. He and his associates had set out in the 1950's to discover when and why major changes in fertility occurred in premodern Europe, particularly the beginnings of effective birth control. Henry's technique of "family reconstitution," correlating the records of all the births, marriages, and deaths in the families of a particular community over a long span of time, enabled historians to learn things about the most intimate aspects of the lives of people who left no other trace.[29]

Led by Philip Greven, family historians in the United States discovered that the structure of early New England families and communities was much more stable and deeply rooted in the European past than scholars had previously supposed.[30] This was exciting news, suggesting new relations between American and European history; but its significance was muffled by further research that turned inward to probe the emotional texture of different types of families and the roles of different members of the family circle in various regions of the country, various periods, and various segments of society. Histories of childhood, adolescence, old age, spinsterhood, and the life cycle, all within an American setting, proliferated. Greven shifted from the trans-Atlantic perspective of his first book to a strictly American study of character formation in three types of families—and now was widely criticized for taking no account of regional variations or temporal changes in the family patterns that he described.[31] While historians of the family tried to organize their efforts through an association and a scholarly journal of their own, research on family-based values spilled out in a bewildering variety of directions.

[29] E. A. Wrigley, "Population, Family and Household," in *New Movements in the Study and Teaching of History*, ed. Martin Ballard (1970), pp. 93-104.
[30] Philip Greven, *Four Generations: Population, Land, and Family in Colonial Andover, Massachusetts* (1970).
[31] *The Protestant Temperament: Patterns of Child-rearing, Religious Experience, and the Self in Early America* (1977). See also Daniel Blake Smith, "The Study of the Family in Early America: Trends, Problems, and Prospects," *William and Mary Quarterly*, XXXIX (1982), 3-28; Joseph F. Kett, *Rites of Passage: Adolescence in America, 1790 to the Present* (1977); W. Andrew Achenbaum, *Old Age in the New Land: The American Experience since 1790* (1978); *Transitions: The Family and the Life Course in Historical Perspective* ed. Tamara K. Hareven (1978); Carroll Smith-Rosenberg, "The Female World of Love and Ritual: Relations between Women in Nineteenth-Century America," *Signs*, I (1975), 1-29.

Thus, each of the new impulses from the social sciences originated in an intellectual context of consensus and continuity; and at the outset every one of them buttressed the reigning paradigm by providing quantitative demonstrations of long-term regularities in behavior. But each of the major social-scientific endeavors had its own goals and preoccupations. There was no single, coherent social science. Each endeavor moved away from the others—and away from any common body of questions. Eventually even economic history seemed to lose a central motif.[32]

In the midst of this diversity, quantification gained general acceptance as a legitimate and sometimes essential instrument for historians, but its programmatic significance diminished. As its applications became more varied, more familiar, and even conventional in historical research, the mystique it had for enthusiastic practitioners in the 1960's began to fade. After the controversy over *Time on the Cross*, the uncertainty of interpretations built primarily or exclusively on quantitative data was more widely understood. Increasingly refined quantitative methods repeatedly destroyed the hypotheses they proved capable of testing and progressively narrowed the problems under investigation. This led in the late 1970's to warnings of the danger of "a new methodological scholasticism."[33] The most ambitious and expensive of the quantitative projects in American social history terminated in 1981 in a disappointing volume of disconnected essays on a few narrow topics.[34] By then the shrinkage of government funding for social and historical research made the prospects for continuance of such elaborate quantitative work in the foreseeable future doubtful.

It is instructive to compare the diffusion of quantification with the much more limited employment of another methodological persuasion historians borrowed in part from the social sciences. A comparative or (more loosely) international approach emerged in

---

[32] James H. Soltow, "Recent Literature in American Economic History," *American Studies International*, XVI (1978), 5-33.

[33] Lawrence Stone, *The Past and the Present* (1981), p. 43. See also Peter N. Stearns, "Toward a Wider Vision: Trends in Social History," in *The Past Before Us*, pp. 226-29.

[34] Theodore Hershberg, ed., *Philadelphia: Work, Space, Family, and Group Experience in the Nineteenth Century: Essays Toward an Interdisciplinary History of the City* (1981). See also the special book review section devoted to this book in *Journal of Urban History*, VIII (1982), 449-84.

the 1950's as a major influence in reshaping American history. It was stimulated not only by the example of sociologists and anthropologists but even more by rapidly increasing international contacts through Fulbright programs and international meetings, and perhaps most of all by the logic of the postprogressive paradigm. By placing American institutions and society in an internationally comparative context, the historians of an American consensus highlighted what was distinctive and unique about the United States. Yet no logical necessity required that comparative analysis should function that way. Enlarging the scope of inquiry can obviously bring out similarities as well as differences between countries and so lead to the discovery of unsuspected linkages across the usual boundaries of place and time. In 1964 that was one of the principal directions I expected American history to take (p. 232). It has indeed done so, but only along two special tracks.

One track ran southward through the slave regimes of the Western Hemisphere. Stanley Elkins's *Slavery: A Problem in American Institutional and Intellectual Life* (1959) opened this rich line of inquiry. Drawing heavily on the work of the Latin American historian Frank Tannenbaum, Elkins maintained that slavery was so much more oppressive in North America than in the Spanish and Portuguese colonies that it may have had a damaging effect on the slave's personality. David B. Davis, who also became convinced that the problem of slavery transcended national boundaries, pursued its intellectual origins back across the centuries. Against Elkins, Davis argued that the slavery of blacks in the New World was a single phenomenon, differing from one country to another only in inessential ways. Carl Degler thereupon narrowed the comparison to two countries, Brazil and the United States, and carried it forward into postemancipation race relations. Other scholars looked instead at the West Indies.[35] In *White Supremacy: A Comparative*

---

[35] David Brion Davis, *The Problem of Slavery in Western Culture* (1966); Carl N. Degler, *Neither Black nor White: Slavery and Race Relations in Brazil and the United States* (1971); H. Hoetink, *Slavery and Race Relations in the Americas: An Inquiry into Their Nature and Nexus* (1973); David W. Cohen and Jack P. Greene, eds., *Neither Slave nor Free: The Freedmen of African Descent in the Slave Societies of the New World* (1972); Donald L. Horowitz, "Color Differentiation in the American Systems of Slavery," *Journal of Interdisciplinary History*, III (1973), 509-41.

Study in American and South African History (1981) George Fredrickson moved the locus of comparison to a system of race relations more rigidly bifurcated than that of the United States; he provided a careful, step-by-step account of how the two societies diverged. Altogether, a complex literature has grown up. Elkins's original concentration on North American uniqueness has been replaced by a dense intertwining of similarities and differences.

The other principal current of comparative research has spanned the Atlantic, linking the American Revolution to distant antecedents and transforming our understanding of early American political ideas. Here the central figures have been Bernard Bailyn, J.G.A. Pocock, and Bailyn's student Gordon Wood.[36] Their interests have not been overtly comparative in the strict sense of juxtaposing discrete societies to see better how each works. Instead, they set out to clarify a particular idea or event. To do so, they traced its ramifications and alterations outward, across great expanses of space and time, always probing for limits, until a new and wider object of inquiry came into view. Comparison has not been the end, it has rather been the crucial means of a program of research centering on the distinctiveness of the American Revolution.

With important help from the English historian Caroline Robbins, Bailyn demonstrated that an ideology of republicanism, derived from classical antiquity and from the Commonwealth period in seventeenth-century England, was at the heart of the patriot cause in 1776. Pocock's own studies of the same body of ideas, which he called civic humanism, enriched their density and extended their longevity from the Italian Renaissance to nineteenth-century America. A split that Pocock found emerging within this tradition in seventeenth-century England—a division between "Court" and "Country"—suddenly looked very much like the ideological basis of politics in Jeffersonian America. As it gathered accretions from other scholars working on Scotland, England, and the United States,

---

[36] Bernard Bailyn, *The Ideological Origins of the American Revolution* (1967); J.G.A. Pocock, *The Machiavellian Moment: Florentine Political Thought and the Atlantic Republican Tradition* (1975); Gordon S. Wood, *The Creation of the American Republic, 1776-1787* (1969). This last, however, is a complex work, which also incorporated in a fresh way the traditional themes of progressive historiography.

a genuinely new interpretation of what may have been the ideological mainspring of early American politics came into being.[37]

The study of republicanism has been a great anomaly in American historiography during the time of troubles. Among the new
approaches to American history only the republican perspective
offered a positive, appreciative view of an intellectual and political
elite. The study of eighteenth-century America "from the bottom
up" remained the business of other scholars—social historians, for
the most part—who distrusted the elitist bias of Bailyn and Pocock.
The republican school was somewhat exceptional also in treating
an ideology with loving care and giving it decisive significance in
historical change. The critics of the republican school paid it the
unconscious tribute of developing their own supple grasp of early
American ideologies in order to construct an alternative synthesis;[38]
and ideology received careful attention in the study of slavery as
well.[39] There, however, the topics being scrutinized—American
ideas of freedom and of race—were not themselves transformed.
Only in the study of republicanism did the comparative approach
attain its potential for a "rescaling of perspective . . . in which the

[37] John M. Murrin, "The Great Inversion, or Court versus Country: A Comparison of the Revolution Settlements in England (1688-1721) and America
(1776-1816)," in *Three British Revolutions: 1641, 1688, 1776* (1980), pp.
368-453. For a full historiographical assessment see Robert E. Shalhope, "Toward a Republican Synthesis: The Emergence of an Understanding of Republicanism in American Historiography," and "Republicanism and Early American
Historiography," *William and Mary Quarterly*, XXIX (1972), 49-80; XXXIX
(1982), 334-56.

[38] Joyce Appleby, "The Social Origins of American Revolutionary Ideology,"
Journal of American History, LXIV (1978), 935-58, and "What is Still Amer-
ican in the Political Ideology of Thomas Jefferson?" *William and Mary
Quarterly*, XXXIX (1982), 287-309; Gary B. Nash, *The Urban Crucible:
Social Change, Political Consciousness, and the Origins of the American Revolu-
tion* (1979).

[39] Eric Foner, *Free Soil, Free Labor, Free Men: The Ideology of the Republican
Party before the Civil War* (1970); George Fredrickson, *The Black Image in
the White Mind: The Debate on Afro-American Character and Destiny, 1817-
1914* (1971); and the work of David Brion Davis, discussed below. It should
be added that ideology is a subject on which European students of American
history are making valuable contributions, notably: J. R. Pole, *The Pursuit of
Equality in American History* (1978); Giorgio Spini, *Autobiografia Della
Giovane America: La Storiografia Americana dai Padri Pellegrini All'Indipend-
enza* (Turin, 1968); Elise Marienstras, *Les Mythes fondateurs de la nation
américaine* (1977); Yehoshua Arieli, *Individualism and Nationalism in American Ideology* (1964); Gerald Stourzh, *Alexander Hamilton and the Idea of
Republican Government* (1970).

basic unit of discussion is larger than any of the traditional units within which research began."[40] Finally, the study of republicanism stands out in the landscape of recent scholarship as a new formulation of the otherwise largely discredited pursuit of consensus and continuity. As an effort to explain the central event in early American history—and the political culture it produced—in terms of a single configuration of thought, while granting only secondary importance to internal divisions in American society, the republican thesis resembles (though it also supplements and challenges) the Lockean thesis of Louis Hartz.[41]

How can we explain so striking an anomaly? The historiography of republicanism owes nothing to the anti-elitist and pluralist mentality of the Sixties—nothing, that is, but resistance. In contrast to most American historians, who could not escape a need to feel involved in the contemporary world and to make their history address it, Bailyn and Pocock for the most part turned their faces resolutely away from the present, rejected the demand for "relevance," and pursued programs of research they had undertaken in the 1950's. Instead of structuring their history in ways that could directly illuminate present issues, they fixed their attention on origins. Like the imperial school of the early twentieth century, they looked backward to a wider trans-Atlantic world to comprehend the birth of the American republic. The republican world view as Pocock described it was by definition premodern. As other scholars uncover extensive survivals of that world view in nineteenth-century America, more and more of the past takes on a remote, antique appearance: a world we may have lost. Perhaps the accomplishments of the republican school suggest that the study of history can benefit most from the historian's detachment from his own time when its meaning seems to him engulfed in confusion.

In the other domains of American history an internationally comparative perspective produced only isolated forays, which were not

---

[40] Bernard Bailyn, "The Challenge of Modern Historiography," *American Historical Review*, LXXXVII (1982), 13.

[41] The basic opposition of the republican thesis to the emphasis on class conflict in progressive and radical historiography is made clear in Bernard Bailyn's *Lines of Force in Recent Writings on the American Revolution* (XIV International Congress of Historical Sciences, 1975).

followed up. In explanation George Fredrickson has pointed out that the organization of the entire historical profession along lines of intense geographical specialization makes early, serious commitment to comparative work too risky for young scholars. Everyone must establish credentials within a conventional niche and then keep constantly in touch with new developments there.[42] This institutional constraint would surely be less limiting, however, if historians *wanted* to study large, complex structures like nations, classes, and ideologies. On the whole they do not: the bias of pluralism has reinforced the existing pattern of specialization. The messages historians received from the world around them in the 1960's and 1970's brought, first, a tremendous disillusion with large systems of power and belief, then a loss of interest in them. Some valid meaning, it now seemed, was far more likely to be found in more intimate fields of action, where experience retained a human scale. How these contemporary attitudes changed the course of American historiography will be the subject of the remainder of this chapter.

Significantly, the first open break with the historiography of the 1950's—the first concentrated expression in historical writing of a new mood on American campuses—appeared in the field of recent American history, where connections between past and present are almost inescapable. Several historians more or less simultaneously set about redefining the progressive movement of the early twentieth century. The postprogressive scholars of the 1950's, such as Hofstadter and Goldman, had criticized the progressive mind rather sharply; but they had done so, as Hofstadter confessed, "largely from within." They wanted especially to separate what was still living from what was dead in the tradition to which they felt most deeply attached.[43] In postwar historiography the strategy of locating oneself within the people one writes about, examining them with a blend of empathy and detachment, was in fact a fundamental methodological premise (pp. 143–44). The break with the style of the Fifties occurred when some historians decided that any lingering bond of sympathy in treating the United States, its leaders, or its dominant institutions would falsify the cold, harsh truth.

[42] "Comparative History," in *The Past Before Us*, pp. 472-73.
[43] *The Age of Reform: From Bryan to F.D.R.* (1955), pp. 12-13.

The progressives were the makers of modern America. For understanding them—and it—the scalpel of the surgeon would have to replace the painter's brush.

This clinical, external approach took two forms, one Marxist, the other institutionalist. The Marxist version described national progressivism as a seizure of the state by big business seeking to stabilize and rationalize the economy through regulatory legislation. Progressivism was not, as Hofstadter had alleged, "the complaint of the unorganized against the consequences of organization," but just the reverse. Gabriel Kolko stated the case forcefully in *The Triumph of Conservatism: A Reinterpretation of American History, 1900–1916* (1963), and James Weinstein gave it a more elegant formulation in *The Corporate Ideal in the Liberal State, 1900–1918* (1968). Weinstein's mentor, William A. Williams, had already attracted a small but enthusiastic following with a softer kind of Marxism, more idealistic and patriotic. The note of alienation in the new writing on progressivism made it different. For the first time Marxism began to exercise direct and substantial influence within the historical profession.[44]

The non-Marxist critique of progressivism diverged from the Marxist analysis in assigning a crucial role to technical and professional elites rather than an economic ruling class. Both the Marxist and the institutionalist interpretations agreed that popular decision making was by-passed by the very reformers who loudly proclaimed it. Samuel P. Hays argued persuasively that the focus on ideologies such as liberalism had blinded historians to the actual distribution and use of power. In the name of reform, for example, an upper-class elite in the Progressive Era had deliberately and successfully maneuvered to make municipal government more centralized and

---

[44] Michael Merrill and Michael Wallace, "Marxism and History," in *The Left Academy: Marxist Scholarship on American Campuses*, ed. Bertell Ollman and Edward Vernhoff (1982). I regret that I cannot within the limits of this essay deal with the history of American foreign relations, except to say that Marxism, functioning as a critique of recent American foreign policy, was almost the only exciting intellectual influence in the field. Consequently, in the 1970's little work was done on any topic dealing with the period prior to 1918. See N. Gordon Levin, Jr., *Woodrow Wilson and World Politics: America's Response to War and Revolution* (1968); Joyce and Gabriel Kolko, *The Limits of Power: The World and United States Foreign Policy, 1945-1954* (1972); John Lewis Gaddis, "Containment: A Reassessment," *Foreign Affairs*, LV (1977), 873-87.

less democratic. Robert Wiebe's extremely influential synthesis, *The Search for Order, 1877–1920* (1967), sketched the rise of experts and managers who wielded power through mastery of bureaucratic processes. Both scholars wrote an impersonal history, a history without heroes, in which patterns of organization change and those who understand the changes adapt to them effectively. "The system was so impersonal," Wiebe mused, "so vast, seemingly without beginning or end."[45]

For a while there was indeed no end to books on social control. Considering the ubiquity of social control in interpersonal relations, the thesis that reformers of all stripes had been intent on maintaining their own authority over people who might get out of hand was not hard to document. The thesis cast a baleful light on national leaders whom earlier historians had admired for their idealism. It also suggested that whatever consensus the nation had attained was contrived and imposed. Consequently, the social control idea rapidly spread back from the Progressive Era to earlier periods, and in skillful hands it had a telling effect. Michael B. Katz, for example, thrust the history of education in a new direction by contending in *The Irony of Early School Reform: Educational Innovation in Mid-Nineteenth-Century Massachusetts* (1968) that civic leaders fearful of disorder imposed on the working class a school system loaded with indoctrination. Paul Johnson assembled evidence to show that the great religious revivals of the 1820's were in good measure an attempt by employers to regain control of their workmen.[46]

There were, however, limits to the kind and extent of repression that reformers and pious do-gooders could be held responsible for. America's deepest injustice, its most searing inhumanity, arose from racial divisions imbedded in the very foundations of the society, and

[45] p. 165. See also Samuel P. Hays, *American Political History as Social Analysis* (1980), esp. pp. 205-32. An early and prescient comment on the new historiography of progressivism is R. Jackson Wilson's "United States: The Reassessment of Liberalism," *Journal of Contemporary History*, II (1967), 93-105.

[46] Paul A. Johnson, *A Shopkeeper's Millennium: Society and Revivals in Rochester, New York, 1815-1837* (1978); David J. Rothman, *The Discovery of the Asylum: Social Order and Disorder in the New Republic* (1971); Roy Lubove, *The Progressives and the Slums: Tenement House Reform in New York City, 1890-1917* (1965); Paul Boyer, *Urban Masses and Moral Order in America, 1820-1920* (1978).

it was therefore appropriate that the most imposing efforts to strip a patina of consensus from American history fixed on the subject of race. The first major book in this vein, Winthrop Jordan's *White over Black: American Attitudes toward the Negro, 1550–1812* (1968), had been undertaken prior to the eruption of the crisis of the mid-Sixties; it did not answer all the questions about racial domination that crisis posed. Jordan dealt sensitively with sexual exploitation and with the anxieties of transplanted whites over a loss of identity in a new land; but he located the source of race prejudice in attitudes that Englishmen had brought with them across the Atlantic. His work failed to explore the early American social context in a way that might explain Negro slavery as part of a larger paradigm of social control.

Two of the leading American historians undertook the task. Unlike the other major scholars of his generation, Edmund S. Morgan quietly laid aside a large part of the framework of consensus in which his earlier work had been cast. Morgan's *American Slavery, American Freedom: The Ordeal of Colonial Virginia* (1975) presented the social history of the first great Anglo-American colony as an anguishing story of the killing of an inter-racial dream by laziness, brutality, corruption, and above all fear of a rebellious lower class. Slavery, according to Morgan, grew in order to eliminate the danger posed by a terribly exploited white working class. An American consensus, such as it was, rested on economic and racial oppression. In the same year Morgan's colleague at Yale, David B. Davis, adopted a similar approach to a later period. The second volume of Davis's comparative study of the problem of slavery was a huge, involuted meditation on the interrelations between slavery and other forms of social control during the era of the American and French revolutions. Its central point (never so flatly stated) was that abolitionists and their opponents unconsciously collaborated in diverting attention from the growing slavery of capitalism.[47]

It is my impression that both books have been more dutifully respected than actively used. To some, their essential argument seemed tenuous without a fully articulated Marxian interpretation

---

[47] *The Problem of Slavery in the Age of Revolution, 1770-1823* (1975).

which neither author wished to supply. Both books were expressions of disillusion but also of personal involvement: in one case with American freedom, in the other with the anti-slavery movement, which comes down to the same thing. Neither author attained the remoteness from his subject, or the antipathy toward it, that the model of social control seemed to call for. Neither had altogether shed the idealistic holism of the 1950's.

Increasingly during the 1970's the theme of social control seemed one-sided and incomplete. It concentrated too much on the people on top and told too little of what those farther down were doing for themselves. With so much awareness of oppression in the 1970's, historians obviously needed to find the oppressed. Four groups that had earlier appeared only on the margins of American history and had received little notice from professional historians sprang into prominence at the annual meetings and in the lists of doctoral dissertations: blacks, Indians, women, and the white working class. Here, incontestably, were histories worth telling. The stifled, empathic feelings that could not attach themselves to America as a whole or to its dominant sectors poured forth in a flood of books on the outgroups that seemed from a progressive or radical point of view the victims of American history. The task in each case was to show how those who had struggled somehow endured and how those who had not fought nonetheless claimed their own human dignity. These requirements produced much ephemeral work; but they also inspired a few books of great distinction and power, notably Eugene Genovese's *Roll, Jordan, Roll: The World the Slaves Made* (1974) and Anthony F. C. Wallace's *Death and Rebirth of the Seneca* (1970).

For all the outgroups, but most especially for blacks, the overwhelming emphasis was on the inner strength of the group and the vital sources of its pride. John Blassingame wrote a pioneering study of the communal life of the slaves on antebellum plantations. Herbert Gutman discerned in the structures of the black family under slavery certain enduring features derived from Africa which authenticated its sustaining power. Lawrence Levine found in traditional Afro-American folk music and folk tales the origins of an evolving but continuous affirmation of a common identity. James Borchert, reporting on the black alley dwellers of Washington, D.C., in the twentieth century, described how the lowest class of rural migrants maintained a viable community in a hostile environment.[48]

This concentration on what was unique and unsharable in the experience of each outgroup answered the demand for a pluralistic history, but it also prevented serious consideration of what the groups might have had in common. The creation of a distinct scholarly literature for each outgroup (now including Chicanos and others, too) has brought into being a corresponding academic network for reporting new research and discussing common problems. In each network an argument over agenda and priorities has arisen, often with political overtones. In labor history, for example, one side follows David Montgomery in studying the pursuit of power by looking at what happens in the workplace, while the other side accepts Herbert Gutman's concentration on working-class cultures as revealed in ethnic traditions. In women's history somewhat similar issues come up between the study of feminism and the study of domesticity. Yet the debate within each network tends to absorb the attention of its members and to strengthen the divisions we have created between the histories of the various outgroups.[49] Instead of finding the oppressed, many historians have found—a specialty.

At the same time, in the last several years the radical spirit that gave a great impetus to the study of underprivileged elements in American society during the early 1970's has lost some of its strength. Much work on the outgroups continues, and much remains to be done. But the special fascination these groups had for a time has proved to be a phase of a larger movement of historical sympathy away from whatever is overpowering or impersonal and

[48] John W. Blassingame, *The Slave Community* (1972); Herbert G. Gutman, *The Black Family in Slavery and Freedom, 1750-1925* (1976); Lawrence W. Levine, *Black Culture and Black Consciousness: Afro-American Folk Thought from Slavery to Freedom* (1977); James Borchert, *Alley Life in Washington: Family, Community, Religion, and Folklife in the City, 1850-1970* (1980); Leon F. Litwack, *Been in the Storm So Long: The Aftermath of Slavery* (1979). Late in the 1970's some scholars began to explore significant divisions in Afro-American society, but still in an affirmative spirit; see Thomas Holt, *Black over White: Negro Political Leadership in South Carolina during Reconstruction* (1977); Joel Williamson, *New People: Miscegenation and Mulattoes in the United States* (1980).

[49] John Higham, "Current Trends in the Study of Ethnicity in the United States," *Journal of American Ethnic History*, II (1982), 5-15.

into whatever seems closer to home. More than ever before professional historians in the latter half of the 1970's devoted themselves to writing histories of local communities. Throughout the first half of the twentieth century professional historians had moved steadily away from local history, separating themselves disdainfully from the patrician amateurs who kept local historical societies alive and who remained, in their pride and naivete, the undaunted guardians of local names and traditions. Now, suddenly, nearly all the new demands and incentives that reshaped professional historiography in the Seventies converged in a revival of local studies. Was not localness the very antithesis of the national abstractions celebrated by progressive and postprogressive historians alike? Was it not in the close mesh of local experience that great national events themselves acquired a felt reality, as Robert A. Gross's *Minutemen and Their World* (1977) demonstrated? Was not local history the vehicle by which the new political historians brought ethnocultural issues to the fore, and the stage on which the new social historians observed clusters of families and patterns of mobility? Did not the "new labor history" rest chiefly on local studies? Was not the beginning of a new era in black history signaled by Willie Lee Rose's pioneering study of Port Royal?[50] All of these localized labors gained further impetus from anthropology, which became for many U.S. historians in the 1980's the most influential of the social sciences. In fact, it was an anthropologist, Anthony F. C. Wallace, who published in 1978 the most intellectually ambitious of the new local histories, *Rockdale: The Growth of an American Village in the Early Industrial Revolution.*

By 1980 local-community studies occupied something like a preeminent position in American historiography. Although only about 10 percent of the books on American history reviewed in the two leading scholarly journals could be classified as localistic,[51] that figure understates the importance of the genre for two reasons. First, a far larger proportion of the best books—those awarded the top prizes for American history in the late Seventies and early Eighties —were local studies. Second, the underlying appeal of local themes

---

[50] *Rehearsal for Reconstruction: The Port Royal Experiment* (1964).
[51] Kathleen Neils Conzen, "Community Studies, Urban History, and American Local History," in Kammen, *The Past Before Us*, p. 272.

informed additional research that did not fit wholly within a local framework. What pluralist historians pursued was not locality for its own sake but rather an authentic social bond, grounded in concrete, shared experience. Wherever they found such communities, whatever their shape or size, books sprang up. One historian discovered a spirit of community linking the wagon trains that carried emigrants across the vast plains of the trans-Mississippi West. Others encountered it in factories, churches, and agrarian movements.[52]

If some general theory had guided this flood of writings on communities, so that new contributions could test and revise an emerging interpretation of American society, academic historians might well have rejoiced in a happy deliverance from their time of troubles. Such was not, however, the condition or the mood of the early 1980's. The fabric of American local history, so rich, so promising, and so elaborately woven, displayed as yet no coherent design. In less than twenty years the focus of American historiography had shifted from one national community to innumerable little communities, and many historians certainly found in those little worlds an authenticity America itself no longer communicated to them. But the more deeply they imbedded themselves in a particular group or place, the more equivocal any larger scheme of meaning became. The disappointment and bafflement were evident in new appeals for narrative, for synthesis, and for vision.[53]

Thus, the pluralist paradigm (if it deserves so formal a designation) seemed to have reached certain limits, but no replacement had coalesced. At this juncture the most recent tendencies in American historiography tell us little about its future unless they are read in the light of longer rhythms and continuities. A long-term view suggests that both the successes and the failures of professional historians have been shaped by their mediating role. The profes-

---

[52] John D. Unruh, Jr., *The Plains Across: The Overland Emigrants and the Trans-Mississippi West, 1840-1860* (1979); Peter Friedlander, *The Emergence of a UAW Local, 1936-1939: A Study in Class and Culture* (1975); Donald G. Mathews, *Religion in the Old South* (1977); Lawrence Goodwyn, *Democratic Promise: The Populist Movement in America* (1976). Thomas Bender offers a commentary on this literature in *Community and Social Change in America* (1978).

[53] See Stone, *Past and Present*, pp. 74-96; Bailyn, "Challenge," *AHR*, LXXXVII (1982), 1-24; Jonathan Yardley, "The Narrowing World of the Historian," *AHA Perspectives*, XX (September 1982), 21-22.

POSTSCRIPT: OBJECTIVITY REEXAMINED

One of the more striking illustrations of the fragmentation of the historical profession in the 1960's and 1970's was an almost eerie absence of debate on the meaning of history and the fundamental principles of historical inquiry. The intense controversies over objectivity, which had aroused historians in the interwar period, had seemed by the early 1960's to be reaching a partial resolution in which subjectivity and science could be joined. Instead of a new synthesis or a grand theory, however, what ensued was a massive loss of interest in any overall conceptions of historical knowledge. A major stock-taking of "Historical Studies Today," published by *Daedalus* in 1971, still gave some small attention to theoretical questions concerning historical knowledge and causation. The next summing up, a decade later, avoided all such issues. In doing so it simply reflected the silence at annual meetings of the American Historical Association on the big, speculative issues of historical thinking.[1]

In contrast to the historical discipline, the other humanities during those same years were riven by the most intense disputes over aims and methods. While taking various specific forms, the disputes have stemmed from devastating critiques of traditional claims for knowledge as a secure, impersonal grasp of reality. In place of the authority of knowledge, the new theorists have focused on the imaginative power of interpreters or on the coercive power of the institutions and ideologies through which they function. In this view any invocation of an external "reality" becomes suspect, while the pervasiveness of language as the medium and agency of all experience becomes crucial. We have learned therefore to speak in a loosely inclusive way of a "linguistic turn" in Western philosophy.[2]

[1] Felix Gilbert and Stephen R. Graubard, eds., *Historical Studies Today* (1972); Michael Kammen, ed., *The Past before Us: Contemporary Historical Writing in the United States* (1980). See also my review of the latter in *American Historical Review*, LXXXVI (1981), 807–9.
[2] John E. Toews, "Intellectual History after the Linguistic Turn: The Autonomy of Meaning and the Irreducibility of Experience," *American Historical Review*, XCII

At the epistemologically radical edge of this interdisciplinary movement, one historian, Hayden White, has been a major figure. Yet White's influence has been largely confined to literary studies and related humanities programs.[3] The mainstream of the historical profession did turn in a markedly relativistic direction in the 1970's; but the shift occurred on the level of attitudes, without either benefit or hindrance from explicit theorizing. Apparently it came about through the diffuse disillusion we have already observed toward all large systems of authority and belief. History, along with everything else, lost some of its credibility.

A change so lacking in obvious signposts is difficult to follow, and its extent very hard to assess. Fortunately, a revitalization of intellectual history in the 1980's has renewed interest in historical theories and has also sharpened the skills required to deal with ideas whether they appear in group behavior or more formally in major texts. Accordingly, we now have from Peter Novick a big, compelling book tracing the problem of historical knowledge at every level of expression and action within the American historical profession from its beginnings to the present. *That Noble Dream: The "Objectivity Question" and the American Historical Profession* (1988) is both a monument to the paradoxical relativism of today and an extraordinarily intensive history of its antecedents.

Novick's title comes from a bleak presidential address that Theodore Clarke Smith delivered to the American Historical Association in 1934. Responding to sledgehammer attacks that progressive scholars were making on "the ideal of the effort for objective truth," Smith suggested gloomily that, the way things were going, this "noble dream"—the basic creed of the historical profession—might in the coming decades be irretrievably lost. While making no such prediction himself, Novick nonetheless casts his monumental story of change and challenge in a pattern of declension. In his account the ideal of objectivity, from about 1910

(1987), 897–907; Dominick LaCapra and Steven L. Kaplan, eds., *Modern European Intellectual History: Reappraisals and New Perspectives* (1982); Quentin Skinner, ed., *The Return of Grand Theory in the Human Sciences* (1985).

[3] White, *Metahistory: The Historical Imagination in Nineteenth-Century Europe* (1973), and *The Content of the Form: Narrative Discourse and Historical Representation* (1987).

to the present, has undergone increasing attenuation and seems now to rest on very shaky foundations.

This is to note immediately a major difference between Novick's narrative and my own telling of the same story in Part II of this book. Novick employs almost the same periodization that I used: first, the founding of a historical profession in the United States and the articulation of its central norm ("Objectivity Enthroned"); then, the development in the interwar years of a relativist movement that put the older scientific school on the defensive ("Objectivity Besieged"); third, an effort in the 1940's and 1950's to integrate relativist insights into a more flexible orthodoxy ("Objectivity Reconstructed"); and finally, moving beyond my time frame, the widespread discrediting of any unifying ideal in the midst of confusion, fragmentation, and uncertainty ("Objectivity in Crisis"). While Novick and I agree on innumerable particulars, he sees my interpretation of the first three stages as Whiggish and celebratory. Whiggish it was—excessively though understandably so. From the vantage point of the early 1960's, when the study of history was prospering at every level, the story of an evolving professional creed fell persuasively into a pattern of thesis, antithesis, and synthesis. Adding a fourth stage, especially as Novick defines it, throws what came before in a different light. From the disarray of the 1980's, the third stage is easily read as an unmitigated failure, a temporary cooptation rather than a fusion, and the resulting four-stage pattern becomes a sequence of deepening disintegration. We have here an instance of a limit—insuperable though not absolute—that the historical process sets on the truths of historical inquiry.

The methods of the two books as well as the time of their composition contribute to the contrasts between them. Novick writes the history of a "question," i.e., a dispute which is best understood by standing outside the arena to observe how contestants deal with one another in rephrasing a given proposition and restating their many answers. I wrote the history of a belief, so I wanted to get inside the principal players to grasp empathically how each of them felt and perceived a problematic situation. Novick seeks distance; I sought identification. His approach reveals complexities of strategy and maneuver that often escaped me. Mine offered a more sympathetic view of ambiguities within various perspectives and of linkages and continuities between rivals and successors.

Consider, for example, how the two books depict the first generation of professional historians. In writing mine, I had discovered to my surprise how much the early professionals had in common with the leading amateur historians of the late nineteenth century, both in theory and in practice. In contrast to previous historiographers I stressed the professionals' typical acknowledgement of the unattainability of complete objectivity along with their resolute belief in moving toward it and their enthusiastic enlistment in the broad, late-nineteenth-century movement to strengthen tradition and authority in American high culture. Novick, on the other hand, begins not with the cultural aspirations of the early professionals but with a highly restrictive definition of what he calls "the original and continuing objectivist creed" (p. 2). In it he includes the propositions that truth is unitary, that facts are independent of interpretations, and that the "meaning" of events never changes regardless of shifts in attributed significance. From these desiccated absolutes Novick can move easily into the American professionals' intellectual shortcomings, namely their naive understanding of science and their misunderstanding of the German academic model they adopted. Later he notes in passing what I featured, just as I had noted (though perhaps more prominently) the professional egoism he dwells upon.

Concentrating on the argument of the book may fail to convey an adequate sense of its range and richness. The bibliography lists sixty manuscript collections. Novick has also drawn heavily on books, reviews, and speeches through which major historiographical controversies and minor professional scandals were fought out. The book can be read almost as a general history of the historical profession. The principal contribution of Novick's dense description, however, is to highlight the political ideologies professional historians have espoused.

The special ideological service of the first generation was to the deepening of national unity, healing the wounds of the Civil War and overcoming the rampant localism and sectionalism of earlier historical writing. What Novick calls a "deliberate negotiation of a mutually acceptable version of the sectional conflict" (p. 74) came about partly through the low-keyed, unemotional tone that the ethic of objectivity mandated and partly through northern scholars' acquiescence in southern views on race relations. The ideological homogeneity that the American historical community thereby attained, Novick believes, was essential in establishing objectivity as its accepted norm.

The progressive scholars of the early twentieth century who began to question objectivist convictions remained much too confident of the progress of scientific knowledge to push their questions very far. For many, especially among the progressive avant-garde, World War I shattered that confidence. The nationalistic zeal that the war excited plunged them back into the hyperbolic language they had collectively repudiated; and then, in the disillusioned aftermath of the war, it left them perplexed and deeply disturbed over the betrayal of their vaunted objectivity. Fierce scholarly quarrels ensued in the interwar years, particularly over the "war guilt question" and over the causes and consequences of the American Civil War, all of which dramatized the breakdown of an ideological consensus and formed the immediate context of the relativist movement of the 1930's.

Novick provides discriminating, impressively knowledgeable chapters on redefinitions of science and on new philosophical and social-scientific ideas that also impinged on the objectivity question. Nevertheless, ideology remains the center of attention as he turns to the reassertion of a qualified objectivity after World War II. Relativism, Novick tells us, became a prime target in the ideological mobilization against "totalitarianism." The defense of the West called on one hand for reassertion of underlying ideals and supposedly universal human values and on the other hand for pride in disinterested scientific inquiry. Consequently, historians followed a middle-of-the-road course. They claimed a partial autonomy for ideas while foreswearing ideological crusades and denying that the past is best handled as a weapon. There is much truth in Novick's assessment, although labeling such a non-activist position as "ideological mobilization" seems distorting. Fascinated as he is with conflict, Novick almost completely overlooks the enormous fear of conflict that the atom bomb introduced into the post-war world. For many historians, including myself, the retreat from aggressive relativism sprang not from mobilization but from demobilization, i.e., from alarm at the danger ideological fanaticism posed to everyone at that particular juncture in history.

The eruption of sharp dissensus in the 1960's did not immediately bring the objectivity question to the fore. In contrast to the 1920's, when an ideological rift spread downward from the leaders of the profession, carrying with it an explicit epistemological challenge, the upheaval of the Sixties came from below, chiefly from rebellious students. Unencumbered with philosophical baggage, the young radicals spoke in the name of objective truth, which they thought they could discern better than established scholars because they had no vested interests to protect. The new crisis for historical objectivity arose because different groups in the profession no longer agreed on a common agenda and no longer wanted to talk to one another. As the noise level escalated, comity collapsed; and with it went the sense that a diversified community of scholars can resolve arguments by rational means. Novick's discussion of this turning point is a graphic, sympathetic narrative of the rise of a new left in the historical profession, its early scholarly initiatives, and its rapid fragmentation into warring factions.

Gradually historians became aware of new forms of relativist theory, beginning with Thomas Kuhn's concept of the paradigm and extending through movements in literary criticism that repudiate determinate meanings, texts, and authors. As Novick suggests, this variegated epistemological pluralism or subjectivism has undoubtedly confirmed and perpetuated what he calls a crisis in historical theory. But why, if there is a crisis, do so few historians seem to care? Why have the ideas agitating other disciplines not yet aroused among historians a new, urgent debate like that of the 1930's and 1940's? Novick gives us no answer, except to say that sensibilities and interests have become too disparate; the historical profession no longer comprises a community of discourse.

I do not think that will do. The weakening of interaction between our many kinds of historians has not unsettled an underlying sense of a common task. Thomas Haskell has noted "our obstinate tendency to continue striving for objective knowledge . . . even in the face of our own skepticism." This striving still constitutes the great community of historians—a community that remains unswervingly engaged in defending a boundary between histories and fictions. The historian's commitment, Haskell continues, to justifying beliefs "by reference to realities that extend beyond language and communal solidarity is a wholesome discipline and a deeply human practice, the value of which is quite independent of the likelihood that it will ever yield incontrovertible Truth."[4] That center still holds, and the multilayered honesty of Novick's disillusioned book is an unintended testimonial to it.

[4] Thomas L. Haskell, "The Curious Persistence of Rights Talk in the 'Age of Interpretation,' " *Journal of American History,* LXXIV (1987), 996, 1011.

INDEX